Revision

WorkBook

Equity and Trusts

Second Edition

ALISON BAXTER, BA (Oxon)
Revised and updated by M. Harris, MA, LLM (Cantab)

HLT Publications

HLT PUBLICATIONS
200 Greyhound Road, London W14 9RY

First Edition 1991
Second Edition 1992

ISBN 0 7510 0002-7

British Library Cataloguing-in-Publication.

A CIP Catalogue record for this book is available from the
British Library.

Printed and bound in Great Britain.

CONTENTS

CONTENTS

ACKNOWLEDGEMENT

Some questions used are taken or adapted from past University of London LLB (External) Degree examination papers and our thanks are extended to the University of London for their kind permission to use and publish the questions.

Caveat

The LLB answers are not approved or sanctioned by the University of London and are entirely our responsibility.

They are not intended as 'Model Answers', but rather as Suggested Solutions.

The answers have two fundamental purposes, namely:

a) To provide a detailed example of a suggested solution to an examination question, and

b) To assist students with their research into the subject and to further their understanding and appreciation of the subject of Law.

INTRODUCTION

This Revision WorkBook is aimed to be of help to those studying equity and trusts. Its coverage is not restricted to any one syllabus but embraces all the core topics which can be found in university and polytechnic examinations.

Students will hopefully find it useful not only at examination time but also as a helpful summary of and introduction to the subject when studying it for the first time.

The WorkBook has been designed specifically to address common problems suffered by students when studying any legal subject. All examination based courses consist of four main processes, all of which may cause problems for some students. The WorkBook can be of help with each of these processes.

a) *Acquisition of knowledge*

This is achieved by individual work - attending lectures and reading the relevant textbooks and source materials such as cases and articles. The WorkBook is not intended to be a textbook and is in no way a substitute for one. However, the 'key points' and 'recent cases and statutes' sections will help students to direct their study to the important areas within each topic.

b) *Understanding*

Whilst difficulties in understanding a topic or particular point are best solved by a teacher's explanation, the WorkBook offers 'flowcharts' at the beginning of each chapter which usefully show how the various aspects of and cases within a topic fit together. This is the key to understanding for many students.

c) *Learning*

The process of learning is also a highly individual one. As a rule, however, students find it much easier to learn a single structure than pages of words. The 'flowcharts' provide a structured summary of each topic and this will be an aid to those who find learning a problem.

d) *Applying the knowledge to the question*

This is, perhaps, the most common problem of all. The WorkBook includes examination questions and answers covering many possible question variations within each topic. All such 'model answers' are of a length which a student could reasonably be expected to produce under the time restraints of an examination. In addition, the WorkBook specifically addresses the problem in two ways:

   i) Problem questions

   These require a logical and structured approach which many students find difficult. To assist them in overcoming this, problem checklists are included for most topics. These can be applied to any problem question on the topic and if so applied will produce the requisite structured answer which will include all relevant material. The checklists are applied in the model answers given to show how this system works.

ii) Essay questions

Although such a formula cannot be used for any given essay question on a topic, students can, with practice, learn how to approach and structure these too. To assist in this task, each chapter (where relevant) includes at least one full model answer preceded by a detailed skeleton solution outlining the essay.

In this revised 1992 edition a new final chapter has been inserted which contains the complete June 1991 University of London LLB (External) Law of Trusts question paper, followed by suggested solutions to each question. Thus the student will have the opportunity to review a recent examination paper in its entirety, and can, if desired, use this chapter as a mock examination - referring to the suggested solutions only after first having attempted the questions.

STUDYING EQUITY AND TRUSTS

Students often embark on the study of equity and trusts with a sense of dread or, at best, resignation. It is seen as both difficult and boring. Admittedly, some of the principles are quite complicated and difficult to grasp initially, but this is true of most areas of the law. It is a myth, however, that the law of trusts is boring. The subject raises many interesting moral, political and general issues - in particular, the political aspect of charitable trusts (chapter 6) and the division of jointly owned property under resulting and constructive trusts (chapter 12). Indeed equity and trusts have something for everyone. For those students who are dissatisfied with the fact that the law never produces concrete answers, trusts comes closer to doing so than any other area of the law - it is a very analytical subject. For those students who prefer more abstract discussions about whether the law is 'fair', the subject raises this question in many areas such as that of charitable trusts.

In equity and trusts, in particular, there exists no substitute for hard work. A student who hopes to do well must not limit his study to textbooks. Knowledge of source material is vital - statutes and cases (judgments; *not* just headnotes!). There has been little recent development in the area. However, the recent changes that have occurred have been almost revolutionary - in particular, Lord Denning's new type of constructive trust (chapter 12) - and must be known and fully understood by the student.

The subject divides itself quite neatly into two parts, as does this book. The first half - the principles of trusts - is based mainly on the development of case law. The role of the trustee in the second half, on the other hand, derives itself primarily from statute although cases do offer important interpretation. Students tend to find the principles of trusts more complicated but more interesting than the law regarding the trustee's role. It is important to remember, however, that most syllabuses will require knowledge and understanding of both aspects of the subject.

REVISION AND EXAMINATION TECHNIQUE

(A)   REVISION TECHNIQUE

Planning a revision timetable

In planning your revision timetable make sure you don't finish the syllabus too early. You should avoid leaving revision so late that you have to 'cram' - but constant revision of the same topic leads to stagnation.

Plan ahead, however, and try to make your plans increasingly detailed as you approach the examination date.

Allocate enough time for each topic to be studied. But note that it is better to devise a realistic timetable, to which you have a reasonable chance of keeping, rather than a wildly optimistic schedule which you will probably abandon at the first opportunity!

The syllabus and its topics

One of your first tasks when you began your course was to ensure that you thoroughly understood your **syllabus**. Check now to see if you can write down the **topics** it comprises from memory. You will see that the chapters of this WorkBook are each devoted to a syllabus topic. This will help you decide which are the key chapters relative to your revision programme. Though you should allow some time for glancing through the other chapters.

The topic and its key points

Again working from memory, analyse what you consider to be the key points of any topic that you have selected for particular revision. Seeing what you can recall, unaided, will help you to understand and firmly memorise the concepts involved.

Using the WorkBook

Relevant questions are provided for each topic in this book. Naturally, as typical examples of examination questions, they do not normally relate to one topic only. But the questions in each chapter *will* relate to the subject matter of the chapter to a degree. You can choose your method of consulting the questions and solutions, but here are some suggestions (strategies 1-3). Each of them pre-supposes that you have read through the author's notes on key points and question analysis, and any other preliminary matter, at the beginning of the chapter. Once again, you now need to practise working from *memory*, for that is the challenge you are preparing yourself for. As a rule of procedure constantly test yourself once revision starts, both orally and in writing.

Strategy 1

Strategy 1 is planned for the purpose of *quick revision*. First read your chosen question carefully and then jot down in abbreviated notes what you consider to be the main points at issue. Similarly, note the cases and statutes that occur to you as being relevant for citation purposes. Allow yourself sufficient time to cover what you feel to be relevant. Then study the author's *skeleton solution* and skim-read the *suggested solution* to see how they compare with your notes. When comparing consider carefully what the author has included (and concluded) and see whether that agrees with what you have written. Consider the points of variation also. Have you recognised the key issues? How relevant have you been? It is possible, of course, that you have referred to a recent case that *is* relevant, but which had not been reported when the WorkBook was prepared.

Strategy 2

Strategy 2 requires a nucleus of *three hours* in which to practise writing a set of examination answers in a limited time-span.

Select a number of questions (as many as are normally set in your subject in the examination you are studying for), each from a different chapter in the WorkBook, without consulting the solutions. Find a place to write where you will not be disturbed and try to arrange not to be interrupted for three hours. Write your solutions in the time allowed, noting any time needed to make up if you *are* interrupted.

After a rest, compare your answers with the *suggested solutions* in the WorkBook. There will be considerable variation in style, of course, but the bare facts should not be too dissimilar. Evaluate your answer critically. Be 'searching', but develop a positive approach to deciding how you would tackle each question on another occasion.

Strategy 3

You are unlikely to be able to do more than one three hour examination, but occasionally set yourself a single question. Vary the 'time allowed' by imagining it to be one of the questions that you must answer in three hours and allow yourself a limited preparation and writing time. Try one question that you feel to be difficult and an easier question on another occasion, for example.

Mis-use of suggested solutions

Don't try to learn by rote. In particular, don't try to reproduce the *suggested solutions* by heart. Learn to express the basic concepts in your own words.

Keeping up-to-date

Keep up-to-date. While examiners do not require familiarity with changes in the law during the three months prior to the examination, it obviously creates a good impression if you can show you are acquainted with any recent changes. Make a habit of looking through one of the leading journals - *Modern Law Review, Law Quarterly Review* or the *New Law Journal*, for example - and cumulative indices to law reports, such as the *All England Law Reports* or *Weekly Law Reports*, or indeed the daily law reports in *The Times*. The *Law Society's Gazette* and the *Legal Executive Journal* are helpful sources, plus any specialist journal(s) for the subject you are studying.

(B)   EXAMINATION SKILLS

Examiners are human too!

The process of answering an examination question involves a *communication* between you and the person who set it. If you were speaking face to face with the person, you would choose your verbal points and arguments carefully in your reply. When writing, it is all too easy to forget *the human being who is awaiting the reply* and simply write out what one knows in the area of the subject! Bear in mind it is a person whose question you are responding to, throughout your essay. This will help you to avoid being irrelevant or long-winded.

The essay question

Candidates are sometimes tempted to choose to answer essay questions because they 'seem' easier. But the examiner is looking for thoughtful work and will not give good marks for superficial answers.

The essay-type of question may be either purely factual, in asking you to *explain the meaning* of a certain doctrine or principle, or it may ask you to *discuss* a certain proposition, usually derived from a quotation. In either case, the approach to the answer is the same. A clear programme must be devised to give the examiner the meaning or significance of the doctrine, principle or proposition and its origin in common law, equity or statute, and cases which illustrate its application to the branch of law concerned.

The problem question

The problem-type question requires a different approach. You may well be asked to advise a client or merely discuss the problems raised in the question. In either case, the most important factor is to take great care in reading the question. By its nature, the question will be longer than the essay-type question and you will have a number of facts to digest. Time spent in analysing the question may well save time later, when you are endeavouring to impress on the examiner the considerable extent of your basic legal knowledge. The quantity of knowledge is itself a trap and you must always keep within the boundaries of the question in hand. It is very tempting to show the examiner the extent of your knowledge of your subject, but if this is outside the question, it is time lost and no marks earned. It it inevitable that some areas which you have studied and revised will not be the subject of questions, but under no circumstances attempt to adapt a question to a stronger area of knowledge at the expense of relevance.

When you are satisfied that you have grasped the full significance of the problem-type question, set out the fundamental principles involved. You may well be asked to advise one party, but there is no reason why you should not introduce your answer by:

'I would advise A on the following matters ...'

and then continue the answer in a normal impersonal form. This is a much better technique than answering the question as an imaginary conversation.

You will then go on to identify the fundamental problem, or problems posed by the question. This should be followed by a consideration of the law which is relevant to the problem. The source of the law, together with the cases which will be of assistance in solving the problem, must then be considered in detail.

Very good problem questions are quite likely to have alternative answers, and in advising A you should be aware that alternative arguments may be available. Each stage of your answer, in this case, will be based on the argument or arguments considered in the previous stage, forming a conditional sequence.

If, however, you only identify one fundamental problem, do not waste time worrying that you cannot think of an alternative - there may very well be only that one answer.

The examiner will then wish to see how you use your legal knowledge to formulate a case and how you apply that formula to the problem which is the subject of the question. It is this positive approach which can make answering a problem question a high mark earner for the student who has fully understood the question and clearly argued his case on the established law.

Examination checklist

1 Read the instructions at the head of the examination carefully. While last-minute changes are unlikely - such as the introduction of a *compulsory question* or *an increase in the number of questions asked* - it has been known to happen.

2 Read the questions carefully. Analyse problem questions - work out what the examiner wants.

3 Plan your answer *before* you start to write. You can divide your time as follows:

    (a)   working out the question (5 per cent of time)

    (b)   working out how to answer the question (5 to 10 per cent of time)

    (c)   writing your answer

    Do not overlook (a) and (b)

4 Check that you understand the rubric *before* you start to write. Do not 'discuss', for example, if you are specifically asked to 'compare and contrast'.

5 Answer the correct number of questions. If you fail to answer one out of four questions set you lose 25 per cent of your marks!

Style and structure

Try to be clear and concise. Basically this amounts to using paragraphs to denote the sections of your essay, and writing simple, straightforward sentences as much as possible. The sentence you have just read has 22 words - when a sentence reaches 50 words it becomes difficult for a reader to follow.

Do not be inhibited by the word 'structure' (traditionally defined as giving an essay a beginning, a middle and an end). A good structure will be the natural consequence of setting out your arguments and the supporting evidence in a logical order. Set the scene briefly in your opening paragraph. Provide a clear conclusion in your final paragraph.

TABLE OF CASES

TABLE OF STATUTES

PART ONE
THE PRINCIPLES OF
TRUSTS

1   CLASSIFICATION OF TRUSTS

1.1   Introduction

1.2   Key points

1.3   Question

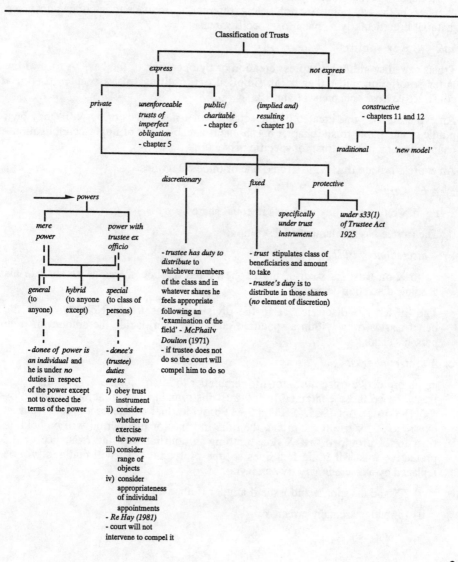

Classification of Trusts

express — not express

private — unenforceable trusts of imperfect obligation - chapter 5 — public/ charitable - chapter 6 — (implied and) resulting - chapter 10 — constructive - chapters 11 and 12

traditional — 'new model'

discretionary — fixed — protective

powers

mere power — power with trustee ex officio

general (to anyone) — hybrid (to anyone except) — special (to class of persons)

- *donee of power is an individual* and he is under *no* duties in respect of the power except not to exceed the terms of the power

- *donee's (trustee) duties are to:*
i) obey trust instrument
ii) consider whether to exercise the power
iii) consider range of objects
iv) consider appropriateness of individual appointments
- *Re Hay (1981)*
- court will not intervene to compel it

- *trustee has duty to distribute* to whichever members of the class and in whatever shares he feels appropriate following an 'examination of the field' - *McPhail v Doulton (1971)*
- if trustee does not do so the court will compel him to do so

- *trust* stipulates class of beneficiaries and amount to take
- *trustee's duty* is to distribute in those shares (*no* element of discretion)

specifically under trust instrument — under s33(1) of Trustee Act 1925

1.1 Introduction

This chapter aims simply to provide an overview of the trust concept by showing the different types of trust which can exist. The relationship between trusts and powers is also considered, as is the nature of a trustee's duties under a trust and a donee's duties under a power as these topics do not fit neatly anywhere else in the book. An understanding of these things is a vital prerequisite to the study of the rest of the law of trusts. They are unlikely, however, to be examined except as a minor part of a question on another topic. As a result, no questions have been included in this chapter. In the key points section below, references are made to later chapters when material is particularly relevant to a specific area.

1.2 Key points

Trusts can arise either by express creation or by operation of the law. A trust of the latter description will either be an (implied or) resulting trust - chapter 10 - or a constructive trust - chapters 11 and 12.

An express trust - one created by the settlor, either inter vivos or by will - may be a public or charitable trust - chapter 6 - an unenforceable trust of imperfect obligation - chapter 5 - or a private trust for specific person(s).

An express private trust will fall into one of three categories:

a) *A fixed trust*

   eg to X on trust for my nephews in equal shares.

   The trustee has no element of discretion.

b) *A discretionary trust*

   eg to X on trust for such of my nephews and in such shares as he shall in his absolute discretion determine.

   The trustee has discretion as to the division of the trust. He may select the beneficiaries from within a specified class and then decide the amount of each person's share.

c) *A protective trust*

   eg on protective trusts to X for life remainder to Y absolutely. The terms of the trust will be those contained in the trust instrument or, if none, as provided by s33(1) Trustee Act 1925. Section 33(1) provides that whenever a protective trust exists, to X for life (or shorter), then the income for that period will be held on trust for X provided that X does nothing in conflict with the existence of the protective trust. If he in fact does so, the protective trust will end and will be replaced by a discretionary trust in favour of:

   i) X and his spouse and issue if any; or if none

   ii) X and the remainderman Y.

The importance of the distinction between discretionary and fixed trusts is of primary importance in the sphere of certainty of objects - chapter 2. Although this distinction is straightforward to draw, the distinction between discretionary trusts and powers is more confusing and also important (although less so since *McPhail* v *Doulton* [1971] AC 424). The courts use the term discretionary trust and trust power interchangeably to mean the same thing. However, clearly a difference does exist between trusts and other forms of powers and it must be recognised in order to determine the nature of the trustee's obligations regarding a trust or a donee's obligations regarding a power.

a) *Fixed trust*

Clearly the nature of the trust means that the trustee is under an obligation to distribute the trust property in accordance with the terms of the trust. There is no element of discretion.

b) *Discretionary trust*

The trustee has a discretion as to the manner of distribution but a duty to actually distribute - *McPhail* v *Doulton* [1971] AC 424. There is a related duty to survey the range of objects before making the distribution. In an exhaustive discretionary trust, the trustees must actually distribute, but if the trust is non-exhaustive, they have a power to accumulate part or all of the trust property instead of distributing it.

c) *Powers*

    i) Mere power - donee is not a trustee.

        There are no duties in relation to the power except not to act beyond the authority conferred by it.

    ii) Power where the donee is a trustee.

        Although in general terms a power imposes no obligation on the donee, it was pointed out in *Re Hay* [1981] 3 All ER 786, that by virtue of his fiduciary position as a trustee, albeit ex officio, means that certain obligations will be imposed upon him. Apart from the fact that, as with a mere power, the trustee must not exceed his authority, he must also survey the range of beneficiaries from time to time and consider whether to exercise the power bearing in mind the range and the appropriateness of individual appointments.

        Unlike trusts, if no appointment is made, the court will not step in and enforce the power.

    iii) Power in the nature of a trust.

        This is sometimes referred to as a trust power, or a power with a trust in default of appointment.

        eg to X for life with power to appoint the remainder among X's children in such shares as X shall think fit.

If X fails to make an appointment, the property will either revert on resulting trust to the settlor or pass to X's children in equal shares. The crucial factor is the intention of the original settlor. If he intended that X's children would benefit in any event, and that X merely had a discretion to fix the shares, the property will pass to X's children in equal shares, if no appointment is made, as in *Burrough* v *Philcox* (1840) 5 My & Cr 72. If the settlor intended that X's children would benefit if and only if X exercised the power in their favour, the property reverts to the original settlor if X fails to make appointment, as in *Re Weekes' ST* [1897] 1 Ch 298. This latter situation is sometimes referred to as a mere power, in contrast to the power in the nature of a trust, or trust power, in the *Burrough* v *Philcox* case. If the instrument contains a gift in default of appointment, the power must be a mere power.

1.3 Question

By his will, a testator who died last year left certain valuable land to his trustees upon trust to sell the same and invest the proceeds in investments authorised by law and to pay the income thereof to Daphne for life and subject thereto to hold the capital and income upon trust for such one or more of Daphne's children and if more than one in such shares as Daphne should by deed appoint. The testator left his residuary estate to his son, Eric.

Advise the trustees in the event of Daphne dying tomorrow leaving three children but without having made any appointment, for whom they should hold the capital and income of the trust fund.

University of London LLB Examination
(for External Students Law of Trusts June 1990 Q 4(b)(ii)

Skeleton solution and comment

A standard type of problem on this area. Students are not expected to come to a definite conclusion whether a trust power or mere power is created, but to set out the two possibilities and state the appropriate test to be applied.

- Who is entitled to the property?
- If trust power - children take in equal shares.
- If mere power - reverts to testator's estate on resulting trust.
- Rest depends on intention of settlor.

Suggested solution

This problem turns on the true nature of the 'power' granted to Daphne by the testator's will. If, indeed, it is, on its true construction, merely a power of appointment that power would be extinguished on Daphne's death so that the property concerned, not being appointed, would go on resulting trust to the testator's estate.

It may possibly be, however, that, on the true construction of the testator's instructions, Daphne has been granted not a simple power but 'a power in the nature of a trust', ie a 'trust-power' which is in reality a trust. If this is the correct conclusion such trust must be enforced but since Daphne obviously cannot make a selection between the potential beneficiaries the court will enforce the trust on the footing of the maxim 'equality is equality' and will thus divide the property equally between the three children. See in this context *Burrough v Philcox* (1840). As Lord Cottenham pointed out in this case, where there appears to be a general intention to benefit a class, subject to a power of selection, and for some reason no selection is made, the court will carry out the testator's intention and divide the property equally between the possible beneficiaries.

The difficulty with a case like this is in deciding whether a power simpliciter or a trust-power is involved and this, as indicated above, is a matter of construction. Since a trust is imperative the settlor, if he did intend a trust, would not have contemplated that the trust might not be carried out so would not have provided for a gift-over in default of appointment. If he has made such a provision it follows that he must have been contemplating a power of appointment only. On the other hand, if there is no gift over in default of appointment, as in *Burrough* v *Philcox* supra, the disposition in question may or may not amount to a trust power; it still remains a matter of construction. In *Burrough* v *Philcox* the disposition was held to be a trust-power but in *Re Weekes' Settlement* (1897), where likewise there was no gift over, on the wording used the court was unable to spell out a trust-power, merely a power. So, on failure to exercise that power by the donee, the potential objects were entitled to nothing. See also *Re Combe* (1925).

But although, as stated above, the presence of a gift over will preclude a trust-power, this is not so if the gift over is a gift of residue. This was made clear in *Re Brierley* (1894), where it was pointed out that a gift over which precludes the finding of a trust-power must be in regard to specific property and not to residue. In the present problem, the power given to Daphne could be a trust power rather than simply a power of appointment. The test is whether the testator intended Daphne's children to benefit in any event or whether he intended them to benefit only if Daphne exercised the power in their favour. The distinction is notoriously difficult to draw, it will be necessary to consider the exact words used in the will.

2 THE THREE CERTAINTIES

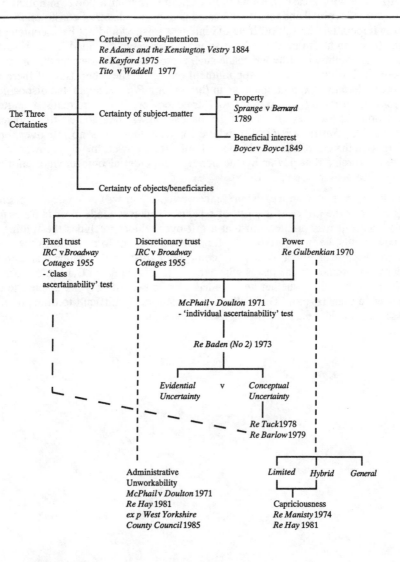

Certainty of words/intention
Re Adams and the Kensington Vestry 1884
Re Kayford 1975
Tito v *Waddell* 1977

The Three
Certainties

Certainty of subject-matter

Property
Sprange v *Bernard* 1789

Beneficial interest
Boyce v *Boyce* 1849

Certainty of objects/beneficiaries

Fixed trust
IRC v *Broadway Cottages* 1955
- 'class ascertainability' test

Discretionary trust
IRC v *Broadway Cottages* 1955

Power
Re Gulbenkian 1970

McPhail v *Doulton* 1971
- 'individual ascertainability' test

Re Baden (No 2) 1973

Evidential Uncertainty   v   *Conceptual Uncertainty*

Re Tuck 1978
Re Barlow 1979

Administrative
Unworkability
McPhail v *Doulton* 1971
Re Hay 1981
ex p West Yorkshire County Council 1985

Limited   *Hybrid*   *General*

Capriciousness
Re Manisty 1974
Re Hay 1981

2.1 Introduction

The three certainties is one of the most conceptually difficult areas of the law of trusts. Much of the difficulty stems from the problems involved in distinguishing between trusts and powers (see chapter 1). At first sight, the topic seems to be a jumble of different rules; once understood it will be seen that the topic is strictly structured with the various rules fitting neatly into place.

2.2 Key points

a) *Certainty of words/intention*

Language must be sufficiently mandatory to infer intention to impose a trust; precatory words will generally not be sufficient - *Re Adams and the Kensington Vestry* (1884) 27 Ch D 394. The test is whether there was an intention to impose a legally binding obligation as opposed to a morally binding one.

The words 'in trust for' are indicative but not conclusive of the existence of a trust - *Tito* v *Waddell* [1977] Ch 106. All circumstances are relevant: eg opening of separate bank account is a helpful indication of intention - *Re Kayford* [1975] 1 All ER 604.

b) *Certainty of subject-matter*

   i) Property - the property subject to the trust must be certain

   Sprange v *Barnard* (1789) 2 Bro CC 585

   - testatrix left £300 to her husband for his sole use and at his death the remaining part of what was left which he did not use to be divided between her brother and sister. It was held that this was an absolute gift to her husband and not a trust as no certainty as to what would be left on his death.

   Re Golay [1965] 1 WLR 1969

   - 'reasonable income' was sufficiently certain as the court could determine what is reasonable.

   ii) Beneficial interest - the size of the beneficial interests must be certain

   Boyce v *Boyce* (1849) 16 Sim 476

   - testator left several houses on trust for his wife for life and on her death to convey one to his daughter A as she might choose and the remaining houses to his daughter B. A died before making a choice. As a result the trust was void for uncertainty of B's beneficial interest.

   (There will be no such uncertainty if it is possible to apply the maxim 'equity is equality').

c) *Certainty of objects/beneficiaries*

i) Fixed trusts

The test is the 'class ascertainability' test in *IRC* v *Broadway Cottages Trust* [1955] Ch 20 - the whole range of objects must be ascertained or ascertainable in the light of the circumstances at the date the instrument came into force. It must be possible to draw up a complete and exhaustive list of all beneficiaries.

ii) Powers

The test is the 'individual ascertainability' test in *Re Gulbenkian* [1970] AC 508 (affirming *Re Gestetner Settlement* [1953] Ch 672) - must be able to say with certainty whether any given individual is or is not a member of the class.

The class of beneficiaries can be as wide as the testator wishes except that it must not be 'capricious' - *Re Manisty* [1974] 1 Ch 17; *Re Hay* [1981] 3 All ER 786.

iii) Discretionary trusts

Until 1971, the test was the 'class ascertainability' test as for fixed trusts. However, in *McPhail* v *Doulton* [1971] AC 424, it was held that the test was the same as that for powers - the 'individual ascertainability' test.

In *Re Baden's Deed Trusts (No 2)* [1973] Ch 9 a distinction was drawn between 'evidential' and 'conceptual' uncertainty. See also *Re Tuck's ST* [1978] Ch 49; *Re Barlow's WT* [1979] 1 All ER 296.

Even if a discretionary trust passes the 'individual ascertainability' test, it will nevertheless be void if it is 'administratively unworkable' - *McPhail* v *Doulton* (1971); *R* v *District Auditor, ex parte West Yorkshire Metropolitan County Council* (1985) 26 RVR 24.

2.3 Analysis of questions

The main way in which an examiner will test understanding of the three certainties is as part of a problem question - either as a sub-question or as an aspect which requires consideration in a problem primarily on another topic. Areas which are commonly combined with the three certainties in this way are secret trusts (chapter 8); charitable trusts (chapter 6); and trusts of imperfect obligation (chapter 5). See chapter 22 for an example of a typical such 'combination' question.

2.4 Questions

Problem checklist

a) Is there certainty of words/intention?

If not, donee takes absolutely.

b) Is there certainty of subject-matter?

    i) property?

    If not, the trust fails.

    ii) beneficial interests?

    If not:

- If possible to apply maxim 'equity is equality', the court will do so and divide the property equally between beneficiaries.

- If not possible, resulting trust for donor's estate.

c) Is there certainty of objects/beneficiaries?

Is the provision a fixed trust, discretionary trust or power?

    i) fixed trust?

    Does it satisfy 'class ascertainability' test?

    ii) discretionary trust?

    Does it satisfy 'individual ascertainability' test? Can one say with certainty of any given individual whether he is or is not within the class?

    (NB. Distinction between evidential and conceptual uncertainty).

    iii) power?

    Does it satisfy 'individual ascertainability' test?

    If so, if it is a special power - is it 'capricious'?

If objects are not certain within (i), (ii) or (iii), there will be a resulting test for the donor's estate.

Question 1

Tom has recently died. Consider the validity of each of the following bequests contained in his will:

i) £10,000 to my brother Ian knowing that he will look after and provide for mother;

ii) The contents of my wine cellar to Bert for his own personal consumption only and whatever is left at his death to go to my nephew Fred;

iii) £10,000 to my sister Kate on trust to distribute the money amongst my friends and relations as she shall think most appropriate.

iv) £20,000 to my trustees on discretionary trust to apply the income for the benefit of such persons in England (excluding my wife and children) as my trustees shall, in their absolute discretion, determine.

Would your answer differ in (iii) if the bequest had been 'to be divided by her in equal shares between my friends and relations'?

Question prepared by author

Skeleton solution and comment

This problem, although not a past examination question, helpfully incorporates almost every aspect of the three certainties which is likely to be examined. In an examination the student should be prepared to tackle any of the points included in this question.

• This gift raises a problem of certainty of words/intention.

• Certainty of subject-matter - the property comprised in the trust - is in issue here.

• This is a discretionary trust and the point which requires consideration is whether the objects/beneficiaries are sufficiently certain. The variation suggested at the end of the question changes the trust into a fixed trust and thus the test for certainty of objects will be different.

• This is also a discretionary trust and the issue is also certainty of objects. More specifically, however, the gift raises the question of administrative unworkability.

Suggested solution

i) What needs to be decided here is whether this provision creates an absolute gift in Sam's favour or whether in fact it creates an express trust for the benefit of the testator's mother of which Sam is simply a trustee. The answer will depend on whether the words 'knowing that ...' onwards show sufficient certainty of intention. If the language is thought to be sufficiently mandatory to infer an intention on the testator's part to impose a trust, then a trust will be imposed on Sam - *Re Adams and the Kensington Vestry* (1884). If it is not, then a trust will only be imposed if other evidence shows that this was Tom's intention. If *Re Steele's WT* (1948) is followed then this intention will be inferred if Tom has used words which have previously been held to be sufficiently certain. In view of the fact that similar phrases such as 'in full confidence that' have been held not to impose a trust, it is unlikely that 'knowing that ...' will be sufficiently certain. As a result the provision will be construed as an absolute gift to Ian and he will be under no obligation - other than a moral one, to use the money for their mother.

ii) The question here is whether the words 'and whatever is left ...' onwards create a trust in favour of Fred. The issue is whether the property to be comprised in such a trust is sufficiently certain. If it is not then no valid trust will have been created and Bert will take the whole amount of wine absolutely. The facts are very similar to those in the early case of *Sprange* v *Barnard* (1789) in which a testatrix left money to her husband for his sole use and at his death the remaining part of what was left which he did not use to be divided between her brother and sister. It was held that the subject-matter of the trust was uncertain and thus the trust failed. By analogy to that case the purported trust here will be void and Bert will take all of the wine absolutely.

iii) With regard to this gift, clearly the intention and the subject-matter are certain. The potential problem is whether the objects of the trust - the beneficiaries - are certain. The provision attempts to create a discretionary trust and thus, following

McPhail v *Doulton* (1971) the test used to determine whether the objects are certain is that laid down for powers in *Re Gulbenkian* (1970). The test is known as the 'individual ascertainability' test, that is to say whether it can be said with certainty if a given individual is or is not a member of the class in question. In applying this test, the court in *Re Baden's Deed Trusts* (1973) drew a distinction between 'evidential' and 'conceptual' uncertainty. A class of objects will fail the individual ascertainability test if it is conceptually uncertain. It has been held that the term 'relations' is conceptually certain and the court has defined the term. The word 'friend', though, appears to give rise to conceptual uncertainty - what one person means by the word may be wholly different from what another means and it would be impossible for the court to attempt to offer an all-encompassing definition of the term. However, it is possible that the court would take a different view in the light of *Re Barlow's WT* (1979) where the word 'friend' was held to be sufficiently certain in relation to a power. However in the case, there was held to be no obligation on the executors to survey the range of objects. Kate should be able to make a sensible survey of the whole range of objects before making a distribution. It is difficult to see how she can do this if the class of objects is conceptually uncertain. It seems likely that in practice the term would in fact not be conceptually certain. The objects are uncertain and there will be a resulting trust to Tom's estate.

If the bequest had been 'to be divided by her in equal shares between my friends and relations', the trust would be fixed rather than discretionary. The result of this is that a different test for certainty of objects must be applied - that in *IRC* v *Broadway Cottages Trust* (1955). This is the 'class ascertainability' test; the whole range of objects must be ascertained or ascertainable. Unless circumstances suggest otherwise, it is very unlikely that all of Tom's friends could be ascertained even if his relations could. The resulting uncertainty of objects would mean that the trust is void and again there is a resulting trust to Tom's estate.

iv) This is also a discretionary trust and the issue is once again certainty of objects. Applying the *Re Gulbenkian* test, it would seem that the class of objects will pass the individual ascertainability test, being conceptually certain. However, the courts have made it clear that even if this is the case, a trust may nevertheless fail if it is 'administratively unworkable'. This concept was introduced in *McPhail* v *Doulton* (1971) and reiterated in *Re Hay* (1981) in which Megarry VC suggested that if the trust had not been void anyway, it would have been void as administratively unworkable if it is so wide that it forms nothing like a class. The concept was applied in *R* v *District Auditor, ex parte West Yorkshire Metropolitan County Council* (1985) and would clearly apply to the trust here so as to render it void for uncertainty. The trustees will hold the money on resulting trust for the estate.

Question 2

Distinguish between a trust and a power and consider the place of the discretionary trust in the context.

University of London LLB Examination
(for External Students) Law of Trusts June 1988 Q1(a)

Skeleton solution and comment

This question requires consideration of both the basic distinctions between trusts and powers outlined in chapter 1, and of the three certainties as since *McPhail* v *Doulton* (1971) the tests for discretionary trusts and powers have become the same and this suggests that the gaps between the two concepts has narrowed.

The length and depth of the answer presupposes that the question is a whole one rather than half of a mixed question. As half of a mixed question it would have to be shortened accordingly.

• Introduction - the traditional approach.

• The classifications of trusts and powers.

• Comments on and criticisms of the courts' and commentators' classifications.

• The effect of the decision in *McPhail* v *Doulton* (1971) on the distinction.

• The distinction between the duties imposed by trusts and by powers.

• Conclusion.

Suggested solution

The traditional approach to the distinction between trusts and powers is that a trust is imperative, a power discretionary. Whether or not this remains true, this approach is too simplistic to be of any real use. There is not a single trust concept or a single type of power; many variations of each exist.

Two main classifications of an express private trust exist - a fixed trust and a discretionary trust. Powers divide themselves in two ways. Firstly, a power may be general (the donee can appoint in anyone's favour, including his own), hybrid (the donee can appoint in anyone's favour except for named persons) and special (possible appointments are limited to a specific class of persons). Secondly, the donee of the power maybe a trustee ex officio or a mere individual (a mere power). Whilst, strictly speaking, it is true that all types of powers are voluntary - no appointment need be made - whereas both types of trust are imperative - a distribution must be made or the court will interfere - it is doubtful whether any other practical distinction remains between the two middle concepts - the discretionary trust and the special power with a trustee ex officio. Indeed, in view of the practical elimination of the distinction by the courts, it is debatable whether this arbitrary distinction should in fact remain.

The problem of distinguishing between trusts and powers and of the place of discretionary trusts in the context is not helped by further classifications put forward by the courts and by commentators. Two terms, in particular, which are used are 'trust powers' and 'powers with trusts in default of appointment'. The former term is used by the courts to mean the same thing as a discretionary trust and it is submitted that the two terms refer to the same concept - the trustee has a discretion as to how distribution is to be made but a duty to distribute in that if he does not do so, the court will step in and enforce the trust. P H Pettit in *Equity and The Law of Trusts* (1989) distinguishes between a 'trust power' and a 'power with a trust in default of appointment' and similarly concludes that a 'trust power' is simply different terminology for a discretionary trust. He also concludes, however, that a 'power with a trust in default of appointment' is a different species of power which has elements of a trust. It is respectfully submitted that this further classification not only creates more unnecessary confusion but is also, in practice, illusory. As will be seen, the only remaining distinction between a special power with a trustee ex officio and a discretionary trust is that a trustee under a discretionary trust is under a duty to distribute in that if he does not do so, the court will do so. A power with a trust in default of appointment has, in fact, the same result. The donee has a discretion regarding appointment. However, if he does not appoint the court will step in and do so. Thus, it is submitted, the middle distinction is between discretionary trusts and powers with a trustee ex officio; there is nothing in between.

The similarity between these two concepts stems from the decision in *McPhail* v *Doulton* (1971). Prior to this case the test for the certainty of objects was the same for both fixed and discretionary trusts and was that laid down in *IRC* v *Broadway Cottages Trust* (1955) - that due to the imperative nature of a trust, it must be possible to ascertain all the potential beneficiaries. A different test existed for powers - the *Re Gestetner Settlement* (1953) test affirmed in *Re Gulbenkian* (1970) that it is only necessary to be able to say with certainty whether any given individual is or is not a member of the class. The test was wider because powers were not considered to be imperative. In *McPhail* v *Doulton* (1971), however, the court decided that discretionary trusts were, in fact, very similar in nature to powers and thus, that the same test for certainty of objects should apply to both. It, therefore, held accordingly - the test to be the existing test for powers in *Re Gulbenkian* (1970). Thus, in the sphere of the three certainties, no important distinction exists between discretionary trusts and powers, although a distinction remains between fixed trusts and powers. A discretionary trust may fail even though it has certainty of objects if there is administrative unworkability - *R* v *District Auditor, ex parte West Yorkshire Metropolitan County Council* (1985) - but it has been said that a power will never fail merely because it is very wide - *Re Manisty's ST* (1974).

The only area, therefore, in which a distinction between trusts and powers can exist is that of the trustee's duties under a discretionary trust and those of a donee under a power, and the related question of what will happen if no appointment or distribution is made. The position was considered in *McPhail* v *Doulton* (1971) and *Re Hay* (1981). It is clear from *McPhail* v *Doulton* (1971) that a trustee under a discretionary trust is under an obligation to distribute the trust property and to act responsibly in doing so - he must survey the range of objects and consider carefully how to exercise his discretion before doing so. If he does not distribute, the court will enforce the trust and compel him to do so. *Re Hay* (1981) considers the position of the donee of a power. If the donee is a mere individual, he is under no duties whatsoever except that he must not act beyond the authority conferred by the power. If, however, he is a trustee ex officio then he must act as a fiduciary in that he must survey the range of beneficiaries periodically and consider whether to exercise the power. If he does not exercise it, the court will not interfere. Thus, in effect, the only distinction between a discretionary trust and a special power with a trustee ex officio is that only in the former case will the court step in in the event of the trustee not distributing. The discretion is blurred by the fact that the trustee of a discretionary trust may well have a power not to make a distribution at all. If he fails to distribute in exercise of this power the court will not interfere unless he exercises the power improperly.

In conclusion it can be seen that the distinction between trusts and powers is not as simple as the traditional imperative - discretionary approach. Whilst there is a vast difference between a fixed trust and a mere power, the difference becomes much less pronounced when comparing a discretionary trust and a power and in particular when considering the former and a power with a trustee ex officio - the only distinction is to be found in the effect of no appointment or distribution.

Question 3

Advise whether a valid and enforceable trust has been created by Grimstone in each of the following circumstances:

a) He conveyed his seaside villa, Sandcastles, to his brother, Sam, absolutely. Immediately prior to doing so, he orally informed Sam that he wished Sam to hold Sandcastles upon trust for his (Grimstone's) secretary, Fiona, absolutely.

b) He transferred shares in a public company worth £50,000 to his sister, Sarah, and at the same time orally informed Sarah that he was confident that she would use the income from the shares for the education and benefit of Sarah's daughter, Sally.

c) He sent a cheque for £20,000 to his son and daughter-in-law, Stephen and Stella, payable to them. Prior to doing so, he had orally informed Stephen, but not Stella, that he intended to give them £20,000 to be distributed by them amongst such charities as they should think fit. Stephen informed Stella of this two weeks after the cheque had been paid into their joint account.

d) He handed £10,000 to his nephew, Stanley, for the express purpose of enabling Stanley to pay his children's school fees at Greyfriars School. Before the fees were paid, Stanley was adjudicated a bankrupt with debts of £100,000. The £10,000 given to him by Grimstone is Stanley's only asset.

University of London LLB Examination
(for External Students) Law of Trust June 1990 Q 2

Skeleton solution and comment

This question has been included here since it is very largely concerned with certainty of intention, although it does contain a minor issue on formalities and an analogy can be drawn with secret trusts.

a) • Formality - land s53(1)(b).

• Equally will not allow a statute to be used as an instrument of fraud.

• Certainty of intention - trust or moral obligation?

b) • Certainty of intention.

• Disposition of capital if trust in favour of Sally?

c) • Certainty of intention.

• Gift or resulting trust.

• Compare secret trust for rules on communication.

d) • Certainty of intention.

• Gift for a particular purpose only.

Suggested solution

a) The first point to note regarding this transaction is that for an *express* trust *inter vivos* concerning any interest in land, s53(1)(b) of the Law of Property Act 1925 requires that a declaration of trust concerning land (including leaseholds) must be manifested and proved by some writing signed by a person who is able to declare such trust.

Section 53(1)(b) does not require the declaration of trust actually to be in writing, merely to be evidenced in writing. Thus, for example, the necessary written evidence might be found in correspondence, see *Forster* v *Hale* (1798), or in a telegram, see *McBlain* v *Cross* (1871). On the facts made available here, however, it does not appear that anything more than an oral declaration of trust has been made - which would not satisfy s53(1)(b).

However, there is an extremely important maxim of equity that equity will not allow a statute to be an engine of fraud. Thus, if it could be shown that Grimstone conveyed Sandcastles to Sam on the clear understanding that Sam should hold the property for the benefit of Fiona and Sam received it on that footing, the court would probably be prepared to impose a trust (ie a constructive trust) to this effect. Cases in which the court has been prepared to enforce a trust in respect of land despite the lack of written evidence include *Davies* v *Otty (No 2)* (1865); *Rochefoucauld* v *Bousted* (1897) and *Bannister* v *Bannister* (1948). See also, in this context, *Binions* v *Evans* (1972) and *Re Sharpe* (1980).

The above cited cases show clearly that the court will, despite non-compliancy with s53(1)(b), impose a trust when justice demands this. Relating this to the present problem, the court would have to be satisfied that Sam had led Grimstone to believe (possibly even by his silence) that he, Sam, would hold the property on trust as requested.

But even if the obstacle presented by s53(1)(b) can be overcome, it does appear that the words Grimstone has used are 'precatory words' (ie 'wish') and, if this is the correct construction, would be insufficiently certain for the imposition of a trust.

This point is discussed in more detail in part (b), infra, but it is appropriate to state at this point that in *Re Hamilton* (1895) the word 'wish' was held not to be sufficiently imperative for the imposition of a trust. On this footing, Sam would take beneficially. However each case must be judged in its own context. Although the word wish may sound vague, Grimstone did apparently say that Sam was to hold the property 'upon trust' for Fiona and the use of the word trust does sound more definite. Given that Sam would owe no moral obligation to Fiona, it seems more likely that Grimstone intended to impose a legally binding obligation on Sam.

b) In this case the property involved is not land or any interest therein so the question of compliance with s53(1)(b) does not arise in declaring an inter vivos trust, although, obviously, evidence of the oral delcaration of trust would be required. The main problem here, however, is that 'precatory words' appear to have been used in attempting to create a trust.

It is axiomatic that express trusts must comply with the 'three certainties' set out by Lord Langdale MR in *Knight* v *Knight* (1840), viz certainly of words, certainty of subject matter, certainty of objects. Whereas the latter two certainties appear to be present in regard to this gift, it is quite likely that Grimstone's statement that he was 'confident' that Sarah would use the income for Sally's education would not be regarded as sufficiently imperative to create a trust in favour of Sally.

However, what is important is the donor's intention to create a trust and the court must be convinced of this intention from the words used and the context of their use. Usually, words such as 'in full confidence', 'feeling confident', 'desire', 'wish', 'request' will be judged to be too imprecise to create a trust: see eg *Re Adams and the Kensington Vestry* (1884); *Mussoorie Bank* v *Raynor* (1882); *Re Diggles* (1888); *Re Hamilton* (1895); *Re Johnson* (1939).

On the other hand, taking the instrument as a whole (or where, as here, there is no instrument, considering all the relevant surrounding circumstances), sometimes an intention to create a trust can be discerned by the court from what, prima facie, are precatory words. See in particular the conclusion of the House of Lords in *Comiskey* v *Bowring-Hanbury* (1905).

In the present question the words used would probably be regarded as too uncertain to create a trust, in which case Sarah, though under a moral obligation to use the income for Sally's education and benefit, would be under no legal obligation. It could be argued that Grimstone would have felt it unnecessary to impose a legal obligation on Sarah and would have been content to rely on a moral obligation. If there is a trust, it seems that Sally is entitled only to the income and that there would be a resulting trust of the capital in favour of Grimstone.

c) It is submitted that this problem can be solved by following, by analogy, the principle in *Re Stead* (1900), although this case was concerned with secret trusts arising out of wills and not inter vivos trusts.

In *Re Stead*, Farwell J showed that a promise made by one of several prospective joint tenants before a will is made that the relevant property would, when received, be held for the benefit of another party, would be binding on the other joint tenants (the position differs with regard to tenants in common). In this case, Stephen and Stella, being joint payees of the sum of £20,000 and having paid the cheque into their joint account, appear to be joint tenants in regard to the £20,000 received. It appears that Stephen has, at least by implication, agreed to hold the money received on discretionary trusts for charity. Since this is personal property no problem under s53(1)(b) arises. Certainly, therefore, Stephen's share will be bound, and, if the principle in *Re Stead* is extended, so will Stella's. Even if this principle is not extended to this situation it would appear that Stella (assuming she is unwilling to use the fund as Grimstone requires) will hold her share on a resulting trust for Grimstone if, as seems at least possible, an intention on the part of Grimstone could be deduced that if the fund were not used for the purpose he had specified it should be returned to him.

d) Since the sum of £10,000 was given by Grimstone to Stanley expressly to pay Stanley's children's school fees, and since it appears that Stanley acquiesced in receiving the money for this purpose, he would receive it as trustee on the terms indicated. No question of compliance with s53(1)(b) would arise and, of course, there would be no need for the word 'trust' to appear in connection with the transaction.

This fund would, therefore, on receipt, be the subject of a trust in favour of Stanley's children. Compare the positions in *Re Kayford* (1975), in which money paid to a company in advance by customers and held by the company in a separate bank account, was held on trust for individual customers, and so free from the claims of the company's general creditors. Although in this problem there is no indication that Stanley has placed the fund in a separate account, the express instructions received by Stanley from the donor, presumably agreed to by Stanley (see supra), would in any event be likely to create a trust. Assuming then a trust has arisen, where a trustee is adjudicated bankrupt it is clear that any funds or other property which he holds on trust cannot be claimed by his trustee in bankruptcy: see s283(3)(a) of the Insolvency Act 1986, formerly s38(1) of the Bankruptcy Act 1914.

3 FORMAL REQUIREMENTS

3.1   Introduction

3.2   Key points

3.3   Analysis of questions

3.4   Question

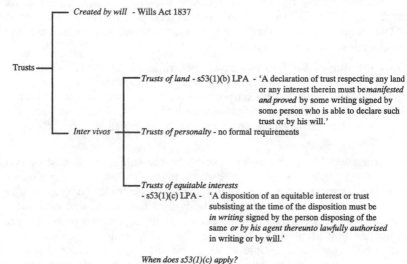

Created by will - Wills Act 1837

Trusts

Inter vivos

Trusts of land - s53(1)(b) LPA - 'A declaration of trust respecting any land or any interest therein must be *manifested and proved* by some writing signed by some person who is able to declare such trust or by his will.'

Trusts of personalty - no formal requirements

Trusts of equitable interests
- s53(1)(c) LPA - 'A disposition of an equitable interest or trust subsisting at the time of the disposition must be *in writing* signed by the person disposing of the same *or by his agent thereunto lawfully authorised* in writing or by will.'

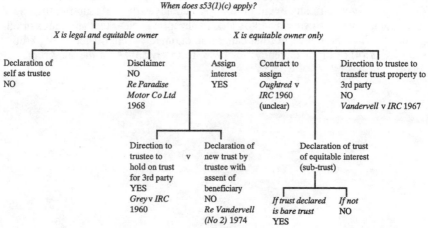

When does s53(1)(c) apply?

X is legal and equitable owner

X is equitable owner only

Declaration of self as trustee
NO

Disclaimer
NO
Re Paradise Motor Co Ltd 1968

Assign interest
YES

Contract to assign
Oughtred v *IRC* 1960 (unclear)

Direction to trustee to transfer trust property to 3rd party
NO
Vandervell v *IRC* 1967

Direction to trustee to hold on trust for 3rd party
YES
Grey v *IRC* 1960

v

Declaration of new trust by trustee with assent of beneficiary
NO
Re Vandervell (No 2) 1974

Declaration of trust of equitable interest (sub-trust)

If trust declared is bare trust
YES

If not
NO

20

3.1   Introduction

The words 'formal requirements' and in particular the phrase 's53(1)(c)' commonly provide subject-matter for students' nightmares. In fact, it is this fear which often creates the obstacle in understanding this topic. Rather like learning to ride a bicycle, s53(1)(c) requires a lot of time and (mental) energy to master, but once done it will appear to be simplicity itself and will never be forgotten.

3.2   Key points

Law of Property Act 1925 (LPA) s53(1)(b) and s53(1)(c) apply only to express trusts (ie not constructive, implied or resulting trusts - s53(2)) created inter vivos. The formal requirements for trusts created by will are governed by Wills Act 1837.

a) *Trusts of land*

Section 53(1)(b) applies:

  i)   There must be written evidence of the trust (the trust itself need not be in writing) at the time of or subsequent to the trust being declared; and

  ii) The writing must be signed by the settlor.

b) *Trusts of personalty*

No formal requirements are necessary provided there is clear intention to create a trust.

c) *Trusts of equitable interests*

Section 53(1)(c) provides that a 'disposition' of an equitable interest must be in writing and signed by the person disposing or by his authorised agent. Thus, if a transaction concerning an equitable interest constitutes a 'disposition' the requirements under s53(1)(c) must be satisfied.

If X is both the legal and the equitable owner:

  i)   If he declares himself trustee of or assigns the equitable interest, there is no 'disposition' but instead the creation of an equitable interest.

  ii) If he disclaims the property, there is no disposition within s53(1)(c) - *Re Paradise Motor Co Ltd* [1968] 2 All ER 625.

If X is the equitable owner only:

  i)   If he assigns the interest to a third party, clearly there is a 'disposition' and so s53(1)(c) applies.

  ii) If he directs the trustee (legal owner) to hold the equitable interest on trust for a third party, there is a 'disposition' within s53(1)(c) - *Grey v IRC* [1960] AC 1.

     NB: However, following *Re Vandervell's Trusts (No2)* [1974] Ch 269, if the trustee declares a new trust with the assent of the beneficiary, there is no such 'disposition'.

iii) If he contracts to assign his equitable interest to a third party, it is unclear whether the requirements under s53(1)(c) must be satisfied.

See *Oughtred* v *IRC* [1960] AC 206 and *Re Holt's Settlement* [1969] 1 Ch 100.

iv) If he declares a trust of the equitable interest (a sub-trust):

- if the trust declared is a bare trust and the trustee (X) has no active duties to perform, the result is that the equitable interest is, in effect, transferred by X to the third party and so s53(1)(c) applies.

- if X has some active duties to perform, there is no 'disposition' of the equitable interest but rather the creation of a 'sub-equitable interest' and so s53(1)(c) does not apply.

- if he directs the trustee (legal owner) to transfer the trust property to a third party (ie to transfer the legal estate), s53(1)(c) does not apply - *Vandervell* v *IRC* [1967] 2 AC 291.

3.3 Analysis of questions

The topic often appears in examination papers as an aspect of, rather than a whole, problem question. It is commonly combined with a question on resulting trusts (chapter 10) or completely and incompletely constituted trusts (chapter 4). Section 53(1)(c) is, however, a complicated area and so a whole problem question or an essay question is always a possibility. Either will demand a good understanding of all the relevant and difficult cases. For an example of a 'combination' question see chapter 21.

3.4 Question

On 1st January 1985, Peter transferred, with the appropriate formalities, Greenacre to Gerald, £200,000 to Herbert, and 20,000 shares in X Ltd to Ian.

None of the transferees gave any consideration and no words of gift were used by Peter. On 2nd February, Peter declared himself a trustee of his interest in Greenacre for Amy for life, remainder to Brian. On 3rd March, Peter telephoned Herbert and directed him to hold the £200,000 on trust for Amy for life, remainder to Brian. On 4th April Peter met Ian and directed him to transfer the shares to Mark beneficially. On 5th May, Peter told Nick, who owed him £30,000, not to repay the £30,000 but to hold it on trust for Amy. Nick agreed to do this.

Peter has recently died leaving all his property to the Feline and Canine Homes, a registered charity.

Amy and Brian seek your advice as to whether any of the trusts set up in their favour are valid and enforceable. Mark seeks your advice as to his rights to the 20,000 shares in X Ltd. Advise Amy, Brian and Mark.

University of London LLB Examination
(for External Students) Law of Trusts June 1985 Q1

Skeleton solution and comment

This question concerns several transactions and it must be decided whether each was valid - in other words was the transaction a 'disposition' under s53(1)(c) and, if so, was s53(1)(c) complied with? A good answer should deal with each transaction separately, otherwise confusion will result.

- The transfer of Greenacre, £200,000 and shares. Do the transferees hold on resulting trust for Peter?

- Declaration by Peter concerning Greenacre - is it a 'disposition' within s53(1)(c)? *Grey* v *IRC* (1958).

- Direction to Herbert regarding £200,000. Section 53(1)(c) applies and must be satisfied - *Grey* v *IRC* (1960).

- Direction to Ian regarding shares - effect of *Vandervell* v *IRC* (1967) is that s53(1)(c) does not apply.

- Direction to Nick - assignment of chose in action (see chapter 4).

- Conclusion.

Suggested solution

When Peter made transfers on 1st January 1985 of Greenacre to Gerald, £200,000 to Herbert and 20,000 shares in X Ltd to Ian, the appropriate legal formalities were complied with so the legal title in this property passed to Gerald, Herbert and Ian respectively. But, as none of the transferees gave any consideration and no words of gift were used by Peter, the position at that stage was that all the property transferred was probably held on resulting trusts for Peter. In *Dyer* v *Dyer* (1788) it was established that where property is purchased by A who directs that it be conveyed into the name of B, without any indication of the reason for such conveyance, a resulting trust arises. But this authority does not completely cover the present situation since it seems Peter was the owner of the property before he made the transfers rather than a purchaser. The case is one of transfer into the name of another. In the case of personalty it is now settled that a name transfer into the name of another will cause a resulting trust to arise: see *Re Vinogradoff* (1935). But, in the case of realty the position is far from clear. Under s60(3) LPA 1925 it is provided that a resulting trust shall not be implied in the case of a voluntary conveyance merely because 'the property is not expressed to be conveyed for the use or benefit of the grantee'. In *Hodgson* v *Marks* (1971) the Court of Appeal regarded it as 'debatable' whether a resulting trust arose where there was a voluntary conveyance to another in the light of s60(3). The textbooks are divided on the issue. Snell (28th Edition) takes the view that no resulting trust can arise whilst Underhill (12th Edition) takes the contrary view. It is submitted that a resulting trust does arise on a voluntary conveyance of land since any other result would be at odds with the purpose of the 1925 legislation to assimilate the law as to realty and personalty and, also, because s60(3) is concerned primarily with getting rid of pre-1925 conveyancing technicalities, rather than affecting the law on resulting trusts as such. Nevertheless, the position as to whether there is or is not a resulting trust affecting Greenacre here will be considered.

On 2nd February 1985 Peter declared himself to be a trustee of his interest in Greenacre for Amy for life, remainder to Brian. This declaration would suggest that Peter did not intend an outright disposition of Greenacre to Gerald. But, if the Court should come to a contrary conclusion, ie that Gerald was entitled to Greenacre absolutely, then Peter's declaration would be useless and no disposition would have flowed from it. But, if Gerald is regarded as holding Greenacre on a resulting trust for the benefit of Peter then the issue arises whether Peter's declaration had to satisfy any formal requirements in order to be effective. Peter was dealing with the equitable interest he possessed under the resulting trust so this is a case which falls to be considered under s53(1)(c) and not s53(1)(b) of the LPA 1925. Under s53(1)(c) a 'disposition' of an equitable interest must be in writing and signed, by the person disposing of the same or his agent. The central issue is whether Peter was making a 'disposition' within s53(1)(c) when he declared a trust of his interest in Greenacre. The position on this is unclear and turns upon whether Peter transferred his equitable interest on the creation of the subtrust for Amy and Brian. In *Grey* v *IRC* (1958) Upjohn J suggested at first instance, that a 'declaration of trust' was included in the term 'disposition' in s53(1)(c). But it has been suggested that this would only apply if the effect of the declaration of trust was such that the equitable owner became a mere bare trustee with no active duties to perform after the declaration. Here the equitable interest would pass to the beneficiary in whose favour the declaration of trust of the equitable interest had been made. But, if the equitable owner has active duties to perform under the trust which he declares of his equitable interest, the position is, arguably, different because there is no outright assignment of the equitable interest, but rather, the creation of a sub-trust. As Peter declared his trust for Amy for life remainder to Brian it is not clear from this alone that he had any duties to perform. Thus, the conclusion must be that if Peter made his declaration of trust in writing under s53(1)(c) the trust is effective in any event. But if his declaration of trust is not in accordance with s53(1)(c) then the declaration is only effective if it is one to which s53(1)(c) does not apply for the reasons stated above.

On 3rd March Peter telephoned Herbert and directed him to hold the £200,000 upon trust for Amy for life, remainder to Brian. This is a case of an equitable owner directing his trustee to hold the equitable interest upon trust for another and such a declaration must be in writing, in accordance with s53(1)(c), in order to be valid. See *Grey* v *IRC* (1960) where the House of Lords held that a direction by A to his trustees to hold his interest upon trust for B had to comply with s53(1)(c). As Peter told Herbert of his wishes over the telephone, s53(1)(c) was not satisfied and thus there was no effective trust of the £200,000 for Amy and Brian. The £200,000 is held upon resulting trusts for Peter's estate, now that he is dead, and will pass under the terms of his will to the Feline and Canine Homes.

On 4th April Peter told Ian to transfer the 20,000 shares in X Ltd to Mark beneficially. In this case s53(1)(c) does not have to be satisfied according to the House of Lords decision in *Vandervell* v *IRC* (1967). In that case it was pointed out that s53(1)(c) did not apply where there was a transfer by the legal owner which carried with it the equitable interest in the property because s53(1)(c) was intended to deal with cases where the equitable interest alone was being disposed of so as to avoid fraudulent transactions concerning the same.

On 5th May Peter told Nick who owed him £30,000 to hold this sum upon trust for Amy. This was a declaration of trust in respect of a chose in action - a legal chose in action and thus did not need to comply with the formalities of s53(1)(c). But, in order to make an assignment of a chose in action completely effective at law the provisions of s136 of the LPA 1925 ought to be satisfied, ie the assignment should be in writing and signed by the assignor, it should be absolute and written notice given to the debtor. The present assignment, it seems, was not in writing. Thus, it can only take effect in equity if at all. See *William Brandt's & Sons* v *Dunlop Rubber* (1905). As Amy has given no consideration for the assignment it is submitted that there is no effective transfer of the interest in the debt to her because she is a mere volunteer. See *Milroy* v *Lord* (1862). Thus, if Peter were to direct Nick to pay the debt to him instead of at some later date, there is nothing that Amy could do to stop this. In the Australian decision in *Olsson* v *Dyson* (1969) it was held that property assignable at law could not be regarded as effectively assigned in equity unless a court could regard the legal owner as bound by his obligation.

In conclusion the position is that there is probably a good declaration of trust of Greenacre for Amy and Brian, the £200,000 goes to the Feline and Canine Homes, the 20,000 shares go to Mark, and Amy has no effective right to the £30,000 debt in equity at present.

4 COMPLETELY AND INCOMPLETELY CONSTITUTED TRUSTS

4.1   Introduction

4.2   Key points

4.3   Analysis of questions

4.4   Questions

4.1   Introduction

Commonly considered to be another 'nightmare', this topic seems, at first sight, to be a maze of cases with no logical route to follow when trying to solve a problem. This is further confounded by the fact that many aspects of the law in this area are by no means settled and have been the subject of much discussion and dispute. The key to mastering the topic is to gain an overall view, to impose on this a structure (such as that contained in the flowchart: see opposite) and finally to insert the case law into the relevant parts. Without some sort of structured view of the subject, students will find it impossible to produce a good answer in an examination.

4.2   Key points

A settlor can create a trust in two ways:

a) *Declaration of self as trustee*

To do so, there must be more than a dramatic gesture; there must be a clear manifestation of the settlor's intention to create a trust - *Jones* v *Lock* (1865) 1 Ch App 25.

Intention may be shown by a combination of words and conduct and the court will look at all the circumstances - *Paul* v *Constance* [1977] 1 WLR 527.

The trust is created by the declaration and no transfer of property is necessary.

b) *By giving property to trustees upon a declaration of trust*

To create a trust in this way, the settlor must intend to do so and must 'do everything which, according to the nature of the property comprised in the settlement, was necessary to be done in order to transfer the property and render the settlement binding upon him' - *Milroy* v *Lord* (1862) 4 De GF & J 264 per Turner LJ.

4 COMPLETELY AND INCOMPLETELY CONSTITUTED TRUSTS

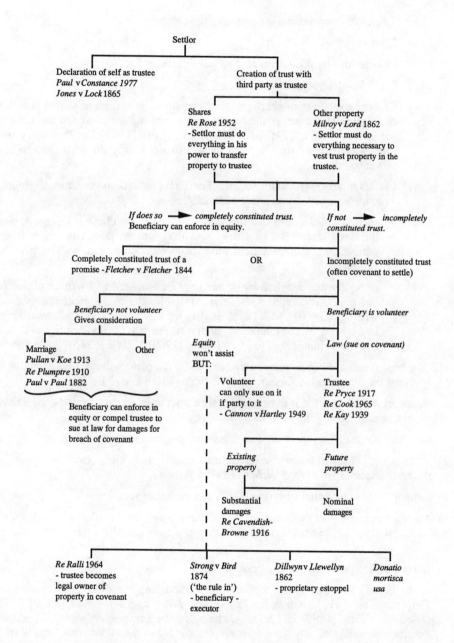

Settlor

Declaration of self as trustee
Paul v Constance 1977
Jones v Lock 1865

Creation of trust with
third party as trustee

Shares
Re Rose 1952
- Settlor must do
everything in his
power to transfer
property to trustee

Other property
Milroy v Lord 1862
- Settlor must do
everything necessary to
vest trust property in the
trustee.

If does so ➞ *completely constituted trust.*
Beneficiary can enforce in equity.

If not ➞ *incompletely
constituted trust.*

Completely constituted trust of a
promise - *Fletcher v Fletcher 1844*

OR

Incompletely constituted trust
(often covenant to settle)

Beneficiary not volunteer
Gives consideration

Beneficiary is volunteer

Marriage
Pullan v Koe 1913
Re Plumptre 1910
Paul v Paul 1882

Other

Equity
won't assist
BUT:

Law (sue on covenant)

Beneficiary can enforce in
equity or compel trustee to
sue at law for damages for
breach of covenant

Volunteer
can only sue on it
if party to it
- *Cannon v Hartley 1949*

Trustee
Re Pryce 1917
Re Cook 1965
Re Kay 1939

*Existing
property*

*Future
property*

Substantial
damages
*Re Cavendish-
Browne* 1916

Nominal
damages

Re Ralli 1964
- trustee becomes
legal owner of
property in covenant

*Strong v Bird
1874*
('the rule in')
- beneficiary -
executor

*Dillwyn v Llewellyn
1862*
- proprietary estoppel

*Donatio
mortisca
usa*

What is necessary depends on the nature of the property:

i) Land - by deed.

ii) Leaseholds - by deed if for at least three years.

iii) Chattels - delivery.

iv) Shares - execution of share transfer form and registration of shares in name of trustee. However, as the registration is outside the power of the settlor, the cases *Re Rose* [1952] Ch 499 and *Re Rose* [1949] Ch 78 qualify the rule in *Milroy* v *Lord* so that the settlor need only do what it is in his power to do.

v) Choses in action (including debts, beneficial interests and contractual rights) - can be assigned at law under s136 LPA or in equity.

• section 136 requires that the whole interest in the chose is assigned; that the assignment is in writing; and that written notice is given from whom the assignor would have been entitled to claim the chose in action.

• in equity, the whole interest need not be assigned and written notice is not necessary. If the chose is equitable, the assignment must be in writing to satisfy s53(1)(c). If it is legal, writing is not necessary but some form of consideration, is due to the maxim that 'equity will not assist a volunteer' - *Olsson* v *Dyson* (1969) 120 CLR 265.

NB If a trust is intended to be created by one mode, the court will not give effect to it by applying the other mode - *Richards* v *Delbridge* (1874) LR 18 Eq 11.

If the settlor has done all that is necessary, then a completely constituted trust exists which can be enforced by the beneficiary in equity.

If the settlor has not, then there are two possible interpretations of what exists:

a) Trust of the benefit of a promise (completely constituted), enforceable in equity by the beneficiary - *Fletcher* v *Fletcher* (1844) 4 Hare 67.

b) Incompletely constituted trust (generally, a covenant to settle).

Whether a beneficiary in this situation has a remedy against a settlor who refuses to settle the property on the trustees (and thereby completely constitute the trust) depends on various factors.

a) *In equity (the remedy of specific performance)*

If the beneficiary has given consideration (including marriage consideration - *Pullan* v *Koe* [1913] 1 Ch 9; *Re Plumptre's Marriage Settlement* [1910] 1 Ch 609; *Paul* v *Paul* (1882) 20 Ch D 742) he will have a remedy in equity. If he has not, then he will generally have no such remedy due to the maxim that 'equity will not assist a volunteer'. This is subject to a number of exceptions:

ii) The rule in *Strong* v *Bird* (1874) LR 18 Eq 315

The donor must intend to make an immediate lifetime gift to the donee which fails for lack of compliance with the appropriate formalities. If the donor continues to intend to make this gift until his death and the donee becomes the executor or administrator of the estate, the gift is perfected.

i) The rule in *Re Ralli's WT* [1964] Ch 288

The rule in *Strong* v *Bird* was extended to trustees. If the trust appears incompletely constituted but the trustee acquires title to the trust property, even if in a different capacity, the trust is constituted.

iii) Proprietary estoppel - *Dillwyn* v *Llewellyn* (1862) 4 De GF & J 517

There are many cases on this topic now and since each case turns on its own facts, it is difficult to generalise. If A makes a representation to B about B's existing of future legal rights and B acts to his detriment in reliance on that representation, an equity arises in favour of B. The court will not allow A to enforce his strict legal rights and devise an appropriate remedy for B.

iv) Donatio mortis causa

The donor, in contemplation of death, intends to make a gift which is conditional on his death and not fully effective until his death. He must transfer 'dominion' over the asset to the donee. He need not comply with the normal formalities for gifts. Thus if the necessary intent is present, a donatio of land may be made by handing over the deeds to the donee.

b) *At law (the remedy of damages for breach of covenant)*

If the beneficiary is party to the covenant, he can sue on the covenant for damages - *Cannon* v *Hartley* [1949] Ch 213. If he is not, then he cannot sue on it due to the contractual rules of privity. Any action on the covenant at common law must be brought within the 12 year limitation period.

The only other possibility, therefore, is for the trustee to sue the settlor on the covenant on the beneficiary's behalf. It is unsettled as to whether this is possible.

It is clear that the trustees will not be able to do so if the subject-matter of the covenant is future property as this is not recognised at law. If, however, the subject-matter is existing property one line of cases suggest that the trustees should not, at least, sue on the covenant - *Re Pryce* [1917] 1 Ch 234; *Re Kay's ST* [1939] Ch 329; *Re Cook's ST* [1965] Ch 902. The case of *Re Cavendish-Browne's ST* [1916] WN 341, on the other hand, suggests that trustees can obtain a remedy for the beneficiary in this way. Furthermore, this case shows that if the trustees do so, they can obtain substantial damages (ie the amount of the beneficiary's loss) and not simply nominal damages (the amount of their own loss). However, this case is poorly reported and its authority is now regarded as doubtful.

4.3 Analysis of questions

Both problem and essay questions are common as are a combination of the two. Due to the complexities of the case law, a structured approach is crucial for a good answer to either type of question. As the topic is very wide, it is particularly important to isolate the relevant issues in the question and to address them alone, rather than to launch into an 'all I know about ...' answer.

4.4 Questions

Problem checklist

a) Is the trust completely constituted?

  i)   Has the settlor effectively transferred property to trustees? *or*

  ii) Has the settlor declared himself trustee of the trust property?

  If so, beneficiary can enforce the trust in equity.

b) If not, has the beneficiary given consideration (marriage or otherwise)?

  If so, beneficiary can enforce the trust in equity.

c) If not, is the beneficiary party to the covenant to settle (if any)?

  If so, beneficiary can sue on the covenant for damages.

d) If not, can a trust of a promise to settle be inferred?

  If so, beneficiary can enforce in equity.

e) If not, can the trustee sue on the covenant on the beneficiary's behalf? (The cases are in dispute). If he can, can he recover substantial or only nominal damages?

f) If not, does the situation fall within one of the exceptions to rule that 'equity will not assist a volunteer'?

  i)   *Re Ralli* (1964) - trustee becomes legal owner of the proposed trust property by some other means.

  ii) The rule in *Strong* v *Bird* (1874) - the beneficiary becomes legal owner of the proposed trust property as executor under the settlor's will.

  iii) Proprietary estoppel.

  iv) Donatio mortis causa.

  If so, the trust can be enforced.

g) If trust cannot be enforced in any of the above ways, the settlor remains legal and beneficial owner of the proposed trust property and the beneficiary has no claim.

Question 1

In 1980 Raymond, a successful author, divorced his first wife and married Tania, his former secretary. In March 1984, on the occasion of the marriage of his eldest son

Alan, Raymond decided to set up trusts for the benefit of each of his three children of his first marriage, Alan, Betty and Charles.

First, Raymond executed a deed to which he and Edward were the only parties containing the following provisions:

'1) I hereby covenant with Edward that I will transfer to Edward within two months of the date hereof 20,000 shares in X Ltd.

2) I hereby direct Edward to hold the said shares upon trust for my younger son Charles.'

Raymond has owned 20,000 shares in X Ltd since January 1984.

Secondly, Raymond covenanted with Tim and Saul to transfer £30,000 to them to hold on trust for his daughter Betty.

Finally, he covenanted with Ian and Henry to transfer all royalties earned on the sale of his books in the United States to be held on trust for Alan and his wife with remainder to the children of the marriage.

In May of this year Raymond sat down at his desk to sign the cheque and share transfer in favour of the various trustees. He filled in the names and amounts payable but then had a heart attack and died without signing the cheque or the share transfer.

By his will, Raymond appointed Tim and Saul as his executors and left all his property to his wife, Tania.

Advise Alan, Betty and Charles.

University of London LLB Examination
(for External Students) Law of Trusts June 1984 Q4

Suggested solution

In this case the issues are concerned with whether each of the trusts is completely constituted or can be completely constituted now that the settlor, Raymond, has died.

The first settlement mentioned is that in favour of Charles. There Raymond covenanted to settle 20,000 shares in X Ltd on Edward for the benefit of Charles. The shares were never transferred to Edward and, in my view, it is not possible to have them transferred now. The proper method of transfer here is to have the share transfer forms executed and the shares registered in the name of the trustee. Raymond clearly intended to do this, but was prevented from signing the share transfer form by his untimely heart attack. Thus, no transfer of the shares took place. The fact that he clearly intended to make a transfer is not enough, there is no equity to perfect an imperfect gift. See *Richards* v *Delbridge* (1874); *Milroy* v *Lord* (1862). It would not be possible to apply the principle in *Re Rose* (1952), which permits the court to perfect an imperfect gift, where the settlor has done all in his power to vest the legal interest in the property in the trustee and something remains to be done by the trustee or a third person. In the present case Raymond had not signed the share transfer thus precluding the application of his principle.

The covenant with Edward was, in effect, to settle property in the future, ie in two

31

months' time. There can be no argument that Raymond assigned a chose in action to Edward in making the covenant, as in *Re Wale* (1956) because he already had the shares registered in his name at the time he made the covenant in March 1984 so the appropriate way to completely constitute the trust was to transfer the shares themselves. Edward might try to sue on the covenant for Charles' benefit but again this is likely to fail. The covenant is voluntary and a court of equity will not give specific performance of it because to do so would be giving by indirect means what the court would not give by direct means; ie enforcement of a covenant in favour of a volunteer. *Re Pryce* (1917). An action for damages for breach of the covenant would also be a waste of time as only nominal damages would be awarded to Edward and Charles could not bring such proceedings as he is not privy to the covenant. See *Re Pryce*.

The covenant made by Raymond with Tim and Saul to settle £30,000 on trust for Betty is also an imperfect gift as Raymond never signed the cheque. Again, there was a clear intention to transfer but the proper formalities had not been fulfilled, ie signing the cheque. See *Richards* v *Delbridge*. For the reasons mentioned above it would not be possible to apply *Re Rose* here either. Raymond had not done all he should to transfer the money to Tim and Saul. It would also be a waste of time to sue on the covenant for either specific performance or damages for the reasons given above. In fact, if the trustees applied to the court for directions on this matter they would be ordered not to sue. See *Re Pryce*; *Re Kay's ST* (1939). However, in Betty's case it might be possible to invoke the rules in *Strong* v *Bird* (1874) since Tim and Saul were appointed executors of Raymond's will. Whether the rule applies here will depend on whether the will was made before or after the covenant was executed and whether it can operate in this case of trustees as opposed to a person who takes the beneficial interest both at law and in equity. Since the trust is of £30,000 the fact that the covenant preceded or succeeded the will should not matter. This point is only of relevance where a specific item of property is the subject matter of the promise and after the promise is made it is dealt with by a will. In such circumstances a continuing intention to give, as required by the rule, would not exist. See *Re Freeland* (1952). There is some doubt if the rule applies to trustees but it was applied to trustees in *Re Ralli's WT* (1964). However, in the Australian case of *Re Halley* (1959), it was suggested that it might not apply in such circumstances. In my view *Re Ralli* would be preferred by the court and Tim and Saul should obtain the £30,000 for the benefit of Betty.

The covenant made by Raymond with Ian and Henry for the benefit of Alan, his wife and children, appears, in the circumstances, to be a marriage settlement. See *Re Densham* (1975). However, the matter may need closer inspection, for as *Re Densham* indicates, it is important that it was conditioned only to take effect on the marriage taking place and to encourage and facilitate the marriage. It is not enough that the creation of the settlement merely coincided with the marriage. If, as seems likely, this is a marriage settlement then all those within the marriage consideration will be able to enforce the transfer of property covenanted to be settled, this will include Alan, his wife and issue. See *Attorney-General* v *Jacobs Smith* (1895).

It may not be necessary to rely on the fact that the settlement is a marriage settlement to ensure that the royalties from Raymond's books pass to the trust. If the royalties are only payable in future then the covenant may be construed as an assignment of the right to receive them so that the trust is completely constituted of this chose in action. See *Re Wale* (1956). Any royalties received after the covenant was executed would therefore belong to the trust and if Raymond's executors hold any of these they must hand them over. But, if it is not possible to regard the covenant in this way, then the marriage consideration will have to be relied upon to enforce transfer of the royalties.

Question 2

'Equity will not assist a volunteer.' Consider the application of this maxim to:

i) completely constituted trusts;

ii) incompletely constituted trusts; and

iii) equitable assignments of legal choses in action.

University of London LLB Examination
(for External Students) Law of Trusts June 1986 Q3

Skeleton solution and comment

This is a common type of question. The potential scope is very wide so the student must present the relevant material concisely.

• Completely constituted trusts - this requires consideration of the cases which underline that once a trust is completely constituted it is enforceable by the beneficiary, notwithstanding that he is a volunteer.

• Incompletely constitued trusts - this requires the student to address the exceptions to the rule that 'equity will not assist a volunteer' as applied to incompletely constituted trusts - in particular - whether the trustee can sue on the covenant on behalf of the volunteer and the rules in *Re Ralli* (1964), *Strong* v *Bird* (1874) and *Dillwyn* v *Llewellyn* (1862).

• The requirements for the assignment of a legal chose in action both in law and equity must be stated as the effect of the maxim here is that if the assignment is only valid in equity a volunteer cannot enforce it - *Olsson* v *Dyson* (1969).

Suggested solution

The maxim 'equity will not assist a volunteer' refers to equity's refusal to give any help to a party who has not given any consideration for a promise to settle property on trust to enforce that promise. It has been expressed in other ways such as 'there is no equity to perfect an imperfect gift'. See *Milroy* v *Lord* (1862).

i) If a trust is completely constituted, that is, the property promised or covenanted to be settled has been conveyed to the trustees by the appropriate method laid down by law, then a volunteer may enforce it. See *Richards* v *Delbridge* (1874). Once the property has been properly conveyed the volunteer is no longer a volunteer vis-à-vis that property because he obtains an equitable interest in it from the moment it is settled. See *Jefferys* v *Jefferys* (1841). This is illustrated by the decision in *Paul* v *Paul* (1882) where a husband and wife asked the court to break up a marriage settlement and permit them to have the capital absolutely since there were no children of the marriage. However, there were ultimate remainders in favour of the next-of-kin of one spouse. As the next-of-kin had a settled interest in the property in the settlement they could not be deprived of it and it was irrelevant that they gave no consideration as the concept of volunteers was now inappropriate. See also *Re Bowden* (1936). However, a volunteer may not enforce the settlement of further property on the trust when some is already settled because equity will only protect the beneficial interest he has already acquired. See *Jeffreys* v *Jeffreys* (1841).

The volunteer can protect his beneficial interest by taking proceedings etc once it is properly settled, the full array of equitable remedies are available to him. See *Paul* v *Paul* (1882).

ii) The maxim 'equity will not assist a volunteer' has its greatest force when applied to cases where a trust is incompletely constituted. If a settlor refuses to honour a covenant to settle property then any party who has given consideration for the covenant may enforce it. Consideration here means both valuable consideration and marriage consideration. See *Pullan* v *Koe* (1913). In the case of marriage consideration the parties who may enforce the covenant include the parties to the marriage and their issue and the children of either party from a former marriage where their interests are inseparable from those of the marriage. See *Macdonald* v *Scott* (1893).

Parties who have not given consideration for the covenant are volunteers and generally cannot enforce it against the settlor. However, there seems to be one exception to this rule and several ways around it. The exception is in *Re Rose* (1952) where the Court held that it would order a conveyance of the legal title at the behest of a volunteer where the settlor had effectively divested himself of the equitable title by doing everything within his power to transfer the property. This exception is frequently met in the context of share transfers where the legal title can only pass when the company registers the volunteer/beneficiary as the new shareholder. The ways around the rule are (i) to sue for damages for breach of covenant, (ii) the application of the rule in *Strong* v *Bird* (1874), (iii) the application of *Re Ralli's WT* (1964) and (iv) under the rule in *Dillwyn* v *Llewellyn* (1862).

A claim for damages for breach of covenant is only maintainable if the covenant was to settle specific existing property. See *Re Cavendish-Browne's ST* (1916). If the covenant is to settle future property it cannot be enforced. See *Re Cook's ST* (1965). This is because future property is recognised only in equity and therefore any claim for enforcement of a covenant concerning such property can only be brought in equity. But if the property is existing property, then the claim in damages can be maintained at law thus avoiding any conflict with equitable rules. It might also be added that a claim by a volunteer for specific performance would also fail because it could only be brought in equity. See *Re Pryce* (1917). An application of the rule in *Strong* v *Bird* (1874) is only possible if a trustee/beneficiary is appointed executor or administrator of the settlor's estate. He may then transfer the promised property from himself qua executor to himself qua trustee/beneficiary. The rule also requires a continuing intention to give up until the settlor's death plus an intention to give presently. See *Re Freeland* (1952). Under *Re Ralli* (1964) a volunteer who acquires the property promised may retain it provided no one else can establish a better title to the property than him. The decision is often closely related to *Strong* v *Bird* (1874). Finally, under *Dillwyn* v *Llewellyn* (1862) a volunteer who has been encouraged to act to his detriment or incur expenditure on the basis of a mistaken belief that he had or would be given the property may acquire an equity in it which a court of equity will protect. See *Crabb* v *Arun District Council* (1976).

iii) A legal chose in action may be the subject matter of a trust. Provided it is assigned to the trustees in a manner recognised at law or in equity the trust may be completely constituted. In *Re Wale* (1956) a chose in action in the form of the right to have a testator's estate properly administered and to obtain a legacy thereunder was considered as assigned at law. But if an assignment of a legal chose in action is not effective at law because it does not satisfy the requirements of s136 of the Law of Property Act 1925, it may nevertheless take effect in equity provided that the assignment was made for valuable consideration. In the Australian High Court decision in *Olsson* v *Dyson* (1969) a husband told his wife to collect a debt he was owed by a friend for herself. The wife wrote to the friend notifying him of the matter and he paid interest on the debt to her thereafter. On the husband's death his executors claimed the debt against the wife and succeeded. This was because the debt had only been orally assigned to the wife and thus did not comply with s136. Thus the assignment was only effective in equity and as the wife was a volunteer she could not obtain the assistance of a court of equity for such assistance would contravene the maxim 'equity will not assist a volunteer'.

Question 3

In 1970, Margery, on the occasion of the marriage of her daughter, Diana, to Henry, executed a settlement under which she (Margery) covenanted with the trustees of the settlement to transfer certain shares worth £100,000 to the trustees upon trust as to one half part thereof for the benefit of Diana's existing two children (by another man), Thomas and Tina, and as to the other half part for the benefit of the future children of the marriage.

Margery died last year without having transferred the shares and leaving all her estate to her son, Charles. Diana and Henry have since divorced, there being two children of the marriage, Sidney and Sara, both of whom are of full age.

Advise Thomas and Tina and Sidney and Sara as to any claims they may have.

University of London LLB Examination
(for External Students) Law of Trusts June 1989 Q3(b)

Skeleton solution and comment

A typical question on this area of law which should not cause any difficulty.

- Incompletely constructed trust generally unenforceable - do any of the exceptions apply?
- Is it a marriage settlement - see *Re Densham*.
- If so, Sidney and Sara within the marriage consideration and can sue: *Pullan* v *Koe*.
- Thomas and Tina - doubtful as not children of the marriage.
- No action on the covenant for breach as outside 12 year limitation period.
- *Fletcher* v *Fletcher* - possible but decision not followed in more recent cases.

Suggested solution

As Margery failed to transfer the shares, which she covenanted with the trustees she would settle, the settlement is incompletely constituted and Thomas and Tina, Sidney and Sara, being volunteers, cannot seek equitable assistance to obtain a transfer of the shares. However, they may be able to avail themselves of the benefit of one of the exceptional cases where a mere volunteer can enforce an imperfect gift.

The first possible way of enforcing the transfer of the shares to the trust is by establishing that it is a marriage settlement. The mere fact that it was made on the occasion of the marriage of Diana in 1970 is not sufficient to make this a marriage settlement. It must also be shown that it was conditioned only to take effect on the marriage taking place and was made for the purpose of or with a view to encouraging or facilitating the marriage. See *Re Densham* (1975). If the settlement can be treated as a marriage settlement it can only be enforced by those who are regarded by equity as being within the marriage consideration. It is clearly established that children of the marriage can enforce such a settlement so that Sidney and Sara could claim half of the shares. See *Pullan* v *Koe* (1913). But, children of a previous marriage are not within marriage consideration unless it can be shown that their interests are so closely intermingled with those of the present marriage as to be inseparable. See *Attorney-General* v *Jacobs-Smith* (1895). The latter rule really only applies to infant children. It is not clear if Thomas and Tina could rely on this rule. If they can, they too can obtain the shares promised but, if not, they will have to seek another method of obtaining their shares. It is unlikely that the interests would be regarded as closely intermingled since each set of children is entitled to a separate half of the trust.

In the event that the settlement is not a marriage settlement or can only be enforced as such by Sidney and Sarah, an alternative method of completely constituting the trust, either wholly or partially, would be to seek damages at law against Margery's estate for breach of the covenant to settle. This action would be doomed to failure because it is statute barred under the Limitation Act 1980, the twelve year limitation period having expired as the covenant was made in 1970. The provisions of the Limitation Act 1980 do not affect the claim to enforce the covenant as a marriage settlement because the property was bound by the marriage settlement and impressed with a trust from the moment the covenant was made. See *Collyer* v *Isaacs* (1881).

The rule in *Fletcher* v *Fletcher* (1844) may provide another way of enforcing Margery's covenant to settle. The trustees of the settlement might seek to establish that the trust was already completely constituted of a chose in action, namely the promise to settle the shares, and that any action to recover the shares for the beneficiaries is one to enforce the rights which they already posses. The difficulty with this method of enforcement is that the courts have seemed rather reluctant to use it in more recent cases to enforce a covenant. See *Re Pryce* (1917). It is difficult to see in *Fletcher* v *Fletcher* itself that there was any intention to declare a trust of the promise and unclear if such a trust should be created by the settlor or by the trustee who has the benefit of the promise. However, the property is not future property so *Re Cook* (1965) does not cause a problem. This case held that there can be no trust of a promise to settle future property. It is suggested that the decision in *Fletcher* v *Fletcher* is unlikely to be followed today.

If the trustees of the settlement were also Margery's executors it might be possible to pursue a claim based on *Re Ralli's WT* (1964), but there is no suggestion in the question that this is so. In conclusion it seems that if the settlement was in consideration of marriage Sidney and Sara will be able to enforce the covenant as being within the marriage consideration, but Thomas and Tina appear to be outside the consideration. If the settlement is not in consideration of marriage, none of the beneficiaries is likely to be able to enforce the covenant as they are all volunteers.

5 TRUSTS OF IMPERFECT OBLIGATION (PURPOSE TRUSTS)

5.1   Introduction

5.2   Key points

5.3   Analysis of questions

5.4   Questions

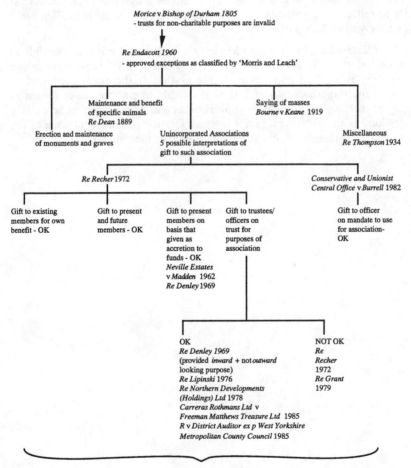

Morice v Bishop of Durham 1805
- trusts for non-charitable purposes are invalid

Re Endacott 1960
- approved exceptions as classified by 'Morris and Leach'

Maintenance and benefit
of specific animals
Re Dean 1889

Erection and maintenance
of monuments and graves

Saying of masses
Bourne v Keane 1919

Unincorporated Associations
5 possible interpretations of
gift to such association

Miscellaneous
Re Thompson 1934

Re Recher 1972

*Conservative and Unionist
Central Office v Burrell* 1982

Gift to existing
members for own
benefit - OK

Gift to present
and future
members - OK

Gift to present
members on
basis that
given as
accretion to
funds - OK
*Neville Estates
v Madden* 1962
Re Denley 1969

Gift to trustees/
officers on
trust for
purposes of
association

Gift to officer
on mandate to use
for association-
OK

OK
Re Denley 1969
(provided *inward* + not *outward*
looking purpose)
Re Lipinski 1976
*Re Northern Developments
(Holdings) Ltd 1978*
*Carreras Rothmans Ltd v
Freeman Matthews Treasure Ltd* 1985
*R v District Auditor ex p West Yorkshire
Metropolitan County Council 1985*

NOT OK
*Re
Recher
1972
Re Grant
1979*

Must be limited to the perpetuity period

5.1   Introduction

This topic divides itself into two parts - firstly, gifts to unincorporated associations and, secondly, the other exceptions to the rule against purpose trusts. The latter part is straightforward and requires knowledge of the case law involved and of the rule against perpetuities. The former part, however, is a controversial and complex area of the law. The student must formulate an opinion on the state of the law based on a thorough knowledge and understanding of the relevant authorities.

5.2   Key points

As a general rule, trusts for non-charitable purposes are void for want of ascertainable beneficiaries - *Morice* v *Bishop of Durham* (1805) 10 Ves 522.

Limited exceptions to this rule do exist, although they are anomalous and exceptional - *Re Astor's ST* [1952] Ch 534. In *Re Endacott* [1960] Ch 232, the classification of exceptions by Morris and Leach in *The Rule Against Perpetuities* was approved:

i) erection and maintenance of monuments and graves

ii) saying of masses

iii) maintenance and benefit of specific animals

iv) gifts to unincorporated associations

v) miscellaneous cases.

Even if a purpose trust falls within one of the exceptions, it must be limited to the perpetuity period. This is lives in being plus twenty-one years and is unaffected by the Perpetuities and Accumulations Act 1964 by s15(4) of the Act.

In addition, the trustees must be willing to carry out the trust.

a) *(i) - (iii) and (v)*

   i) Will be valid provided it is not wasteful and of benefit to no-one - *McCaig* v *University of Glasgow* 1907 SC 231. The monument or grave need not be erected on church ground - *Re Dean* (1889) 41 Ch D 552.

   ii) *Bourne* v *Keane* [1919] AC 815.

   iii) *Re Dean* (1889) 41 Ch D 552.

   v) *Re Thompson* [1934] Ch 342.

In some situations, trusts falling within these exceptions will also be charitable in which case they will be valid as such and it is unnecessary to consider whether they fall within the exceptions to the rule against purpose trusts (see chapter 6).

An invalid purpose trust will not be upheld as a valid power - *IRC* v *Broadway Cottages Trust* [1955] Ch 20.

In *Re Denley's Trust Deed* [1969] 1 Ch 373 it was held that a distinction should be drawn between abstract and impersonal purpose trusts which are void and trusts which though expressed as purpose trusts are directly or indirectly for the benefit of individuals. The latter are valid. However, in *Re Grant's WT* [1980] 1 WLR 360 it was said that these trusts are really not purpose trusts at all but discretionary trusts for individuals.

b) *Unincorporated associations (iv)*

For definition, see *Conservative and Unionist Central Office* v *Burrell* [1982] 2 All ER 1.

Re Recher's WT [1972] Ch 526 states four possible interpretations of a gift to an unincorporated association.

i) As a gift to existing members for their own benefit as joint tenants or tenants in common so that they could agree to divide it and so that any member can claim their share.

Such a gift is valid as an absolute gift (provided the rules do not disallow such a division). As a result, this is not a purpose trust as the members are ascertainable beneficiaries and there are no perpetuity problems.

ii) As a gift to present and future members.

This is prima facie valid and since the Perpetuities and Accumulation Act 1964, it will not fail for perpetuity. Instead, it will operate in favour of those members who are ascertained within the perpetuity period - s15(4) of the Act does not apply as this is not a purpose trust.

iii) As a gift to the existing members beneficially but on the basis that it is given as an accretion to funds and should be dealt with according to the rules of the association by which the members are contractually found inter se.

Such a gift is valid and the gifts in *Re Recher* (1972) and *Neville Estates* v *Madden* [1962] Ch 832 were construed in this way.

There is no perpetuity problem as the gift vests immediately.

iv) As a gift to the trustees or other proper officers of the association on trust to carry into effect the purposes of the association.

The gift will fail for lack of a beneficiary - see *Morice* v *Bishop of Durham* (1805) 10 Ves 522.

Conservative and Unionist Central Office v *Burrell* (1982), offers a fifth interpretation of a gift to an unincorporated association:

v) As a gift to an officer of the association on mandate to use it for the association.

This is not possible if the gift is by will.

5.3 Analysis of questions

Examination questions also tend to follow the discussion used in the introduction and in the key points, although a very general essay question on when purpose trusts will be valid is always a possibility. A variety of questions (both essays and problems) is possible on unincorporated associations, all of which will require, in particular, a full understanding of the '*Denley* v *Grant*' arguments. A common device by the examiner is to combine a question about gifts to such an association with one about its dissolution (implied and resulting trusts - chapter 10). An alternative question may require the student to consider a gift to an association which may or may not be a charity, thus demanding consideration of charitable trusts (chapter 6) too.

The other exceptions to the rule against purpose trusts are generally examined as part of a problem question by using a gift which might be valid either as a charitable trust or as one of these exceptions, or as an express private trust if the three certainties are satisfied (chapter 2). For examples of such combination questions see chapter 21.

5.4   Questions

Type 1: gift to unincorporated association

Problem checklist

a) Can the gift be construed as one of the '*Re Recher* (1972) categories' which does not present purpose trust problems - (i) to (iii) in key points? If so, trust is valid.

b) If not, is *Re Denley* (1969) correctly decided?

Is it a trust for the benefit of individuals?

c) Alternatively, could the trust be valid under the 'mandate theory' in *Conservative and Unionist Central Office* v *Burrell* (1982)?

Question 1

Tom died recently and his will contained the following bequest:

'£50,000 to the Trumpton Social Club to be used solely in the work of constructing the new bar and games room for the club and improving the facilities of the club house.'

The Trumpton Cricket Club is an unincorporated association whose rules freely allow the members to make resolutions and change the rules as they wish.

Advise the executors as to the validity of the bequest.

Question prepared by author, September 1989

Suggested solution

Whether a gift to an unincorporated association such as this is valid depends on the construction of the gift and on the interpretation of the case law in this area.

It is well settled that a gift to an unincorporated association will be valid as an express private trust if it can be construed in one of three of the four ways laid down in *Re Recher's WT* (1972): Firstly, as a gift to existing members for their own benefit as joint tenants or tenants in common secondly, as a gift to present and future members who are ascertained within the perpetuity period; thirdly, as a gift to the existing members beneficially but on the basis that it is given as an accretion to funds and thus should be dealt with according to the rules of the association by which the members are contractually bound inter se - the gifts in *Re Recher* (1972) and *Neville Estates* v *Madden* (1962) were valid by being construed in this way. The gift is clearly not intended to be for the members beneficially and thus, the only possible construction above is the third one. However, in view of the fact that the purpose has been stated, the gift is in fact unlikely to fall within this construction. Rather, it should be properly interpreted in the fourth way under *Re Recher* (1972).

The fourth classification by the court in *Re Recher* (1972) of a gift to an unincorporated association is to the officers of the association on trust for the purposes of the association.

If the gift is interpreted in this way, then it was held in *Re Recher* (1972) that it would be invalid as offending the rule against purpose trusts as stated in *Morice* v *Bishop of Durham* (1805). This proposition was supported in *Re Grant* (1979) although other cases suggest that such a gift may in fact be valid following the decision in *Re Denley's Trust Deed* (1969).

In *Re Denley* (1969) a gift to an unincorporated association for a named purpose was held to be valid. A distinction was drawn by the court between a gift for an 'inward-looking' purpose (one which was for the benefit of the members) and an 'outward-looking' purpose (one which is not directly). A gift for the former type of purpose is, it was said, valid as it is, in fact, a private trust for the benefit of the members expressed differently to but being the same as a gift of the third construction in *Re Recher* (1972) above. This contention was supported in *Re Lipinski's WT* (1976) where a similar gift was upheld, and either expressly or by implication in subsequent cases as recently as *R* v *District Auditor, ex parte West Yorkshire Metropolitan County Council* (1985).

In *Re Grant* (1979) however, *Re Denley* (1969) was criticised and a gift for what seemed to be 'inward-looking' purposes of the association was held to be invalid as a purpose trust. At first sight, therefore, it seems that the gift to the Trumpton Social Club will be valid if *Re Denley* (1969) is correct and invalid if *Re Grant* (1979) is correct. It is submitted however, that despite Vinelott J's comments in *Re Grant* (1979), there is in fact no necessary conflict between the two cases, that the cases can be read together and that, therefore, the gift in question is undoubtedly valid.

An important fact in *Re Grant* (1979) was that the rules of the donee association did not allow the members to control the property given to it. It is well established - *Neville Estates* v *Madden* (1962) - that a gift construed in the third way above as a gift to present members on the basis that it is given as an accretion to funds will only be valid if nothing in the rules prevents the members controlling how the association's property should be used. The same requirement will exist, therefore, in an application of *Re Denley* (1969). Following this line of reasoning, the gift in *Re Grant's WT* (1979) could not have been applied in the same way as the gift in *Re Denley* (1969) as the associations rules were too restrictive. The two cases can be distinguished in this way and there is no necessary conflict between them.

The gift to the Trumpton Social Club will, therefore, be valid following *Re Denley* (1969) as the rules of the association allow the members to control the use of property donated to it. Despite the wording, it is not a purpose trust but rather a trust for the members beneficially subject to the rules.

It would then follow that the gift need not be used by the members solely for the purposes specified. In *Re Lipinski's WT* (1976) it was held that a gift in similar terms could still take effect as a gift to the members beneficially as accretion to the funds and not as a trust for the specified purposes. In that case there was evidence that the testator was fully aware that it might not be possible to carry out the specified purpose and therefore must have intended that the gift could be used in other ways. If Tom knew that the purpose he specified might not be possible to carry out, there would be a strong argument that the decision in *Re Lipinski* (1976) should be followed. If not it is possible that the court might hold that his words do attempt to impose a trust on the money so that it may be used in a particular way only, and the gift cannot then be construed as a gift to the members beneficially and the trust will fail as a private purpose trust.

Type 2: other purpose trusts (non-charitable)

Problem checklist

a) Does the trust fall within the exceptions to the rule against purpose trusts in *Re Endacott* (1960)?

b) Is the trust limited to the perpetuity period?

If the answer to (a) or (b) is no, the trust is not valid as a purpose trust.

NB (a) and (b) will often be preceded by a consideration of whether the trust is a valid charitable trust.

Question 2

a) Discuss the proposition that there must be some identifiable person on whose application (to the court) a trust can be enforced in the context of (i) trusts for non-human objects, and (ii) discretionary trusts.

b) By his will a testator who died last year, after appointing Tug and Tow to be his executors and trustees, left £100,000 upon trust to invest the same and to apply the net income for a period of twenty years (i) as to one half part thereof for the maintenance of the testator's horses and dogs and (ii) as to the other half part for the benefit of such persons who had at any time during his lifetime been employed by him for a period of not less than one year and the children and remoter issue (whether born or to be born) of such employees in such shares as Tug and Tow shall from time to time think fit, and subject thereto to hold the capital and income upon trust for such person (for his or her personal benefit) who shall, at the end of the twenty year period, be the Mayor of London.

Advise Tug and Tow.

University of London LLB Examination
(for External Students) Law of Trusts June 1989 Q2

Skeleton solution and comment

Part (a) (i) of this question calls for an explanation of the rationale behind the court's refusal to uphold non-charitable purpose trusts subject to a number of limited exceptions. This is a fairly straightforward matter. Part (a) (ii) requires an explanation of how the test of certainty of objects works in relation to discretionary trusts. Part (b) of this question raises some issues on purpose trusts and certainty of objects which do not raise anything remarkable. This is a question which a competent student ought to attempt.

a)   i)   Trusts for non-human objects or purpose trusts not enforced because they do not have identifiable or any beneficiaries. The reason behind this is that the courts would not be able to control trustees who ran a trust for purposes as there would be no-one to bring breaches of trust to the court's attention.

       ii)   Discretionary trusts have identifiable objects if they satisfy the test in *McPhail* v *Doulton* [1971] AC 424. Fact that the class of objects may be very large is irrelevant.

b)   i)   Trust for maintenance of testator's horses and dogs for 20 years a valid purpose trust.

       ii)   • Trust for persons employed by testator for not less than one year a valid discretionary trust.

            • Gift over for Mayor of London a valid private trust which satisfies rules on remoteness of vesting.

Suggested solution

a)   i)   The proposition that there must be some identifiable person on whose application (to the court) a trust can be enforced has been regarded as one of the traditional reasons behind the general rule that trusts for non-human objects or purpose trusts are void. This rule does not affect charitable trusts which are often made for non-human objects since the Attorney-General has locus standi to enforce such trusts as was explained by Lord Eldon LC in *Attorney-General* v *Brown* (1818).

It is inherent in many of the rules governing private trusts that they should have human beings as beneficiaries. This can be seen in the tests of certainty of objects in relation to private trusts. When cases have come before the courts involving trusts for non-human objects it has been pointed out that they cannot be upheld because without such objects they cannot be controlled by the court and would be tantamount to absolute ownership by the trustees. In *Morice* v *Bishop of Durham* (1805) Lord Eldon LC pointed out that it must be possible for the Court to review the administration of a trust by the trustees, if necessary. Thus, if the trustee died or was guilty of maladministration the Court should be able to intervene. However, if there were no human objects this could not be done since there would be no-one to bring the matter to the attention of the Court. The result would be that the trustees could do what they like with the trust money without being called to account. See also *Re Endacott* (1960). Obligation and duty are key features of trusts and trusteeship, but it must be possible to enforce the duty.

It is arguable that there are other reasons which lie behind the Court's refusal to enforce purpose trusts and the fact that they do not have human objects may not be the real reason for this. In some cases the purpose has been too uncertain to enable the court to determine what the testator intended. This could be an explanation for the decision in *Morice* v *Bishop of Durhan* where the gift was for 'such objects of benevolence and liberality' as the bishop should 'most approve of'. Another reason may be that in some instances they amount to a delegation of testamentary power. See *Leahy* v *Attorney-General for New South Wales* (1959). Many of the cases which now embody the exceptional categories where, contrary to the general rule, purpose trusts are enforced seem to have been originally upheld because the purposes were specified with a sufficient degree of certainty. See *Re Astor* (1952). However, it may be that, in view of the Court of Appeal decision in *Re Endacott*, it is now too late to argue that purpose trusts should be upheld if specified with sufficient certainty. The exceptional categories still survive this decision but with the caveat that they are not to be extended. In these exceptional cases the problem of controlling the trustees is overcome by the Court accepting undertakings from the trustees to carry them out should they choose to do so. But, if they choose not to do so the trust will fail. See *Re Dean* (1889). There is no reason why the same rule could not be applied to all trusts with purposes specified with sufficient certainty.

ii) In a discretionary trust the beneficiaries do not possess any beneficial interest in the trust property and it does not appear to have been settled where the beneficial or equitable interest lies. The beneficiaries do, however, possess various rights and these can be protected by the Court. See *Gartside* v *IRC* (1968). Thus, the beneficiary has rights to ensure the trustees do not misappropriate capital; to ensure that the trustees exercise their discretion properly and to take and enjoy whatever part of the income the trustee chooses to give.

The problem which may arise in relation to many discretionary trusts is that the class of beneficiaries is so large or they are to be ascertained at a future date with the result that there would appear to be no identifiable person on whose behalf the court can enforce the trust. If the trust can pass the test of certainty of objects laid down in *McPhail* v *Doulton* (1971) an individual should be in a position to determine whether he has a right to make an application to the court. Therefore, the issue of whether the beneficiaries are identifiable or not is resolved as part of the issue of certainty of objects.

b) The bequest of £100,000 to Tug and Tow for the objects stated in this problem may be divided into three parts, namely, the purpose trust for the horses and dogs, the discretionary trust for the employees and their issue and the gift in remainder to the Mayor of London.

As regards the purpose trust for the testator's horses and dogs this is valid. Although purpose trusts are, as a general rule, void they can be upheld in some exceptional cases. One such case which is well recognised is where the purpose is to provide for the maintenance of a particular animal or group of animals. Thus, in *Re Dean* (1889) a trust for the maintenance of the testator's horses and hounds was upheld. But, even in the exceptional categories, it is necessary to show that the trust is limited in perpetuity and that the trustees are prepared to execute it. The present gift is limited in perpetuity since it only permits maintenance of the horses and dogs for a period of twenty years. This is well within the maximum twenty-one year period which is allowed in these cases. See *Re Astor* (1952). As regards the trustees executing the trust, there is no indication that they are prepared to do so. If they should undertake to carry it out the court will allow the trust to run. But, should they refuse to do so it would seem that the income of the trust would pass to those entitled under the residuary estate of the testator for the next twenty years as the gift over for the benefit of the Mayor of London does not, on its terms operate until the end of the 20 year period.

The second aspect of this gift involves a discretionary trust for the benefit of such persons who had at any time during the testator's lifetime been employed by him for a period of not less than one year and their children or remoter issue. The appropriate test of certainty of objects is that laid down in *McPhail* v *Doulton* (1971), namely, whether it can be said whether a given person is or is not a member of the class of objects. In determining whether this test is satisfied in this case it is necessary to examine the terms of the trust. The main difficulty will be in evidential certainty rather than conceptual certainty. The terms of the trust do not involve any conceptual uncertainty since it is clear what an 'employee' is and there cannot be any doubt about the condition that they must have been employed by the testator for not less than one year. But, as stated, there may well be evidential uncertainty in that the potential beneficiaries may have difficulty in establishing their claim. In *Re Baden (No 2)* (1973) Sachs LJ took the view that evidential uncertainty would never defeat a disposition and that once the gift was conceptually certain it became a question of fact to be determined on the evidence whether an individual was within the class of objects and, if not proved, then he was not within it. Accordingly this gift is valid and should be applied as directed.

The gift provides that at the end of the twenty year period the capital and income should be held for the benefit of the person who shall then be the Mayor of London. This gift is a valid private trust but it cannot be charitable as it is for the personal benefit of the person who shall then be Mayor of London rather than to assist him in his office. Two points arise for consideration on this gift. First, the gift will only take effect in twenty years time. This will not defeat it under the rule that an interest in property, if not vested at its creation must vest, if it vests at all, within twenty-one years from the date of creation. See *Cadell* v *Palmer* (1833).

Second, the person who will benefit under the gift will not be known until shortly before the gift vests. This will not defeat the gift since a trust is not uncertain merely because the actual person entitled to the trust property cannot be known in advance of the date of distribution; it is sufficient if the trust provisions ensure that upon that date the beneficiaries can be ascertained. See *Re Hain's Settlement* (1961).

Question 3

See chapter 21 for a combination question.

6 CHARITABLE TRUSTS

6.1   Introduction

6.2   Key points

6.3   Recent cases

6.4   Analysis of questions

6.5   Questions

6.1   Introduction

Charitable trusts is a very wide topic and one which students generally find interesting. Much of the material comprises of numerous cases which simply decide whether a particular object is charitable and which raise no real difficulties. This is not true, however, of the requirement of public benefit - a complicated area involving theoretical concepts which many students find difficult to grasp. It cannot, unfortunately, be avoided as questions on charitable trusts invariably require the student to consider the problems raised by the cases in this area which must, therefore, be digested and fully understood.

6.2   Key points

The status of 'charitable trust' has several advantages over that of 'private trust':

a) *Tax advantages*

Charities are largely exempt from income tax, corporation tax and capital gains tax. Inheritance tax is not chargeable on gifts to charities and transfers, conveyances and leases to charities are exempt from stamp duty.

b) *Certainty of objects (see chapter 2)*

If there is a clear intention to give property for charitable purposes, the trust will not fail for uncertainty of objects.

c) *The rule against perpetual trusts*

This does not apply to charitable trusts which may continue for ever.

d) *The rule against remoteness of vesting*

The rule applies to charitable trusts except where a gift is made to one charity with a gift over to another on the occurrence of certain events - *Re Tyler* [1891] 3 Ch 252.

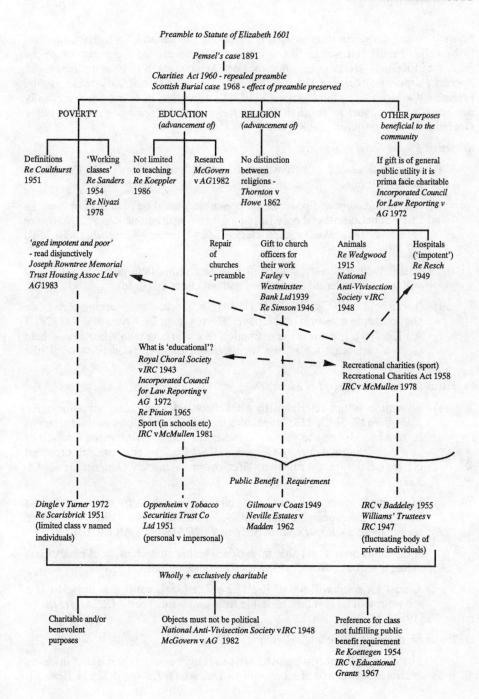

Preamble to Statute of Elizabeth 1601

Pemsel's case 1891

Charities Act 1960 - repealed preamble
Scottish Burial case 1968 - effect of preamble preserved

POVERTY	EDUCATION (advancement of)	RELIGION (advancement of)	OTHER purposes beneficial to the community

| Definitions Re Coulthurst 1951 | 'Working classes' Re Sanders 1954 Re Niyazi 1978 | Not limited to teaching Re Koeppler 1986 | Research McGovern v AG 1982 | No distinction between religions - Thornton v Howe 1862 | If gift is of general public utility it is prima facie charitable Incorporated Council for Law Reporting v AG 1972 |

'aged impotent and poor' - read disjunctively Joseph Rowntree Memorial Trust Housing Assoc Ltd v AG 1983

Repair of churches - preamble

Gift to church officers for their work Farley v Westminster Bank Ltd 1939 Re Simson 1946

Animals Re Wedgwood 1915 National Anti-Vivisection Society v IRC 1948

Hospitals ('impotent') Re Resch 1949

What is 'educational'? Royal Choral Society v IRC 1943 Incorporated Council for Law Reporting v AG 1972 Re Pinion 1965 Sport (in schools etc) IRC v McMullen 1981

Recreational charities (sport) Recreational Charities Act 1958 IRC v McMullen 1978

Public Benefit Requirement

Dingle v Turner 1972 Re Scarisbrick 1951 (limited class v named individuals)

Oppenheim v Tobacco Securities Trust Co Ltd 1951 (personal v impersonal)

Gilmour v Coats 1949 Neville Estates v Madden 1962

IRC v Baddeley 1955 Williams' Trustees v IRC 1947 (fluctuating body of private individuals)

Wholly + exclusively charitable

Charitable and/or benevolent purposes

Objects must not be political National Anti-Vivisection Society v IRC 1948 McGovern v AG 1982

Preference for class not fulfilling public benefit requirement Re Koettegen 1954 IRC v Educational Grants 1967

There is no statutory definition of what is charitable. In general, for a charitable trust to be valid it must fall within 'the spirit and intendment' of the preamble to the Statute of Elizabeth 1601 as classified by Lord Macnaughten in *Commissioners for Special Purposes of Income Tax* v *Pemsel* [1891] AC 531. Strictly speaking, the preamble was repealed by the Charities Act 1960. However, its effect was specifically preserved by the court in *Scottish Burial Reform and Cremation Society Ltd* v *Glasgow City Corporation* [1968] AC 138.

a) *Trusts for the relief of poverty*

   i)   Poverty does not mean destitution, rather 'going short' - *Re Coulthurst* [1951] Ch 661.

   ii) 'Aged, impotent and poor' in the preamble should be read disjunctively so that a beneficiary need only fit one of these descriptions - *Joseph Rowntree Memorial Trust Housing Association Ltd* v *Attorney-General* [1983] 1 All ER 288.

        (NB if the beneficiary is aged or impotent rather than poor, then the trust will be valid under the fourth head and not under this head).

   iii) It was held in *Re Sanders' WT* [1954] Ch 265 that the working classes do not constitute a section of the poor. However, in *Re Niyazi's WT* [1978] 3 All ER 785 a gift for the construction of a working men's hostel was held to be a valid charitable trust for the relief of poverty in view of all the circumstances.

b) *Trusts for the advancement of education*

   i)   Education is not restricted to a teacher-student in class situation - *Re Koeppler* [1986] Ch 423. It includes the improvement of a useful branch of human knowledge and its public dissemination - *Incorporated Council of Law Reporting* v *Attorney-General* [1972] Ch 73 - and research provided certain conditions are fulfilled - *McGovern* v *Attorney-General* [1982] Ch 321.

   ii) Many things are considered to be of educational value - from a search for the Bacon - Shakespeare manuscripts - *Re Hopkins' WT* [1965] Ch 669 to choral singing - *Royal Choral Society* v *IRC* [1943] 2 All ER 101.

        If the court do not feel able to decide whether something is of educational value, it will use expert evidence - *Re Pinion* [1965] Ch 85.

        A trust for sport will not of itself be educational, but if it is for sport in a school it will be a valid charitable trust under this head - *IRC* v *McMullen* [1981] AC 1.

c) *Trusts for the advancement of religion*

   i)   The court will not distinguish between religions unless a religion involves doctrines subversive of all morality - *Thornton* v *Howe* (1862) 31 Beav 14.

Indeed the law 'assumes that any religion is at least likely to be better than none' - *Neville Estates Ltd* v *Madden* [1962] Ch 832 per Cross J.

ii) Gifts for the maintenance or repair of churches and churchyards are charitable by clear analogy to the preamble.

iii) Whether a gift to a church officer as the holder of that office will be charitable, depends on the wording of the gift. *Farley* v *Westminster Bank Ltd* [1939] AC 430 - a gift to vicars and churchwardens for 'parochial work' was held not to be wholly and exclusively charitable as it could include work which is not, strictly speaking, for religious purposes.

Re Simson [1946] Ch 299 - a gift to a vicar 'to be used for his work in the parish' was held to be charitable.

d) *Trusts for other purposes beneficial to the community*

The trust must be for public purposes beneficial to the community or for the public welfare *and* it must be charitable within the 'spirit and intendment' of the preamble - *Attorney-General* v *National Provincial Bank* [1924] AC 262. However, the emphasis was reversed in *Incorporated Council for Law Reporting* v *Attorney-General* [1972] Ch 73 where it was said that if a purpose is shown to be beneficial to the community or of general public utility, it is prima facie charitable and it is for those who oppose its charitable status to show that the object is not within the spirit and intendment of the preamble.

Trusts which have been held charitable under this 'fourth head' fall into three main categories:

i) Animals

Trusts in favour of animals generally or a class of animals (not specific animals - see chapter 5) are charitable on the ground that they promote public morality by tending to discourage cruelty - *Re Wedgwood* [1915] 1 Ch 113.

However, not all such trusts will be charitable. In *Re Grove-Grady* [1929] 1 Ch 557, the court felt that the law had gone far enough in affording charitable status to such gifts and refused to hold a refuge for all animals to protect them again human molestation, charitable. And in *National Anti-Vivisection Society* v *IRC* [1948] AC 31 the plaintiff institution was held not to be charitable as it was not in the public interest.

ii) Hospitals

Gifts to hospitals are charitable as for the relief of the impotent in the preamble even if a charge is made to patients - *Re Resch's WT* [1969] 1 AC 514 - provided that it is not a profit-making body.

iii) Recreational charities

A trust simply to promote sport is not charitable - *Re Nottage* [1895] 2 Ch 649. However, since the Recreational Charities Act 1958 recreational facilities can be charitable subject to the fulfilment of the conditions under the Act.

The Public Benefit Requirement

Even if a trust is prima facie charitable, it will not be a valid charitable trust unless it can also be shown to be for the public benefit. (This requirement does not apply to trusts for the relief of poverty).

a) *Trusts for the relief of poverty*

The public benefit requirement does not apply - *Dingle* v *Turner* [1972] AC 601. However, a distinction must be drawn between a gift to a limited class and a gift to particular individuals. The former gift would be a valid charitable trust; the latter would not - *Re Scarisbrick* [1951] Ch 622.

b) *Other trusts*

Judgments in some cases suggest that there is a single test to determine whether the public benefit requirement is satisfied, which applies to all three remaining heads. The decisions themselves, however, show that this is not the case.

   i) Trusts for the advancement of religion

       Following *Gilmour* v *Coats* [1949] AC 426 and *Neville Estates Ltd* v Madden [1962] Ch 832 a trust will satisfy the public benefit requirement if the members of the beneficiary organisation live in (rather than outside) the community.

   ii) Trusts for the advancement of education; trusts for other purposes beneficial to the community

       Two different tests exist:

       • *Oppenheim* v *Tobacco Securities Trust Co Ltd* [1951] AC 297 - the possible beneficiaries must not be numerically negligible and the quality which distinguishes them from other members of the public must not depend on their relationship to a particular individual. It must be an impersonal and not personal quality.

       • *Williams' Trustees* v *IRC* [1947] AC 447 and *IRC* v *Baddeley* [1955] AC 572 - the possible beneficiaries must constitute a section of the public as contrasted with 'a fluctuating body of private individuals' or 'a class within a class'.

The trust must be wholly and exclusively charitable.

In other words, under the terms of the trust it must not be possible to apply the trust property for non-charitable purposes.

If the gift is to an organisation, the organisation and thus the gift will not be charitable if some of the purposes of the body are non-charitable - generally, political - *National Anti-Vivisection Society* v *IRC* (1948); *McGovern* v *Attorney-General*

[1982] Ch 321 - and more than simply incidental to the body's main charitable purposes.

If the gift is for apparently charitable purposes, it will not be a valid charitable trust if the gift is worded in such a way that the trust property could be applied for non-charitable purposes. In particular, this may be the case where the gift includes a preference to benefit a limited class which fails to satisfy the public benefit requirement - *Re Koettegen's WT* [1954] Ch 252; *IRC* v *Educational Grants Association* [1967] Ch 123. The court will look at the reality of the situation.

A recent case, *Re Hetherington (dec'd)* [1989] 2 All ER 129 suggests, however, that if a gift could be carried out in a way which would satisfy the public benefit requirement but could also be carried out in a way which would not, the gift will be construed as a gift to be carried out only by the methods which satisfied the requirement and would thus be a valid charitable trust.

6.3 Recent cases

Re Hetherington (dec'd) Gibbs v McDonnell [1989] 2 All ER 129.

6.4 Analysis of questions

Charitable trusts often crop up in problem questions which may also require the student to consider the cy-pres doctrine (chapter 7), non-charitable purpose trusts (chapter 5) and the requirements for an express private trust (chapter 2). In particular, if a potential charitable trust is not valid as such, the student is expected to then, at least briefly, consider its validity as one of the last two. If the student fails to do so, the question is incomplete. Essay questions are also possible, although less common, and generally require the student to address and express an opinion on a controversial aspect of the topic such as political trusts or the public benefit requirement.

6.5 Questions

Problem checklist

a) Is the trust prima facie charitable within the preamble as classified by *Pemsel's case* (1891) - ie does it fall within one of Lord Macnaghten's categories?

   If not, go to (e).

b) Is it political?

   If so, go to (e).

c) Is the relevant public benefit requirement satisfied? If there is a preference for a class, the relevant class which must satisfy the requirement is the class which is the subject of the preference - *IRC* v *Educational Grants Association* (1967). If not, go to (e).

   i)   if for relief of poverty, no requirement except that in *Re Scarisbrick* (1951).

   ii) if for advancement of religion, the test is that in *Gilmour* v *Coats* (1949) and *Neville Estates Ltd* v *Madden* (1962).

    iii) if for other 'heads', various possible tests (see key points).

d) Is the trust wholly and exclusively charitable?

    If not, go to (e).

e) If the trust does not satisfy the above requirements, it will only be valid in two situations:

    i) valid non-charitable purpose trust (chapter 5); or

    ii) express private trust if three certainties are satisfied (chapter 2).

Question 1

Consider the validity and effect of the following provisions in the will of Terence, who has recently died.

1) £500,000 to my Trustees upon trust to use the capital and income to establish a centre in England for (a) the formation of an informed international public opinion and (b) the promise of greater co-operation between the United Kingdom and other Commonwealth states in general.

2) £750,000 to be invested and the income applied towards the relief of need suffered by employees and ex-employees of the National Coal Board as a result of strikes.

3) £30,000 to my Trustees upon trust to use the income for such period as the law allows for the maintenance of my pet tortoise, Emmy.

4) The residue of my property upon trust for such charitable or benevolent purposes as my Trustees may select.

University of London LLB Examination
(for External Students) Law of Trusts June 1985 Q5

Suggested solution

1) This trust is potentially charitable as for the advancement of education. Two problems, though, may prevent it from being charitable as such - the purposes may be too vague and the second purpose may be considered to be political. A similar gift was under consideration in *Re Koeppler* (1986) except that in that case the gift was made to a body ('Wilton Park') for such purposes. It was held by the Court of Appeal that the gift was not political in the sense used in *McGovern* v *Attorney-General* (1982), nor did the vague nature of the purposes prevent the gift from taking effect as a charitable trust. However in *Re Koeppler* (1986) an important aspect of the decision was that the gift was construed as for the purposes of Wilton Park. The court, therefore, looked to what these purposes actually were and concluded that they were charitable as for the advancement of education, and that the stated purposes in the gift were merely the ultimate aims and aspirations of the testator. These aims were not of themselves charitable, but this did not affect the charitable nature of the gift as a whole.

Consequently, although the provision in question appears to be similar to that in *Re Koeppler* it can be distinguished when as here the stated purposes are not incidental as in *Re Koeppler*, but rather from the core of the gift. As such, they are not charitable and thus the gift fails as a charitable trust.

Clearly, the gift cannot be a valid private trust as there are no ascertainable beneficiaries. Nor is it valid as a non-charitable purpose trust as it does not fall within any of the exceptions to the rule against purpose trusts in *Re Endacott* (1960). It will therefore be held by the trustees on resulting trust for the testator's estate.

2) This is a valid charitable trust for the relief of poverty. The main object of the gift is to relieve need and is not in any way political. The relief of poverty was identified as a separate head of charity by Lord McNaughten in *Pemsel's* case (1891) and for the purposes of charity law poverty does not mean destitution. As Lord Simonds said in *IRC* v *Baddeley* (1955) poverty does not connote 'grinding need or utter destruction' and that 'relief' consists a need of some sort 'the means to provide for some necessity or quasi necessity'. Thus the 'relief of need' in this case would seem to connote the relief of poverty for charitable purposes.

But it is not enough that the gift be for a charitable object viz. poverty. If the gift has political objects it cannot, it seems, be upheld as charitable. In *McGovern* v *Attorney-General* (1981) political objects were held to include, inter alia, furthering the interests of a political party, procuring or opposing changes in the law, whether in England or abroad, procuring the reversal of government policy or a particular decision of a governmental authority either in England or abroad. Taking these matters into consideration it seems that there are no political objects in the present trust. The main purpose of the trust is the relief of need and not the attaining of political or quasi-political objects through a strike. The fact that the charitable object of the trust is or can be closely identified with a political object does not seem to matter. In *McGovern* v *Attorney-General*, Slade J considered that the objects of relieving prisoners of conscience could be charitable but not seeking their release by, for example, campaigns for changes in the law or government policy either in England or abroad, which would have this effect. The relief of prisoners of conscience may be closely identified with a political object but, as stated, it is not in itself a political object. Likewise, the relief of need amongst employees and ex-employees of the National Coal Board as a result of strikes is not a political trust, even if the strikes are political in nature.

A factor which will not affect the validity of the trust in this case is the public benefit requirement. This applies to all charitable trusts other than those for the relief of poverty so that if there is a nexus in the trust limiting it to a class of people by reference to a particular quality of common factor, it will be regarded as a private trust. See *Oppenheim* v *Tobacco Securities* (1951). But the public benefit requirement was not considered necessary in a trust to relieve poverty amongst the employees and ex-employees of a particular company in *Dingle* v *Turner* (1972). Although this exception was described as anomalous in *Dingle* v *Turner* and one which would not be extended by analogy, it is one which can be invoked here since there is no material ground on which the present case is distinguishable.

3) This trust is not charitable because it is for the maintenance of a particular animal. In charity law a trust for the welfare and benefit of animals generally or a particular species of animal is charitable if it involves a benefit to the community. See *Re Wedgwood* (1915). Thus, a trust for the provision of a dog's home or a hospital for sick animals is charitable. See *Re Douglas* (1887); *University of London v Yarrow* (1857). There is no benefit to the community in the maintenance of a particular animal, such a trust is in the nature of a private trust. See *Re Grove-Grady* (1929).

If the present trust is to be upheld as a private trust this is only possible if it falls within one of the exceptional cases to the rule that non-charitable purpose trusts are void. This rule can be traced back to the decision of Sir William Grant MR in *Morice v Bishop of Durham* (1805) and rests on the fact that there are no objects under such a trust in whose favour the court can decree performance. But, by exception, trusts for the maintenance of particular animals may be enforced provided that they are limited in perpetuity and also, it seems, that there is somebody prepared to give the court an undertaking that they will carry out the terms of the trust. Thus, trusts for the maintenance of cats, dogs, horses, etc have been upheld. See *Re Dean* (1889). But, as stated, the gift must be limited in perpetuity and this means a perpetuity period of 21 years or such other period as was permissible under the law as it stood prior to the enactment of the Perpetuities and Accumulations Act 1964. See section 15(4) of the 1964 Act. A perpetuity period is not set out in the present gift but this is not fatal since phrases which by implication limit the gift in perpetuity will do. Thus, a gift, as here, to carry out the non-charitable purpose for 'as long as the law allows' will be deemed to limit the gift in perpetuity. This can be concluded from decisions such *Pirbright v Sawley* (1896), where the gift was upheld as valid when it was for the maintenance of a grave for 'so long as the law for the time being permitted'. See also *Re Hooper* (1932). Without this limitation the present gift would probably fail since judicial notice of the longevity of tortoises in deciding if the gift would breach the perpetuity rule would not assist. In *Re Haines* (1952) judicial notice was taken of the lifespan of a cat so as to hold that a gift for the maintenance of cats would not breach the perpetuity rule. Admittedly 21 years is more than the lifespan of the average cat, but this cannot be said for tortoises. But, in conclusion, the gift is a good non-charitable purpose trust for a maximum period of 21 years.

4) This gift is not charitable since it fails to meet an essential element of charitable status, namely, that a charitable trust must be wholly and exclusively charitable. See *McGovern v Attorney-General* (1981). If a trust which comprised both charitable and non-charitable objects were permitted to take charitable status, then many of the tax and other fiscal advantages which are given to charitable trusts could be indirectly fed into non-charitable objects. In addition the trustees would be placed in some difficulty because they would not know what part of the trust their duties as charitable trustees applied to.

A gift for 'charitable or benevolent' objects is not wholly and exclusively charitable because the trustees have been given an alternative, ie to apply the gift for charitable objects or for benevolent objects. A gift for charitable objects alone would be wholly and exclusively charitable but a gift for benevolent objects alone would not. As Lord Simonds said in *Chichester Diocesan Fund and Board of Finance* v *Simpson* (1944) the word benevolent 'has a range in some respects far less wide than legal charity, in others somewhat wider'. Thus, not all benevolent objects are necessarily charitable objects. The gift cannot be construed as a gift for charitable objects of a benevolent nature since this would ignore the importance of the word 'or' in the gift, such a construction might be applicable if the word 'and' had been used instead of 'or'. The conclusion that must follow, as followed in *Chichester Diocesan Fund and Board of Finance* v *Simpson*, is that the present gift is not charitable, and, cannot be upheld as a non-charitable purpose trust since it is within none of the exceptions to the rule that such trusts are void. Consequently, as this is a residuary gift the residuary gift fails and therefore the next-of-kin of the testator, Terence, will benefit under the intestacy rules.

Question 2

a) In what major respects do charitable trusts enjoy special treatment and privileges as compared with non-charitable trusts?

b) Consider the validity and effect, if any, of the following dispositions:

   i) A gift by will of £10,000 'to the Vicar of my Parish Church knowing that he will apply it for worthy and deserving objects';

   ii) A gift by cheque of £10,000 by an old student of Blanktown University in favour of the President of the Students Union 'to be used to further the Union's objects';

   iii) A gift of £20,000 cash sent to Bob Geldof 'to be applied for the relief of the starving and poor in East Africa'.

University of London LLB Examination
(for External Students) Law of Trusts June 1986 Q6

Skeleton solution and comment

This question is mainly concerned with charitable trusts. Part (a) is a straightforward essay on the privileges and special treatment accorded to charitable trusts. It is something which should present no difficulty as all the textbooks deal with this. Part (b) sets out some fairly typical problems on the validity of gifts with particular reference to whether or not they are charitable. An average student should be able to obtain good marks on this uncomplicated question.

a) Charitable Trusts - special treatment and privileges given to charitable trusts as compared with private trusts - no need to satisfy certainty of objects requirement - possibility of cy-pres application if charity fails - modifications to rule against perpetuities - tax privileges given to charities.

b) • £100,000 to Vicar of my Parish Church 'for worthy and deserving objects' - not charitable, does not satisfy need to be wholly and exclusively charitable - probably an absolute gift to vicar as no imperative words creating a trust are used.

• £10,000 to Blanktown University Students Union 'to further the Union's objects' - a good charitable trust for advancement of education if, as probable, Union only exists to provide ancillary services at University. See *London Hospital Medical College* v *IRC* (1976).

• £20,000, to Bob Geldof 'for relief of starving and poor in East Africa', - a good charity for the relief of poverty - no objection that this work is being carried out abroad.

Suggested solution

a) Charitable trusts are in their nature public trusts and, thus, are accorded privileges and special treatment which do not apply to private trusts. The three certainties which apply to private trusts are not all applicable, the rules against perpetuity are modified, charitable trusts can be modified if they become obsolete and exemption and relief is given in respect of certain taxes and rates.

A charitable trust will not fail for lack of certainty of objects, a requirement essential in all private trusts save for those anomalous cases where non-charitable purpose trusts are upheld. See *McPhail* v *Doulton* (1971). So long as a gift to charity shows a clear intention that it should be applied exclusively for charitable purposes it will be upheld. Thus, a gift merely for 'charitable' purposes or 'charitable and deserving purposes' are good since it is clear that they are devoted exclusively to charity. See *Re Sutton* (1885). In cases where no particular charitable objects are specified the court will, on an application, apply a scheme for the use of the funds under the cy-pres doctrine. In some cases gifts for charitable objects which cannot be attained or have been attained so far as is practicable are exempt from the doctrine of resulting trusts. This will arise where a general charitable intention can be found so as to apply a cy-pres scheme or under ss13 and 14 of the Charities Act 1960.

The rule against perpetuities is applied to charitable trusts in a modified form. These are two aspects to this rule, namely, the rule against inalienability and the rule against remoteness of vesting. The rule against inalienability does not apply to charitable trusts so that a gift to a charity is not void merely because the subject matter thereof will be inalienable in perpetuity in the charity's hands. See *Chamberlayne* v *Brockett* (1872) The rule against remoteness of vesting only applies to charitable trusts in a modified form. Under this rule a gift must vest in a trust within the perpetuity period. If a gift is made to a non-charity and followed by another gift to a charity the gift must vest in the charity in the perpetuity period otherwise it is void. See *Re Lord Strathenden and Campbell* (1894). But if a gift is made to one charity and followed by a gift over to another charity the rules as to remoteness of vesting do not apply. See *Royal College of Surgeons* v *National Provincial Bank* (1952).

If a private trust should fail because it is obsolete, ie those for whose benefit it was intended no longer exist or its purposes have been fulfilled, there will be resulting trusts for the settlor or donor. See *Cunnack* v *Edwards* (1896); *Re West Sussex Constabulary Trusts* (1971). In the case of charitable trusts a cy-pres application can be made under s13 of the Charities Act 1960 and, in appropriate cases, the objects of the trusts may be altered under the Charities Act 1985.

Another privilege given to charitable trusts is the exemption and relief from rates and taxes. The income of a charity is exempt from income tax, corporation tax and capital gains tax insofar as it is applied for charitable objects. See *IRC* v *Educational Grants Association* (1967). Transfers, conveyances and leases to charities are exempt from stamp duty. See s129 Finance Act 1982. Relief is given from liability to Value Added Tax where a charity raises funds by the sale of goods etc. See VAT (Charities) Order 1973. Finally, there is no liability to inheritance tax in respect of gifts to charities. See Inheritance Tax Act 1984.

b)   i)   A gift of £10,000 'to the Vicar of my Parish Church knowing that he will apply it for worthy and deserving objects' is not a charitable trust. Although a gift virtute officii to a person who discharges charitable functions in his office is charitable, this rule only applies insofar as there is nothing in words added to the gift which would negative any implication that the gift is to be devoted exclusively to the charitable functions of that office. Thus, a gift to a vicar 'for such objects connected with the church as he shall think fit' is consistent with the exclusively charitable nature of the gift. But, a gift to a vicar 'for parochial institutions or purposes' could legitimately be applied for non-charitable purposes. See *Re Eastes* (1948); *Re Stratton* (1931). In the present case the vicar has a discretion to apply the gift for non-charitable objects as 'worthy and deserving objects' may be either charitable or non-charitable. See *Re Saxone Shoe Co Ltd's Deed* (1962).

As this gift is not charitable the next issue is whether it can be regarded as a valid gift to the Vicar on some private trusts or as an outright gift to him or void. It would seem that the words used do not impose a trust on the Vicar, 'knowing that he will apply it' are arguably mere precatory words, which do not create a trust. See *Re Adams and the Kensington Vestry* (1884). Thus, the gift should be treated as an absolute gift to the Vicar subject to a moral obligation.

ii)   A gift of £10,000 to the President of Blanktown Students Union 'to be used to further the Union's objects' is probably a good charitable trust. The position of a students union attached to a university or college was considered by Brightman J in *London Hospital Medical College* v *IRC* (1976) and also by Scott J in *Attorney-General* v *Ross* (1985). In the first case Brightman J considered that a students union standing alone was not charitable under the general law as it was nothing more than a club to provide athletic and social activities for its members. But, he added, that if the union existed solely to further, and did further, the educational purposes of the college and the work of the college was charitable, then the union was also charitable. Thus, if Blanktown University is charitable and its Students Union exists solely to further the educational purposes of the University, it will be entitled to treat the £10,000 cheque as a donation to charity.

The fact that the students union may confer personal benefits on its members will not affect the charitable status of the donation. Further, even if the students union has a radical outlook and sometimes indulges in ultra vires and non-charitable activities, these will not be relevant in determining whether or not it is a charity. See *Attorney-General* v *Ross*.

iii) A gift of £20,000 to Bob Geldof 'to be applied for the relief of the starving and poor in East Africa' would appear to be a good charitable trust for the relief of poverty. The reference to 'starving and poor' would suggest that the objects of the gift have to 'go short' in the ordinary acceptation of that term. See *Re Coulthurst* (1951). Thus, a starving person has to go short of food and the reference to 'poor' undoubtedly imports poverty. There is no need to satisfy the public benefit test in this case as trusts for the relief of poverty are exempt from this. See *Dingle* v *Turner* (1972). It is no bar to charitable status that the objects of the gift are all abroad. This matter was considered by the Charity Commissioners in their Annual Report in 1963 and they concluded that the relief of poverty was charitable even if done abroad. In other areas the court has been prepared to permit the charities work to be carried out abroad, for example, in *Re Robinson* (1931) where the gift was for German soldiers in Germany disabled by the War.

Question 3

By his will, a testator who died last year, made the following gift:

i) '£10,000 to A upon trust to distribute it amongst such persons or charitable objects as he shall select';

ii) '£20,000 to B upon trust to apply the income in maintaining my Labrador dog and Siamese cat and subject thereto to apply the capital in promoting research into population of the United Kingdom';

iii) '£50,000 to C upon trust to purchase a suitable site near Birmingham for a football field for the use of all the inhabitants of Birmingham'.

Consider to what extent, if at all, these gifts are valid and enforceable.

University of London LLB Examination
(for External Students) Law of Trusts June 1988 Q4

Skeleton solution and comment

A typical question which raises issues of certainty of objects and private purpose trusts as well as charitable trusts.

i) This gift is void and unenforceable. It cannot be charitable as it is not wholly and exclusively charitable since it gives the trustees a choice to apply it either to 'persons' or 'charitable objects'. The former does not encompass a charitable object. The gift cannot be upheld as an express private trust as it is so wide as not to refer to anything like a class of objects. It cannot be a valid non-charitable purpose trust as it is too vague.

ii) This gift cannot be charitable as it is for the benefit of specific animals and, thus, confers no public benefit. It is a purpose trust as in *Re Dean* (1889). A gift for the benefit of particular animals can only be a purpose trust if limited in perpetuity and someone interested in the money is willing to carry out the trust. The present gift is not limited in perpetuity as required under s15(4) of the Perpetuity and Accumulations Act 1964. However, the court may take judicial notice of the fact that cats do not live longer than 21 years and it may also take judicial notice of the age of the dog and that it could not possibly live longer than 21 years. See *Re Haines* (1952). The gift over for research can only be upheld as a charitable trust, if at all.

iii) This gift cannot be upheld as an express private trust as the class of objects is so large as to be administratively unworkable. See *McPhail* v *Doulton* (1971). The gift does, however, seem to be a valid charitable trust under the Recreational Charities Act 1958 as it satisfies the public benefit requirement and appears to be in the interests of 'social welfare'. The fact that the trust is limited to providing facilities for a particular sport does not seem to be objectionable as there is nothing in the 1958 Act itself forbidding this and the case law seems to support it. See *Re Morgan* (1955).

Suggested Solution

i) This gift of '£10,000 to A upon trust to distribute it amongst such persons or charitable objects as he shall select' cannot be upheld as a charitable trust. This is because it does not satisfy the requirement that a gift for charitable objects must be wholly and exclusively charitable. By this requirement the trustee of a charitable trust should not be able, under the terms of the trust, to apply all or any part of the trust funds for non-charitable objects and, thus, conferring on these non-charitable objects the considerable tax privileges enjoyed by charitable objects. See *Chichester Diocesan Fund and Board of Finance* v *Simpson* (1944). The gift to A gives A a discretion in applying the £10,000 to either 'persons' or to 'charitable objects'. The use of the word 'or' in the context of this gift has the effect, as was pointed out in the *Chichester Diocesan* case, of giving an alternative in applying the fund between the objects which are joined or separated by it. If each of these objects was in itself charitable, for example, 'charitable or educational', then the gift could be upheld as wholly and exclusively charitable as was done in *Re Ward* (1941). But, where one of the objects is non-charitable the trustee could properly apply the fund for a non-charitable object. The reference to 'persons' in the gift to A does not encompass a charitable object. Instead, it indicates a benefit to individuals without regard to charity and to charitable objects. See *Re Hood* (1931).

61

The gift of £10,000 to A cannot be upheld as a valid express private trust since it fails to satisfy the requirement of certainty of objects. The reference to 'charitable objects' is a reference to purposes rather than ascertainable beneficiaries and the reference to 'persons' is so hopelessly wide that it does not refer to anything like a class of objects and is administratively unworkable. It is similar to the example given by Lord Wilberforce in *McPhail* v *Doulton* (1971) of a gift for the benefit of all the residents of Greater London.

The gift of £10,000 to A is void and will pass to those entitled to the residue of A's estate or, if there is no residuary gift, to the testator's next of kin on intestacy. It is not possible to save it by omitting the word 'or' as such a step was rejected by the court in *Re Horrocks* (1939) and the Charitable Trusts (Validation) Act 1954 has no application as it does not apply to trusts coming into effect after 15 December 1952.

ii) A true construction of this gift would appear to be that the income of the £20,000 is to be applied to maintain the testator's Labrador dog and Siamese cat for so long as they or each of them shall live and then to apply the capital for the stated purpose.

A trust for the benefit of animals may be classified as either a non-charitable purpose trust or a charitable trust but it cannot be treated as an express private trust as it is inherent in the test of certainty of objects that there should be human beings as beneficiaries thereunder. See *Re Astor's ST* (1952). In order to be treated as a charitable trust a gift must be for the benefit of animals generally or a species of animal generally and satisfy the public benefit requirement. See *Re Wedgewood* (1915). The gift for the testator's dog and cat cannot be charitable as it is for the benefit of specific animals and confers no public benefit. Instead it is a purpose trust and similar to cases such as *Re Dean* (1889) where the testator left funds for the maintenance of his horses and hounds.

A purpose trust for the maintenance of animals may be upheld as valid contrary to the general rule that purpose trusts are void provided it satisfies two conditions, namely, i) that the trust does not offend the rule against perpetual duration of trusts and ii) there is some person interested in the money who is willing to carry it out. In relation to the first condition it must be shown that the gift will not run for longer than 21 years from the date it took effect in the absence of any perpetuity period being specified. See s15(4) Perpetuities and Accumulations Act 1964. If there is no limitation on the duration of the trust the court will not add one and the gift may fail. See *Re Compton* (1946). There is no limitation as to the duration of the purpose trust for the testator's dog and cat which would suggest that it is liable to failure. However, it may be possible to imply a perpetuity period here by taking judicial notice of the the lifespan of the animals in question. In *Re Haines* (1952) judicial notice was taken of the fact that cats do not live longer than 21 years and there a gift for the maintenance of the testatrix's cats upheld even though it was not specifically limited in duration. If the present gift was limited to the testator's cat this case could be applied. However, it may not be possible to do so if judicial notice cannot be taken of the lifespan of a Labrador dog being less than

21 years. Expert evidence on this point would be appropriate and/or details of the dog's age so as to show that it could not possibly live for another 21 years. Even if judicial notice is taken of the lifespan of the dog as being 21 years or less the purpose trust can only be upheld if B or those interested in the £20,000 are prepared to carry out the purpose trust since it seems that the court will not order those charged with the purpose trust to execute it. See *Re Hooper* (1932).

If the purpose trust for the cat and dog is held to be invalid or B refuses to carry it out or if it is valid and comes to an end on the death of the dog and cat the £20,000 may then be applicable in promoting research into the population of the United Kingdom. This gift can only operate if it is valid and the only method by which it could be so upheld is if it can be treated as charitable. It cannot be an express private trust as it includes all persons comprising the population of the United Kingdom as potential objects and is so wide as not to form a class of objects. See *McPhail* v *Doulton* (1971). It cannot be a purpose trust as it couched in terms which are so indefinite and vague that the trustees could not execute them and it does not fall within any of the categories where the court has been prepared to uphold purpose trusts. See *Re Astor's ST* (1952).

As regards charitable status the gift can only be upheld if its object can be treated as charitable in law. The object in this case would appear to be research into population. The addition of the term 'research' in this gift would suggest that it is primarily of an educational nature and should be treated as for the advancement of education. In *Re Hopkin's WT* [1965] Ch 669 it was held that a trust for research could be charitable under this head provided that three conditions were met including that the area of proposed research involved a useful subject of study and the knowledge acquired would be disseminated to others. In *Re Shaw* (1957) a trust for research into a new phonetic alphabet was held not charitable as it merely tended to the increase in human knowledge. However, later cases such as *Re Bestermann* (1984) and *McGovern* v *A-G* (1982) have been more liberal. A trust for research need not be confined to research carried out in an educational institution and the court will assume, unless there is evidence to the contrary, that the results of the research will be made known to the public at large. It is likely that this is a valid charitable trust for the advancement of education.

iii) The gift of £50,000 to C to purchase a suitable site near Birmingham for a football field for the use of all the inhabitants of Birmingham can only be upheld as valid if it is charitable. It cannot be an express private trust as the objects, viz the inhabitants of Birmingham, are so wide as not to form a class. See *McPhail* v *Doulton* (1971). It cannot be treated as a non-charitable purpose trust as it does not fall within any of the exceptional categories where such trusts are upheld.

As regards charitable status, the gift seems to be primarily for the purchase site for a football field rather than for the promotion of mere sport. If it were for the promotion of mere sport, for example, to encourage football by providing prizes and trophies, it could not be upheld. See *Re Nottage* (1895). The provision of recreational facilities which may be used for sports or particular sports may be charitable under the Recreational Charities Act 1958 if provided in the interests of social welfare and they satisfy the public benefit requirement. Under as s1(2) of the 1958 Act if the facilities have the object of improving the conditions of life for the persons for whom they are primarily intended and, inter alia, those persons have need of such facilities by reason of their youth, age, poverty or social and economic circumstances then the requirement of 'social welfare' is fulfilled. This gift would probably improve conditions of life for the young inhabitants of Birmingham and the need for such facilities for youth could probably be established. As the facilities are for all the inhabitants of Birminghan the public benefit test is satisfied as this at least represents a section of the community. See *Oppenheim* v *Tobacco Securities* (1951).

The only difficulty which may arise here is that the gift is confined to providing facilities for football and it may be said that one of its consequences is to promote football by being so limited. See *Re Hadden* (1932). The case law would appear to support the view that it is acceptable to give charitable status to a gift which provides facilities which can be used for only one sport. Thus gifts for the provision of a swimming pool and for the provision of an ice rink have been held to be charitable. See *Re Morgan* (1955). But, it is noteworthy that the House of Lords did not refer to this matter in *IRC v McMullen* (1981) even though the opportunity arose to do so. Further, there is nothing in the terms of the Recreational Charities Act 1958 which suggest that recreational facilities promoting particular sports are excluded. Thus, it seems that this is a good charitable trust.

7 THE CY-PRES DOCTRINE

7.1   Introduction

7.2   Key points

7.3   Analysis of questions

7.4   Questions

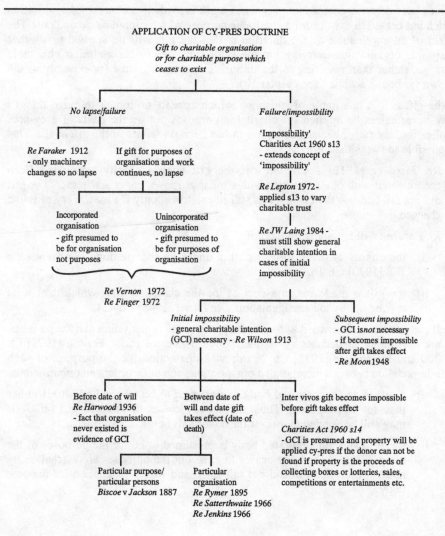

APPLICATION OF CY-PRES DOCTRINE

*Gift to charitable organisation
or for charitable purpose which
ceases to exist*

No lapse/failure

Re Faraker 1912
- only machinery
changes so no lapse

If gift for purposes of
organisation and work
continues, no lapse

Incorporated
organisation
- gift presumed to
be for organisation
not purposes

Unincorporated
organisation
- gift presumed to
be for purposes of
organisation

Re Vernon 1972
Re Finger 1972

Failure/impossibility

'Impossibility'
Charities Act 1960 s13
- extends concept of
'impossibility'

Re Lepton 1972 -
applied s13 to vary
charitable trust

Re JW Laing 1984 -
must still show general
charitable intention in
cases of initial
impossibility

Initial impossibility
- general charitable intention
(GCI) necessary - *Re Wilson* 1913

Subsequent impossibility
- GCI is *not* necessary
- if becomes impossible
after gift takes effect
- *Re Moon* 1948

Before date of will
Re Harwood 1936
- fact that organisation
never existed is
evidence of GCI

Between date of
will and date gift
takes effect (date of
death)

Inter vivos gift becomes impossible
before gift takes effect

Charities Act 1960 s14
- GCI is presumed and property will be
applied cy-pres if the donor can not be
found if property is the proceeds of
collecting boxes or lotteries, sales,
competitions or entertainments etc.

Particular purpose/
particular persons
Biscoe v *Jackson* 1887

Particular
organisation
Re Rymer 1895
Re Satterthwaite 1966
Re Jenkins 1966

7.1 Introduction

An understanding of charitable trusts (chapter 6) is a prerequisite to studying the cy-pres doctrine as the two topics are closely related. At first sight, the cases and statutory material concerning the topic appear to be relatively straightforward. Complexities do exist, however; notably in distinguishing whether a gift has been saved by an application of the cy-pres doctrine or whether in fact the gift did not fail at all. This distinction, although many students find it difficult to draw, must be grasped before the cy-pres doctrine as a whole can be mastered.

7.2 Key points

The cy-pres doctrine comes into play when a gift is made to a charitable organisation which has ceased to exist or for a charitable purpose which cannot be carried out. The effect of an application of the doctrine is that the gift will be applied to another charitable organisation carrying out the same purposes or for a similar charitable purpose, rather than resulting to the donor via a resulting trust (or possibly to the Crown via bona vacantia - see chapter 10).

If the gift is to a charitable organisation which appears no longer to exist, the gift may nevertheless be applied for charitable purposes not on the basis of a cy-pres application, but rather because there has in fact been no failure of the gift at all. This is possible in two situations:

a) *Re Faraker* [1912] 2 Ch 488 - if the gift is to a charity which has been consolidated with other charities with similar purposes under a scheme. The gift did not fail because the charity was still in existence, only the machinery of it had changed.

   Re Faraker will not apply, though, if:

   i) the charity is liable to termination under its constitution - *Re Stemson's WT* [1970] Ch 16.

   ii) the gift is made for an aspect of the the charity's work which cannot be carried out by the amalgamation - *Re Lucas* [1948] Ch 424.

b) If the gift can be construed as for the purposes of the organisation and the purposes are now being carried out by another body. The cases of *Re Vernon* [1972] Ch 300 and *Re Finger* [1972] Ch 286 drew a distinction for the purpose of such interpretation between incorporated organisations and unincorporated organisations.

   i) a gift to an incorporated body is presumed to be for the body itself rather than for its purposes. Thus, if the body ceases to exist the gift fails. (It may still be applied cy-pres if the conditions below are fulfilled).

   ii) a gift to an unincorporated body is presumed to be for the purposes of the body. Thus if the body ceases to exist but the purposes are carried on by another body the gift did not fail at all and would be applied for the new body.

If the gift has, however, failed (a case of 'impossibility') the possibility of cy-pres application arises.

(Since the Charities Act 1960 s13 the concept of 'impossibility' has been a very wide one enabling, in effect, the terms of gifts to be varied if they are impractical - as was done in *Re Lepton* [1972] 1 Ch 276. It has been underlined, however, that s13 expressly preserves the need for general charitable intention in cases of initial impossibility - *Re J W Laing* [1984] Ch 143).

The gift may be applied cy-pres if the case is one of initial impossibility and general charitable intention is proved and if it is a case of subsequent impossibility in which case there is no need to prove a general charitable intention.

a) *Initial impossibility*

If a gift is initially impossible - becomes impossible before the gift takes effect - it can be applied cy-pres if the donor can be shown to have had a general charitable intention:

i) if the gift becomes impossible before the date of the will.

In *Re Harwood* [1936] Ch 285 it was held that a gift to a body which had never existed showed a general charitable intention.

ii) if the gift becomes impossible between the date of the will and the date the gift takes effect (date of death):

- if the gift is for a particular purpose but can be construed as a gift to benefit a particular group of persons with only a desire for a particular mode which is impossible, the gift will be applied cy-pres for those persons in other ways - *Biscoe* v *Jackson* (1887) 35 Ch D 460.

- if the gift is for a particular organisation then if the organisation is simply the machinery for carrying out a purpose which the gift is intended for, then the gift can be applied cy-pres for that purpose via another body - *Re Rymer* [1895] 1 Ch 19. Whether the organisation was simply the machinery will be influenced by other gifts in the will from which a general charitable intention maybe inferred - *Re Satterthwaite's WT* [1966] 1 WLR 277 and *Re Jenkins' WT* [1966] Ch 249.

iii) if an inter vivos gift becomes impossible before the gift takes effect.

Charities Act 1960 s14 - if property is given for a specific charitable purpose, general charitable intention will nevertheless be presumed and the property will be applied cy-pres if the donor cannot be found or if he executes a written disclaimer. It will be presumed that the donor cannot be found if the property is the proceeds of collecting boxes or lotteries, sales, competitions or entertainments, etc.

b) *Subsequent impossibility*

A gift is subsequently impossible if it becomes impossible after the gift takes effect - *Re Moon's WT* [1948] 1 All ER 300. The gift will be applied cy-pres and there is no need to find a general charitable intention.

7.3   Analysis of questions

Questions on the cy-pres doctrine are commonly combined with those on charitable trusts (chapter 6), either as distinct parts of the question or as a problem on a gift to a charitable organisation which then ceases to exist - was the gift valid as a charitable trust and if so, can it be applied cy-pres? The main difficulty for the student attempting a question on this topic deciding whether a gift has in fact failed at all. If it has not, there is no need to consider whether a cy-pres application is possible.

7.4   Questions

Problem Checklist

a) Has the gift in fact failed? - *Re Faraker* (1912); *Re Vernon* (1972) and *Re Finger* (1972)?

b) If so, is it a case of initial or subsequent impossibility?

c) If initial, is there a general charitable intention (or will one be presumed by the Charities Act 1960 s14)? If so, the gift will be applied cy-pres.

d) If subsequent, the gift will automatically be applied cy-pres.

Question 1

Edmund, an eccentric but wealthy dancer, who was very fond of cats, has just died in Holborn, London. By his will made in 1975, after appointing Howard and Keith to be his executors and trustees, he made the following bequests:

1) £50,000 to the Holborn School of Dancing;

2) £60,000 to the Holborn Cat Hospital, London.

No dancing school by the name of the Holborn School of Dancing has ever existed in London. The Holborn Cat Hospital was an incorporated charity establishment for the treatment of sick cats. It was in existence when Edmund made his will but was wound up in 1978 and its works taken over by the National Animal Hospital, a registered charity.

Advise Howard and Keith.

University of London LLB Examination
(for External Students) Law of Trusts June 1984 Q6(b)

Suggested solution and comment

The main issue here is whether either of the gifts in Edmund's will can be saved from lapse under the cy-pres doctrine. If not they will fall into residue or pass to the next-of-kin on intestacy.

As regards the gift of £50,000 to the Holborn School of Dancing, this is to an organisation that never existed. Such a gift can be applied cy-pres if its object is charitable. On this I have no doubt. If the encouragement of classical drama and acting is charitable being for the advancement of education (see *Re Shakespeare Memorial Trust* (1923)) or encouraging interest in the works of a particular composer (see *Re Delius' WT* (1957)), I fail to see how the teaching of dancing could be regarded otherwise. These are all cases where there is a raising of the arts and artistic taste, a matter which was clearly regarded as charitable by Lord Greene MR in *Royal Choral Society* v *IRC* (1943). In these circumstances the gift being to an organisation which never existed will be applied cy-pres as in *Re Harwood* (1936). In that case a gift to a peace society which never existed was applied cy-pres as a case of initial impossibility on the basis that the testator was indicating a general charitable intention by pointing to a fictitious example.

The gift of £60,000 to the Holborn Cat Hospital, London was to an established charity which was wound up in 1978, before Edmund's death, and is, therefore, a case of initial impossibility. See *Biscoe* v *Jackson* (1887). Before this gift can be applied cy-pres it is necessary to show that there is a general charitable intention in it and that it is not a specific gift for a specific purpose only. *Re Rymer* (1895). It seems to me that there is no evidence one way or the other on this when one reads the gift. However, the courts have gone far to find a general charitable intention and one rule of construction adopted to this end is that a gift to an unincorporated charity is prima facie a gift to its purposes rather than to it beneficially. See *Re Vernon's WT* (1972). Unfortunately, this will not help in the present case as the Cat Hospital was an incorporated charity. There seems to be little prospect of finding the necessary general charitable intention here and if this is so, the gift will lapse. I can only suggest that the executors and trustees read the will to see if it suggests a general charitable intention.

Question 2

In what circumstances, if any, may trust moneys be applied cy pres?

University of London LLB Examination
(for External Students) Law of Trusts June 1987 Q5(a)

Skeleton solution and comment

This is a very general question. In an answer the student is required to give a precis of the law relating to cy-pres. This must necessarily be very concise due to the time constraints (this is only half of a question).

- Introduction

  When cy-pres applies; contrast with non-charitable trusts; requirement of general charitable intention.

- Distinction between initial and supervening impossibility.

- Initial impossibility - whether gift has in fact failed; requirement of general charitable intention.

- Supervening impossibility.
- Charities Act 1960 ss13 and 14.

Suggested solution

Trust monies may only be applied cy-pres where the trust concerned is charitable in nature and it has failed. In private trusts failure will result in the property being returned on resulting trusts to the settlor in most cases. In charitable trusts the cy-pres doctrine is designed to avoid money given for charitable trusts which fail being returned on resulting trusts if it can be said that there was a general charitable intention behind the gift. If such an intention can be found the money will be applied for the benefit of charitable objects which are similar to those of the original gift.

A gift to a charitable trust may fail because the trust has ceased to exist at the date the gift takes effect, for example, a gift under a Will which comes into operation after the trust went out of existence, or because the trust ceased to exist after the gift took effect and it has not been exhausted by those trusts. The former is known as initial impossibility whilst the latter is known as supervening impossibility.

In cases of initial impossibility, it must be shown that the charitable trust ceased to exist before the gift took effect. Thus, there will be no room for the application of cy-pres where the charity has been amalgamated with other charities and has lost its administrative machinery and name but not its identity as a trust. See *Re Faraker* (1912). It must also be shown that there is a general charitable intention behind the gift and that the donor was not intending it as a specific gift for a specific purpose. See *Re Rymer* (1895) There are often problems in determining if there is a general charitable intention and to this end the court has devised a number of rules which are designed so that the gift can be applied cy-pres. In *Re Vernon's WT* (1972) Buckley J held that a gift to an unincorporated charity without more was prima facie to be construed as a gift for its purposes so that if the charity ceased to exist but its work was still being carried on a cy-pres application could be made. This principle does not apply to incorporated charities as these are considered as taking any gifts to them beneficially. In *Re Satterthwaite's WT* (1966) it was held that a general charitable intention might be drawn from a long list of gifts which had a common charitable theme but included a gift which was unidentifiable as a gift to a known charity, that gift could be applied cy-pres. See also *Re Harwood* (1936).

Supervening impossibility does not require that a general charitable intention be shown to exist behind the gift because once money is effectively dedicated to charitable purposes it is always held for charitable purposes. All that is necessary in supervening impossibility is that it is a gift which took effect and since then the charity has ceased to exist. Thus, in *Re Slevin* (1891) a gift was made by Will to an orphanage. Shortly after the will took effect the orphanage closed but the gift was nevertheless applied cy-pres.

There are also some statutory provisions on initial impossibility. Under s13 of the Charities Act 1960 the court may order that a cy-pres application be made in certain cases even though there is no impossibility in applying the gift. This may be done where, for example, the original purposes have been carried out as far as may be or where they are no longer a practical or useful way of applying the money. Under s14 of the Charities Act 1960 cy-pres is applied to monies from unidentified sources as part of a collection for a charitable purpose which cannot be carried out. The object of this provision is to overcome the difficulties of returning the money to the donors.

8   SECRET TRUSTS

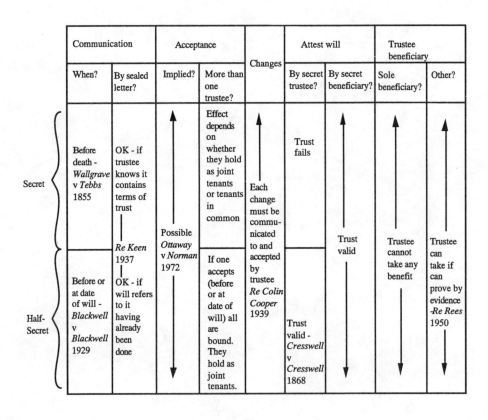

	Communication		Acceptance		Changes	Attest will		Trustee beneficiary	
	When?	By sealed letter?	Implied?	More than one trustee?		By secret trustee?	By secret beneficiary?	Sole beneficiary?	Other?
Secret	Before death - *Wallgrave v Tebbs* 1855	OK - if trustee knows it contains terms of trust *Re Keen* 1937	Possible *Ottaway v Norman* 1972	Effect depends on whether they hold as joint tenants or tenants in common	Each change must be communicated to and accepted by trustee *Re Colin Cooper* 1939	Trust fails	Trust valid	Trustee cannot take any benefit	Trustee can take if can prove by evidence *-Re Rees* 1950
Half-Secret	Before or at date of will - *Blackwell v Blackwell* 1929	OK - if will refers to it having already been done		If one accepts (before or at date of will) all are bound. They hold as joint tenants.		Trust valid - *Cresswell v Cresswell* 1868			

72

8.1   Introduction

Secret and half secret trusts are out-of-date topics in that in reality they are now practically extinct. The rules remain, however, and are straightforward. More complicated are the arguments surrounding the nature of such trusts - express or constructive - and the various rationales which have been put forward on the doctrine. The only way for a student to gain sufficient understanding of these problems is to familiarise himself fully with at least some of the many articles written about them. Cases and textbooks alone will not offer the answers.

8.2   Key points

SECRET   HALF-SECRET

a) *Background*

Wills are public documents and thus any legacies made in them are open to public scrutiny. The doctrine of secret and half-secret trusts evolved to enable legacies to be made privately.

Secret trusts can arise in cases of inter vivos gifts - *Bannister* v *Bannister* [1948] 2 All ER 133 - and in cases of intestacy - *McCormick* v *Grogan* (1869) LR 4 HL 82. However, the main area of their application is trusts created by will.

b) *Nature*

Where

   i) No sign of a trust on the face of the will; or

   ii) Any words in the will attempting to create a half-secret trust fail the test for certainty of intention (see chapter 2)

Where a trust is created on the face of the will, but the beneficiaries are not named. The will must refer to communication having already taken place. If it refers to future communication the trust will be invalid under the 'best evidence rule'.

c) *Communication*

   i) When?

      Testator must communicate fact of trust to secret-trustee at any time during testator;'s lifetime (ie can be done after date of will) - *Wallgrave* v *Tebbs* (1855) 2 K & J 313.

Communication must be before or contemporaneously with making of the will - *Blackwell* v *Blackwell* [1929] AC 318 and *Re Bateman* [1970] 3 All ER 817. If none, trustees hold on resulting trusts for the residuary beneficiary under the will (or, if none, those entitled on intestacy) and never take beneficially themselves.

SECRET	HALF-SECRET
If no communication, secret trustee takes absolutely if he knew nothing of any trust. If the person knew he was to take as trustee but did not know the terms of the trust, there is a resulting trust to the estate.	

ii) Terms

All terms must be communicated (trust property, beneficiaries and how much each is to receive) - *Re Boyes* (1884) 26 Ch D 531. If the fact of the trust, but not the terms, is communicated, the trustee holdson trust for the residuary beneficiary.	Same, except that the fact of the trust will always be communicated in the will.

iii) By sealed letter

If trustee is handed a sealed envelope before death not to be opened until after testator's death, this will satisfy the communication requirement if the trustee knows the envelope contains the terms of trust - *Re Keen* [1937] Ch 236.	If trustee is handed an envelope before or contemporaneously with the date of the will and the will refers to this having already been done, this will satisfy the communication requirement - *Re Keen* (1937).

iv) Nature

Communication must be of a legally binding obligation and not merely a moral obligation - *McCormick* v *Grogan* (1869). In other words, it must satisfy the test of certainty of intention. If no such certainty, trustee takes absolutely. If certainty, but trust fails on another ground, trustee holds on trust for residuary beneficiary.	Same. If words in the will are not sufficiently certain, the only possibility is a fully-secret trust.

SECRET	HALF-SECRET

d) *Acceptance*

i) General

Trustee must expressly or impliedly (*Ottaway* v *Norman* [1972] Ch 698) accept the trust. If the terms of the trust are communicated and the trustee rejects, he holds on trust for the residuary beneficiary. If only the fact of the trust is communicated, the trustee can take absolutely if he rejects - *Wallgrave* v *Tebbs* (1855) 2 K & J 313.

Same. Acceptance must also be before or contemporaneously with the date of the will.

ii) Gift to more that one trustee

- as tenants in common. If one accepts on behalf of all, only the one who actually accepts is bound.

- as joint tenants. If one accepts before the date of the will, all are bound.

If one accepts after date of will, only he is bound and the others can take their share beneficially.

Always take as joint tenants in equity, and thus all will always be bound, since if one accepts after the date of the will, the half-secret trust fails in any event.

e) *Changes*

Each change must be communicated to and accepted by the trustee - *Re Colin Cooper* [1939] Ch 811.

Same.

f) *Revocation*

Following *Re Gardner (No 2)* [1923] 2 Ch 230 this does not appear to be possible as the beneficiary acquires an interest as soon as the trust is communicated and accepted. However, this case has been strongly criticised.

SECRET	HALF-SECRET
g) *Attestation of the will*	
i) By secret beneficiary	
By s15 Wills Act 1837 a witness or their spouse cannot benefit under a will. However, in equity, the beneficiary can take the benefit as the trust operates outside the will - *Re Young* [1951] Ch 344.	Same.
ii) By trustee	
Legacy and trust fail as the trust has nothing to operate on.	Legacy succeeds because there is a trust on the face of the will following *Cresswell* v *Cresswell* (1868) LR 6 Eq 69.
h) *Secret beneficiary predeceases testator*	
Following *Re Gardner (No 2)* [1923] 2 Ch 230 the trust is not defeated as the beneficiary receives his interest when the trust is created.	Same.
i) *Secret trustee predeceases testator*	
Trust fails - *Re Maddock* [1902] 2 Ch 220.	Provided the purpose of the trust is known it should be enforced as equity will not allow trust to fail for want of a trustee.
j) *Secret trustee is also a beneficiary*	
i) Sole beneficiary	
Cannot take under trust - *Re Pugh's WT* [1967] 1 WLR 1262.	Same.
ii) Other	
Re Rees [1950] Ch 204 suggests that trustees can take if can prove evidence other than their own of existence of the gift. Possibly written evidence is required.	

k) *Express or constructive trust?*

Half-secret trust of land must be evidenced in writing under s53(1)(b) LPA - see *Re Baillie* (1886) 2 TLR 660, but in *Ottaway* v *Norman* [1972] Ch 698 a fully secret trust or land was valid without written evidence. This suggests a fully secret trust is constructive but a half-secret trust is express.

l) *Rationales*

   i)   Doctrine of incorporation (half-secret trusts).

   ii) Fraud. It is not necessary to comply with the Wills Act because equity will not allow it to be used as an instrument of fraud.

   iii) Inter-vivos trusts - *Re Gardner (No 2)* [1923] 2 Ch 230.

   iv) Operate outside the will - *Re Young* [1951] Ch 344.

8.3   Analysis of questions

The topic is well suited to problem questions and, as a result, these often appear in examinations. Such questions usually address most aspects of the topic and often overlap with other topics such as formal requirements (chapter 3) and the three certainties (chapter 2). In particular, a student tackling a problem in this area must be familiar with the rules concerning certainty of intention. Students should also be aware of the controversial aspects of the topic such as the possible rationales behind the doctrine of secret trusts as these are often examined in essay questions.

8.4   Questions

Problem checklist

a) Is there any trust on the face of the will?

If not, potential fully-secret trust. If so, if the writing satisfies the rules regarding certainty of intention, potential half-secret trust. If it does not, potential fully-secret trust.

b) Fully-secret trust. Have the rules been satisfied?

If they have not, the trust fails. The 'trustee' will only take absolutely if:

   i)   no communication to him of the trust at all.

   ii) only the fact of the trust was communicated and he rejected it.

In all other circumstances, the 'trustee' will hold the property on resulting trust for the testator's estate.

c) Half-secret trust. Have the rules been satisfied?

If not, the trust fails and the property is always held by the trustee on resulting trust for the testator's estate.

d) Did the 'trustee' attest the will?

If so:

   i)   fully-secret trust - the trust fails.

   ii) half-secret trust - the trust does not fail.

e) Did the beneficiary attest the will?

If so, the trust does not fail.

f) Did the trustee predecease the testator?

If so:

   i)   fully-secret trust - the trust fails.

   ii) half-secret trust - the trust does not fail.

g) Did the beneficiary predecease the testator?

If so, the trust does not fail.

Question 1

By his will executed in 1980, Tristram, who died earlier this year, after appointing Eric and Ernie to be his executors and trustees, made the following dispositions:

i) He devised his main residence, The Oaks, to his friend, Frank absolutely;

ii) He devised his country cottage, Rose Cottage, to his sisters, Hilda and Helga in equal shares;

iii) He bequeathed £50,000 to his brother, Bertram 'in the knowledge that he will give effect to my expressed wishes'.

iv) He devised and bequeathed his residuary estate to the British Museum.

Shortly after executing his will, Tristram orally informed Frank that he wished Frank to hold The Oaks for the benefit of his secretary's (Sonia's) children, Jack and Jill; he also wrote separately to both Hilda and Helga asking them to hold Rose Cottage for the benefit of Sonia. Hilda replied that she would do as Tristram requested but the letter to Helga went astray and Tristram's request never came to her notice.

Prior to executing his will, Tristram had handed Bertram a sealed envelope with instructions that Bertram was only to open it after Tristram's death. The letter inside the envelope (which Bertram has just opened) expresses Tristram's wish that the £50,000 shall be paid to Sonia.

Sonia was one of the witnesses to Tristram's will.

Advise Eric and Ernie as to the distribution of Tristram's estate.

University of London LLB Examination
(for External Students) Law of Trusts June 1987 Q2

Skeleton solution and comment

This is a wide question which requires the student to address several of the rules on and other aspects of both fully-secret and half-secret trusts. In a question such as this, the student's first concern is to spot every issue raised. Once this is done, consideration of these points in a logical way will produce a good answer.

- Disposition to Frank is an attempt to create a fully-secret trust. Consider, therefore, communication and acceptance of the terms and

- whether s53(1)(b) LPA 1925 applies.

- Disposition to Hilda and Helga is also an attempt to create a fully-secret trust. Consider possible effects of two secret trustees on the rules as to communication and acceptance.

- Effect of the secret beneficiary witnessing the will.

- Disposition to Bertram is an attempt to create half-secret trust but as the words fail to impose a trust obligation, the only possibility is, in fact, the existence of a fully-secret trust. Consider in particular the effect of constructive communication.

Suggested solution

The first disposition made by Tristram was of The Oaks to Frank absolutely. Shortly after executing his Will Tristram orally informed Frank that he wished Frank to hold The Oaks for the benefit of Sonia's children. This indicates an attempt to create a fully secret trust as there was no reference to the obligation imposed upon Frank in the Will itself. See *Wallgrave* v *Tebbs* (1855). The communication after the Will is valid as it need only take place during the testator's lifetime, whether before or after the Will is irrelevant. See *Wallgrave* v *Tebbs*. It is unclear whether Frank accepted or rejected the trust obligation imparted to him. If he accepted he is bound to carry the obligation into effect but if he did not then he could take The Oaks beneficially. It is clear from *Wallgrave* v *Tebbs* that a secret trustee who refuses the trust can take beneficially when the testator fails to change his will thereafter as there can be no fraud on the testator by him.

The secret trust imposed upon Frank involved land and this raises the issue whether it is necessary that it should satisfy the provisions of s53(1)(b) LPA 1925. Frank was only orally informed of the terms of the trust. In *Ottaway* v *Norman* (1972) a fully secret trust of a house was upheld even though it was orally communicated to the trustee. The reasons for this are not explained in the judgment but it appears that the explanation may be that fully secret trusts are a species of constructive trust and, therefore, do not require writing because of s53(2) LPA 1925.

Rose Cottage was devised to Hilda and Helga 'in equal shares'. Tristram wrote to both of them asking them to hold the cottage on trust for Sonia but Helga never received her letter. This indicates an intention by Tristram to create another fully secret trust but with two secret trustees. Where there is a fully secret trust with two secret trustees, the trustees may take the property as either joint tenants or tenants in common. See *Re Stead* (1900). Hilda and Helga would appear to be tenants in common as the cottage was devised to them 'in equal shares' suggesting they have separate interests. The rule as to communication in such instances is that each tenant in common must be told of and accept the secret trust in order that his share be bound by it. Hilda is clearly bound on the facts but Helga is not. The decision in *Tee* v *Ferris* (1856) suggests that Helga could take her share beneficially since the share of each tenant in common must be considered in isolation and because acceptance by one tenant in common should not bind the shares of the others. However, there are dicta in the Irish Court of Appeal in *Geddis* v *Semple* (1903) which suggest that the matter should be viewed by asking if the gift to Helga was induced by the undertaking of Hilda and, if so, that her share should be bound by the trust but not otherwise. On any view Helga should be able to claim a half share of the cottage for herself as the will was not made on the faith of the undertaking by Hilda, communication being after its execution.

A further point which arises in relation to the secret trust of the cottage is that Sonia witnessed the Will. As beneficiary under the secret trust she is not within the ambit of s15 of the Wills Act 1837 which prevents a witness or the spouse of a witness benefiting under a Will. In *Re Young* (1951) it was held that the secret trust operated outside the Will and was not affected by s15. Thus, Sonia is entitled to a half share in Rose Cottage.

The bequest of £50,000 to Bertram appears to be an ineffective attempt to create a half secret trust. The words in the Will do not impose a trust obligation upon Bertram as is necessary for a half secret trust. See *McCormick* v *Grogan* (1869). The words appear to be precatory words with no certainty of intention to impose a legally binding obligation on Bertram. A fully secret trust may be considered as arising here if the letter which Bertram received from Tristram imposed upon him an imperative obligation to pay the £50,000 to Sonia. See *Re Snowden* (1979). The requirements of communication and acceptance of the secret trust are satisfied here. There has been a constructive communication of the terms of the trust, if there be one, by handing over these terms in a sealed letter. According to *Re Keen* (1937) the secret trustee need not know the terms of the trust at the time of communication, it is sufficient that he is told that a trust is being imposed and that the means of ascertaining the terms of that trust are given to him then. Thus, if there is a trust obligation in the letter, Sonia will be entitled to the £50,000 and as stated above, her witnessing the Will will not affect her claim. But, if no secret trust obligation was imposed by the letter then Bertram would be entitled to keep the money for himself, he would only have a moral obligation towards Sonia. Bertram would also be able to keep the money for himself if he did not know that the letter contained details of a trust at all.

Question 2

Consider the proposition that the theory underlying the development of wholly secret trusts differs fundamentally from that underlying the development of half secret trusts and that in the light of this difference, the present rules as to communication are in each case justifiable.

University of London LLB Examination
(for External Students) Law of Trusts June 1988 Q2(a)

Skeleton solution and comment

This question requires the student to look at the various rationales of the doctrines of fully-secret and half-secret trusts, to decide which is the most plausible and then to consider whether the rationale selected offers an explanation for the different between the communication rules concerning each type. To answer a question such as this the student must have studied the topic in depth; knowledge of the rules alone will not enable him to produce a good answer. The length and depth of the answer presupposes that the question is a whole one rather than half of a mixed question. As half of a mixed question, the student would be under severe time constraints and the issues discussed below could only be touched upon.

* Introduction: define fully and half secret trusts; state that the rules on communication differ.
* Explain the different communication rules.
* Matthews' rationale - doctrine of incorporation (half-secret) and fraud (fully-secret).
* Other rationales - 'dehors' the will; inter vivos trusts.
* The fraud theory.
* Conclusion - the proposition is wrong.

Suggested solution

The concepts of secret trusts - both wholly and half secret - stem from a necessity to be able to dispose of property privately on death. A will is a public document and thus testators who did not wish anyone to know of the ultimate destination of their property wold on the face of the will create a disposition in favour of X either as an absolute gift (a fully-secret trust) or expressed to be on trust but for unnamed beneficiaries (a half-secret trust). They would communicate the terms of such trust to X outside the will. Despite the fact that such communication did not satisfy the requirements of the Wills Act 1837, equity enforced these trusts on the basis that not to do so would be to allow that statute to be used as an instrument of fraud by those who wished to deny the existence of such a trust. Certain of the rules concerning these trusts differ depending on whether the trust in question is fully-secret or half-secret; notably the rule regarding communication to X of the trust and of its terms.

The position on communication is that in the case of a fully-secret trust, it can take place at any time during the testator's lifetime - *Wallgrave* v *Tebbs* (1855). However, if the trust in question is half-secret, then communication must occur before or contemporaneously with the making of the will - *Blackwell* v *Blackwell* (1929). This distinction has been criticised as purely arbitrary by Holdsworth (1937) 53 LQR 501, although some commentators feel that the reason for the distinction can be explained by reference to the rationales of the doctrine which, in their views, differ for fully-secret and half-secret trusts.

An academic who takes this latter view is Matthews [1979] Conv 360. He feels that the theory underlying half-secret trusts is the probate doctrine of incorporation whereas that underlying fully-secret trusts is a type of fraud. The doctrine of incorporation allows extrinsic evidence to be admitted to probate as part of the will provided that such evidence is in writing and is referred to in the will. To say that this doctrine explains half-secret trusts is, however, misguided in two important respects. Firstly, the intention of the testator is clearly not that the terms of the half-secret trust should be incorporated into the will. To do so would be to cause the terms of the trust to become public, the avoidance of which is why a half-secret trust was originally used. Secondly, the courts do not appear to consider that the terms of the half-secret trust should be in writing. In *Blackwell* v *Blackwell* (1929) itself the terms of the trust were communicated orally and thus, following Matthews' line of reasoning, should have failed as a half-secret trust.

Other possible rationales include the theory that secret trusts are in fact inter vivos trusts and that they operate outside the will. No distinction is drawn between fully-secret and half-secret trusts when putting forward these two theories and thus they would offer no support for the proposition given. In any event both arguments are weak. To say that secret trusts operate outside the will is undoubtedly true - otherwise cases such as *Re Young* (1951) would not have been decided as they were. However, it does not logically follow that this proposition is the theory underlying the doctrines which it clearly is not. The former theory, above, is stronger, especially since the case of *Re Gardner (No 2)* (1923) in which it was held that a secret trust took effect once the terms of the trust had been communicated and accepted and that from that point the beneficiary had an enforceable interest under the trust. This case has, however, been strongly criticised and ignores the revocable nature of wills. If the decision in *Re Gardner (No 2)* (1923) is correct then the result is that once a secret trust has been communicated and accepted, the will cannot be revoked if such revocation would result on there being no gift in the will for the trust to operate on. It is, therefore, respectfully submitted that the decision in the case is wrong.

A far more convincing rationale is the fraud theory which has been supported in many decisions and by many academics. It is well established that equity will not allow a statute to be used as an instrument of fraud, and it has been suggested that this is the reason that equity will enforce secret trusts despite the fact that they do not accord with the requirements of the Wills Act 1837. The problem with the fraud theory, however, is the nature of the fraud it refers to. In the case of a fully-secret trust it is arguable that equity will intervene to prevent actual fraud on the part of the proposed trustee as if no fully-secret trust is found to exist, the trustee would, in accordance with the terms of the will, take the property beneficially. In the case of a half-secret trust, though, the trustee can never take beneficially and thus there is no question of this type of fraud. Instead, not to enforce it would constitute fraud of 'a special kind' - per Lord Buckmaster in *Blackwell* v *Blackwell.* By this is meant fraud in the sense of breaking a promise to the dead and one which the testator relied on.

If the fraud theory is the theory underlying both fully-secret and half-secret trusts as argued, then the theories are the same for both types of secret trusts and do not, therefore, offer any explanation as to the different rules of communication. It is submitted that in respect of this distinction, Holdsworth was correct in saying that it is purely arbitrary and should be abolished.

Question 3

By her will executed in 1986, Tania appointed Alpha and Bravo to be her executors and trustees (in the will referred to as 'my Trustees') and made the following gifts:

 i) My cottage, Ratcatchers, to my Trustees absolutely;

 ii) My London house to my Trustees upon trust to sell the same and to distribute the net proceeds of sale amongst such of my good friends and in such shares as my Trustee shall think appropriate;

 iii) My time-share in Villa Dolce Vita, to my gardener, George;

 iv) All my residuary real estate to my son, Samuel, and all my residuary personal estate to my husband, Harry.

In 1985, Tania had informed Alpha that she would be leaving Ratcatchers to Alpha and Bravo but that she wanted to ensure that her gardener, George, would be entitled to occupy the cottage for the rest of his life; Alpha said he fully understood.

Tania has recently died survived by all the persons mentioned in her will. George was one of the witnesses to Tania's will.

Advise all parties as to their respective beneficial entitlement, if any, in Tania's estate.

University of London LLB Examination
(for External Students) Law of Trusts June 1989 Q1

Skeleton solution and comment

The main issues in this problem are secret trusts and certainty of objects. The former raises a number of complex and, as yet, not clearly answered issues on the position of communication to one of two or more secret trustees and, also, whether fully secret trustees may benefit under their secret trust. The certainty of objects issue does not raise any real difficulties. This question is not difficult and a student who has made a reasonable study of secret trusts should find it well within his/her capabilities.

• Gift of cottage, Ratcatchers to trustees. Valid fully secret trust communicated to and accepted by Alpha. Bravo not informed of secret trust but he is bound by its terms as Alpha told of trust before will made. George witnessed will but not affected by s15 Wills Act 1837 as a beneficiary under a secret trust not affected by this provision.

• Gift of London house on discretionary trusts for 'my good friends'. Trust void because of uncertainty of objects and house will pass to Samuel as residuary realty.

• Gift of time-share in Villa Dolce Vita to George. Gift cannot take effect because of s15 Wills Act 1837. Time-share is personalty and will pass to Harry as residuary personalty.

Suggested solution

The gift of the cottage, Ratcatchers, to the Trustees, Alpha and Bravo, appears to be subject to a secret trust for the benefit of George. This is because Tania informed Alpha, about one year before she made the will that she would be leaving the cottage to Alpha and Bravo but wanted to ensure that George would be entitled to occupy it for the rest of his life. This obligation in favour of George is, in my view, such as to impose a trust. See *Ottaway* v *Norman* (1972).

Although Alpha and Bravo are named as trustees, the gift is expressed as an absolute one. There is an apparent contradiction here. If Alpha and Bravo take as trustees on the face of the will, there is a half-secret trust. Communication is valid since it did take place before the execution of the will - see *Blackwell* v *Blackwell* (1929).

The secret trust in this case is a fully secret trust because the gift to the trustees is an absolute gift on the face of the will with the testatrix's intentions being communicated outside the will. See *Wallgrave* v *Tebbs* (1855). Communication of the terms of the trust was valid since in fully secret trusts it may be made either before or after the execution of the will. See *Wallgrave* v *Tebbs*. One difficulty which does arise in this case is that only one of the trustees, Alpha, was informed by the testatrix of the terms of the trust. In my view, the failure of the testatrix to inform Bravo of the terms of the trust does not affect it's validity. As the trust property is land Alpha and Bravo could only be treated as joint tenants as a legal estate cannot be held by tenancy in common. See ss1(6); 34(1) and 36(2) Law of Property Act 1925. As Alpha accepted the secret trust before the will was made it seems that both he and Bravo are, as joint tenants, bound by the terms of the secret trust. See *Russell* v *Jackson* (1852). Thus, the whole trust property is bound by the secret trust and Bravo cannot take any part of it for himself. Alpha's reply to the testatrix in 1985 that 'he fully understood' was also a sufficient indication of his acceptance because acceptance will be inferred from any mode of action which gives the testatrix the impression or belief that he assents to the request. See *McCormick* v *Grogan* (1869).

Three further issues in relation to this secret trust merit discussion but they do not affect its validity. First, the trust involves land and raises the issue whether it should satisfy s53(1)(b) of the Law of Property Act 1925. The secret trust in *Ottaway* v *Norman* involved a house but Brightman J held the trust valid on parol evidence. However, there was no reference to this provision in the case. As fully secret trusts are treated as constructive trusts rather than express trusts, in that they are enforced to prevent fraud, it may be argued that they are exempt from the formalities of s53(1) (b) by reason of s53(2). If the trust is half-secret it will fail for lack of formality: see *Re Baillie* (1886).

Second, George was a witness to the testatrix's will. Under s15 of the Wills Act 1837 a beneficiary under a will who witnesses that will loses his beneficial interest in order to ensure that he is an impartial witness. This provision does not affect those who are beneficiaries under a secret trust because, as was held in *Re Young* (1951), a beneficiary under a secret trust takes outside the will by reason of the trust imposed on the beneficiary under the will.

Third, George is given a life interest only under the secret trust and the cottage otherwise belongs to Alpha and Bravo. Alpha and Bravo take their interest under the terms of the will and not under the terms of the secret trusts. Provided they are beneficiaries on the face of the will, there is no objection to their taking a beneficial interest under a fully secret trust. If the trust here were a half-secret one, Alpha and Bravo might well not be allowed to bring oral evidence to contradict the terms of the will as in *Re Rees WT* (1950), and on George's death there would be a resulting trust to the estate.

This is an attempt to create a discretionary trust and appears to fail for lack of certainty of objects. The trust must satisfy the test in *McPhail* v *Doulton* (1971) - can it be said with certainty of any given claimant whether he is or is not a member of the class? 'My good friends' appears to be a term which lacks conceptual certainty and cannot be objectively defined, and a description which has no conceptual certainty will cause a trust to fail. There will be a resulting trust to the estate and the house will pass to Samuel who is entitled to residuary realty. There is no conversion as the trust has wholly failed.

The gift to George will fail as George witnessed the will - see Wills Act 1837 s15. The time-share will become part of the residuary personalty and pass to Harry.

In conclusion, the gift of the time-share and the trust of the house will fail and the property will become part of the residuary estate. There appears to be a valid secret trust of the cottage in favour of George, provided this can be shown to be a fully secret trust. If it is a half-secret trust it may fail for non-compliance with s53(1)(b) LPA 1925.

9 SETTING TRUSTS ASIDE

9.1 Introduction

9.2 Key points

9.3 Analysis of questions

9.4 Questions

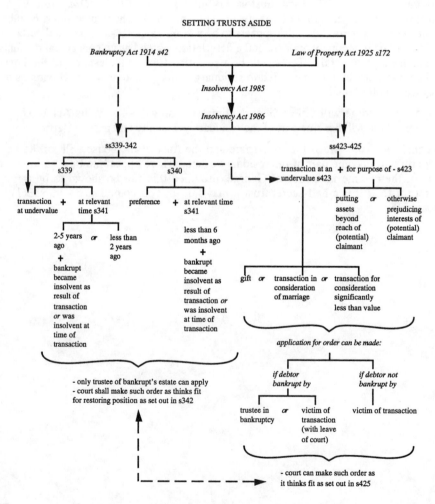

9.1   Introduction

Since the Insolvency Act 1986 most difficulties raised by the topic have disappeared. The law is now wholly contained in the statute which must simply be digested and learnt. The previous law is now only relevant in as much as the student should formulate an opinion as to whether and how the Act has ironed out previous problems and improved the law.

9.2   Key points

Until the Insolvency Act 1986 (replacing the Insolvency Act 1985), the law concerning whether a trust could be set aside in the event of the settlor's bankruptcy was contained in two statutory provisions:

a) *Bankruptcy Act 1914 s42*

The main defects in this provision as noted in the Cork Report on Insolvency Law and Practice (1982) Cmnd 8558 were that the section only covered settlements, so that gifts fell outside its provisions. In addition, it did not cover all transactions at an undervalue; only those for merely nominal consideration or less. The section has now been replaced by ss339-342 Insolvency Act 1986.

b) *Law of Property Act 1925 s172*

This provision contained many defects as outlined in the Cork Report. Notably, the section required an intention to defraud creditors, the meaning of which was unclear.

The section has now been replaced by ss423-425 Insolvency Act 1986.

The Insolvency Act 1985 and then the Insolvency Act 1986 replaced the above provisions:

a) *Sections 339-342*

These sections allow the court to make an order regarding a transaction at an undervalue or a preference by a bankrupt provided that certain conditions are fulfilled. Only the trustee of the bankrupt's estate can apply for such an order:

   i)   transaction at undervalue

        By s339 this is either a gift, a transaction in consideration of marriage or a transaction for consideration 'significantly less' than the value. Such a transaction must have been entered into 'at a relevant time', which by s341 means within 5 years of the presentation of the individual's bankruptcy petition. If it is more than 2 years before that date, then the individual must also have been insolvent at that time - as defined by s341(3) - or must have become insolvent as a result of such transaction. In working out whether or not an individual is insolvent, account must be taken of contingent debts.

   ii) preference

        By s340 an individual gives a preference if he puts one of his creditors (etc - as defined in s340(3)) into a position which, on the event of the individual's bankruptcy, is a better position than he would otherwise have been in. The preference must have been exercised 'at a relevant time' within s341 - that is to say, within 6 months of the presentation of the individual's bankruptcy petition. In addition the requirements of the individual's insolvency apply as above.

b) *Sections 423-425*

These sections will be resorted to in the case of a transaction at an undervalue which does not fall within the requisite time limits above. The main difference between the previous and present sets of sections is that for the court to make an order regarding a transaction of an undervalue under s423 it must be satisfied that the transaction was entered into in order to prejudice a potential claimant against him. The advantage of these sections is that there exist no time limits. In addition the power to apply is not restricted to the trustee in bankruptcy; any victim of the transaction can apply although if the individual has been adjudged bankrupt, the victim needs the leave of the court.

9.3 Analysis of questions

As this topic has been the subject of quite recent changes, an essay question about whether the law has improved is a possibility. Problem questions are, however, more common and, if the Insolvency Act 1986 is learnt thoroughly, should prevent no real difficulties. A simple application of the statutory provisions is all that is required.

9.4 Questions

Problem checklist

a) Is the transaction a transaction at an undervalue or a preference?

   If transaction at undervalue, go to (b); if preference, go to (f).

b) Are we advising the trustee in bankruptcy?

   If so, go to (c); if not, go to (e).

c) Does the transaction fall within the definition in s339/423?

   If not, it cannot be set aside; if so, go to (d).

d) Was the transaction made at 'the relevant time'?

   i) Within 2 years of the presentation of the transferor's bankruptcy petition?

       If so the transaction can be set aside under s339(2).

   ii) Between 2-5 years before this date?

       If so the transaction can be set aside (provided the insolvency requirements under s341(3) are complied with) under s339(2).

       If not, go to (e).

e) Was the transaction entered into for a purpose under s423(3)?

If so, it can be set aside under s423(2); if not, it cannot be set aside.

f) Does the preference fall within the definition in s340(3)?

If so, go to (g); if not, the preference cannot be set aside.

g) Was the preference exercised within 'a relevant time'? (See (d) above).

If so, go to (h); if not, the transaction cannot be set aside.

h) Are we advising the trustee in bankruptcy?

If so, the preference can be set aside under s340(2); if not, the preference cannot be set aside.

Question 1

In 1986, Charles, a married man with children and who had made a small fortune in a computer programming business, decided to diversify and to embark upon business in the field of biotechnology.

In 1987, he obtained a divorce from his wife and later in that year married Jane. Shortly before his re-marriage he:

i) Executed a marriage settlement whereby, in consideration of his intended marriage to Jane, he settled £200,000 upon trust for Jane for life remainder to any children he might have by Jane;

ii) Made an outright gift of £100,000 to his son by his first marriage, Dan;

iii) Gave £100,000 to the trustees of the golf club of which he was a member, to be held upon trust to apply the income in awarding trophies and cash prizes to the winners of club golfing tournaments which were held monthly;

iv) Settled his house upon trust for himself for life upon protective trusts and subject thereto upon trust for Jane absolutely.

After making these dispositions, he had enough resources left to meet his ordinary liabilities but proceedings had been commenced against him, which he was vigorously and optimistically defending, for breach of copyright.

In 1989, judgment was given against him in the copyright proceedings (which related to a computer programme) and at the same time his biotechnology business failed. He has now been adjudicated a bankrupt.

Advise his trustee in bankruptcy (with reasons) whether he (the trustee) can have recourse to any of the funds and assets disposed of under (i) to (iv) above.

Adapted from University of London LLB Examination
(for External Students) Law of Trusts June 1986 Q4

Suggested solution

The trustee in bankruptcy may only have recourse to the funds and assets disposed of by Charles shortly before his re-marriage in 1987 if he can make a claim for setting the trusts aside under the Insolvency Act 1986.

i) The marriage settlement falls within the definition of a transaction of an undervalue under s339(3)(b) of the Act. Under s339(1) the trustee in bankruptcy can apply for an order to set the trust aside provided the transaction was entered into at 'a relevant time'. The relevant date for determining whether this requirement is satisfied is the date of the presentation of Charles' bankruptcy petition - 1989. He therefore entered into the transaction two years before this date. It is not clear whether this was more or less than two years before the bankruptcy. If less than two years the marriage settlement may be set aside. This will qualify as 'a relevant time' under s341(1) provided that Charles was either insolvent at the time or became insolvent as a result of the marriage settlement - s341(2). Section 341(2) goes on to provide that this 'insolvency requirement' will be presumed to be satisfied unless the contrary is shown if the transaction is entered into with a person who is an associate. Jane is clearly an associate, and so the presumption is raised. However, the facts suggest that the contrary can be shown; Charles was not insolvent at the time of the transaction and did not become insolvent in consequence of the transaction. His insolvency was rather as a consequence of a judgment against him in 1989 and of the failure of his business at the same time. This approach, though, does not take into account the definition of insolvency for this purpose in s341(3)(b) - that 'the value of his assets is less than the amount of his liabilities - taking into account his contingent and prospective liabilities'. The proceedings against him in 1987 would probably qualify as 'contingent and prospective liabilities' and, thus, it seems likely that the court would make an order to set the trust aside under s339(2).

In the unlikely event that the requirements of s341(2) are not satisfied, the trustee in bankruptcy may apply to have the trust set aside under s423. The court will make an order under this section if it is satisfied that Charles executed the settlement for the purpose of putting the assets beyond the reach of a person who is making, or may at some time make, a claim against him or of otherwise prejudicing the interests of such a person in relation to the claim which he is making or may make - s423(3). In view of the proceedings against him and of the fact that the settlement was made soon after a risky business diversification it is at least arguable that Charles executed the settlement for one of these purposes. If this can be proved, the court will make an order setting the trust aside under s423(2).

ii) The gift to Dan is a transaction at an undervalue under s339(3)(a) and the same considerations apply as in (i) in deciding whether an application by the trustee in bankruptcy for the trust to be set aside will be successful.

iii) As (i) except that no presumption will be raised under s341(2) as the other members of the golf club are unlikely to be considered 'associates'. Should proceedings for the trust to be set aside fail, another possibility is for the trustee in bankruptcy to argue that the gift is, in any event, void as offending the rule against purpose trusts, as stated in *Morice* v *Bishop of Durham* (1805). The gift is one to the trustees of the golf club for specific purposes. Even if it were held to be prima facie valid under the principle in *Re Denley's Trust Deed* (1969), the fact that the income alone is to be used and the gift is not limited to the perpetuity period indicates that it would probably - in any event, fail for this reason.

iv) This settlement clearly qualifies as a transaction at an undervalue under s339(3)(a). The same considerations apply as in (i). In addition, if the trustee in bankruptcy is forced to resort to a remedy under s423, the fact that the life tenant of the settlement is to be Charles himself provides strong evidence that the purpose of the trust was an ulterior one under s423(3). The usual rule is that on the bankruptcy of a life tenant under a protective trust, the life interest comes to an end and there are discretionary trusts for the benefit of the life tenant, spouse and issue, or the life tenant and the person next entitled: Trustee Act 1925 s33. However, if the life tenant is also the settlor, his bankruptcy will not determine his interest: *Re Burroughs-Fowler* (1916). Therefore, even if the trust itself cannot be set aside, the trustee in bankruptcy will be entitled to Charles' life interest.

Question 2

a) In what circumstances will a settlement be voidable on the insolvency of the settlor?

b) In 1989 Simon transferred his shares in a private company of which he was managing director and majority shareholder to P & Q to hold on trust for his wife and children. At that time S was being investigated by the Department of Trade and if the findings had been adverse, he would not have been able to meet his liabilities without the aid of the settled shares. In fact the findings were favourable and in 1990 S set up a new business venture which has now failed and S has gone bankrupt.

Advise P & Q whether the trustee in bankruptcy has any claim to the settled shares.

Adapted from London University LLB Examination
(for External Students) Law of Trusts June 1989 Q8

Skeleton solution

a) Trust voidable on subsequent insolvency of the settlor under either ss339-342 or ss423-425 of the Insolvency Act 1986. Sections 339-342 enable a trustee in bankruptcy to set aside trusts which are 'transactions at an undervalue' or give preference to creditors provided they fell within the time limits in s341. Sections 423-425 enable a trust to be set aside where it amounts to a transaction at an undervalue and was made by the settlor for the purpose of putting assets beyond the reach of his creditors or otherwise prejudicing their interests. There are no time limits on ss423-425.

b) Simon's trustee in bankruptcy might set a trust aside under ss339-342 if it was made less than two years before date of presentation of bankruptcy petition but not if it was made more than two years before date of presentation of bankruptcy petition as conditions in s341 could not be met. If case cannot be dealt with under ss339-342, it can be dealt with under ss423-425 on basis that trust was created by Simon to put some of his assets beyond the reach of his creditors.

Suggested solution

a) A trust will be voidable on the subsequent insolvency of the settlor if it was created in circumstances to which either ss339-342 or ss423-425 of the Insolvency Act 1986 apply. The provisions of ss339-342 are concerned with two types of transaction, namely, transactions at an undervalue and preferences. The provisions of ss423-425 are designed to enable transactions at an undervalue which are intended to prejudice creditors to be avoided.

Sections 339-342 of the Insolvency Act replace s42 of the Bankruptcy Act 1914 and the basic principles in s42 are still adhered to with some modifications. If a trust is created prior to the settlor's insolvency and it amounts to a transaction at an undervalue as defined by s339(3) or a preference as defined by s340(3) it may be voidable on the application of the settlor's trustee in bankruptcy. Transaction at an undervalue is widely defined under s339(3) and would cover most situations involving the creation of a trust. It includes gifts, transactions entered into in consideration of marriage and transactions entered into at a significant undervalue. Thus, all voluntary settlements and marriage settlements are capable of being caught by these provisions. Further, if the settlement was made for value it may be caught if at an undervalue within the terms of s339(3)(c). This covers any settlement where the consideration provided for the creation of the settlement is significantly less than that provided by the settlor. The provisions dealing with preferences are unlikely to have great importance in setting trusts aside. However, they would cover cases where a settlor creates a trust for the benefit of particular creditors at the expense of others or cases where an executory covenant to settle property on a trust is completely constituted by the settlor for the benefit of a particular creditor.

The provisions of ss339-342 do not apply to any trusts created prior to the settlor's insolvency but only those entered into by him at 'a relevant time'. This is defined by s341. In the case of a transaction at an undervalue trusts created within the five year period prior to the date of the presentation of the bankruptcy petition are all caught. See s341(1)(a). But, if the trust was made not less than two years before the date of the presentation of the bankruptcy petition then, under s341(2) it is not voidable unless the settlor was a) insolvent at that time, or b) became insolvent in consequence of the transaction. In the case of trusts created to give a preference 'a relevant time' will, in general, be six months ending with the day of the presentation of the bankruptcy petition.

Sections 423-425 of the Insolvency Act are designed to replace the provisions which were contained in s172 of the Law of Property Act 1925. If a settlor creates a trust with the purpose of placing some or all of his property in it in order to avoid his creditors in the event of his bankruptcy, the trust could be voidable under s423. In order for these provisions to apply it must be shown that the creation of the trust was a transaction at an undervalue. This is defined in terms similar to those in s339(3). Under s423(3) it must also be shown that the object of the settlor in making the trust was to put assets beyond the reach of present or future creditors or to prejudice their interests. But, unlike the provisions of s339-342, there are no time limits placed on transactions falling within s423. It is not necessary to prove that the settlor was intending to defraud his creditors in creating a trust for ss423-425 to apply as was required under s172 of the Law of Property Act 1925.

b) Simon's trustee in bankruptcy could seek to have the settlement of shares made in 1989 set aside, insofar as that is necessary to satisfy the claims of the creditors, under s339-342 of the Insolvency Act 1986. It would appear that the settlement was made voluntarily so that it amounts to a transaction at an undervalue under s339(3)(a), ie it was made on terms that provided for Simon to receive no consideration. Even if it was a marriage settlement it will be regarded as a voluntary settlement. But, in order for it to be set aside the trustee in bankruptcy would have to show that it was made at 'a relevant time'. There are two aspects to this under s341. If the settlement was made less than two years before the date of the presentation of the bankruptcy petition, the trustee in bankruptcy would be able to have it set aside on establishing these facts without more. But, if the settlement was made more than two years before the date of the presentation of the bankruptcy petition, the trustee in bankruptcy would also have to show that Simon was insolvent at the time he made the settlement or became insolvent in consequence of it: see s341(2). On the facts it is not clear when the bankruptcy petition was presented. We are told that Simon would only have been unable to meet his liabilities if the findings of the Department of Trade and Industry investigation had been adverse. Section 341 provides that in determining whether or not Simon was insolvent at the time, account must be taken of contingent liabilities. It is not clear whether the value of his contingent liability should DTI findings be adverse would be sufficient to mean that he was insolvent at the time.

In the event that ss339-342 do not provide the trustee in bankruptcy with recourse to the settled shares, his only option would be to consider ss423-425. There are no time limits on these provisions. The main issue here would be to establish that Simon's purpose in entering the transaction was to put assets beyond the reach of his creditors or to otherwise prejudice their interests: see s423(3). In view of the circumstances in which the settlement was made in 1989 it would not be unreasonable to conclude that Simon's purpose in creating the settlement for his wife and children was to protect their financial position if the investigation of his business activities was adverse and led to his insolvency. Thus, the purpose of the settlement was to put the assets settled beyond the reach of either existing or future creditors. The fact that the settlement was not required for the purpose for which Simon created it is irrelevant since ss423-425 are not dependant for their operation on the eventuality for which the settlement was created coming to pass.

10 IMPLIED AND RESULTING TRUSTS

10.1   Introduction

10.2   Key points

10.3   Analysis of questions

10.4   Question

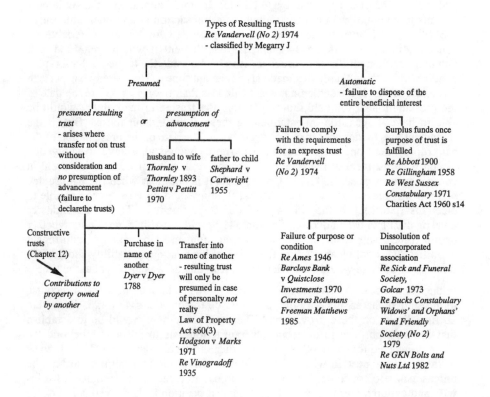

10.1   Introduction

As the flowchart shows, this topic is a very wide one. This is due to the nature of resulting trusts; the concept is used 'whenever there is a gap in beneficial ownership' - per Lord Denning MR in *Re Vandervell (No 2)* [1974] Ch 269. The main area of difficulty is that of matrimonial property which is considered in chapter 12.

10.2   Key points

Although consideration of this topic often refers to implied and resulting trusts, the distinction between the two types of trust appears to be illusory. A distinction does exist, however, between two types of resulting trust - presumed and automatic - as indicated in *Re Vandervell (No 2)* [1974] Ch 269.

a) *Presumed resulting trusts*

If X voluntarily transfers property to Y, not on trust, and there is no presumption of advancement, Y is presumed to hold the property on resulting trust for X.

There will be a presumption of advancement if X is a husband transferring to Y, his wife - *Thornley* v *Thornley* [1893] 2 Ch 229 - or if X is a father transferring property to Y his child - *Shephard* v *Cartwright* [1955] AC 431. In the former situation, the presumption of advancement is now very weak and is easily rebutted - *Pettitt* v *Pettitt* [1970] AC 777.

A presumed resulting trust may arise in three main situations:

    i)   purchase in the name of another.

        A resulting trust will be presumed in the absence of evidence to the contrary - *Dyer* v *Dyer* (1788) 2 Cox Eq 92.

    ii) transfer into the name of another.

        No presumed resulting trust in the case of land, due to s60(3) Law of Property Act 1925 (and see *Hodgson* v *Marks* [1971] Ch 892). There is, though, it seems, a presumed resulting trust if the property is personalty - *Re Vinogradoff* [1935] WN 68.

    iii) contributions to property owned by another.

        This is considered in chapter 12.

b) *Automatic resulting trusts*

If X makes a disposition to Y on trusts which leave some or all of the beneficial interests undisposed of, Y will hold the undisposed of beneficial interests on an automatic resulting trust for X. There exist four main situations in which a resulting trust of this nature will arise:

i) failure to comply with the requirements for an express trust

If this is the case, the settlor has failed to dispose of any of the beneficial interest which is held by the trustees on resulting trust for the settlor. This was the reason that a resulting trust arose in *Re Vandervell (No 2)* (1974).

ii) failure of a purpose or a condition

If a trust is created for a specific purpose which fails or subject to a condition such as the attainment by the beneficiary of a particular age (as in *Re Ames* [1946] Ch 217) which is not fulfilled, then the trustees will hold the property on resulting trust for the settlor. If the situation is one of failure of purpose, the nature of the trust imposed was considered in the two important cases of *Barclays Bank* v *Quistclose Investments* [1970] AC 567 and *Carreras Rothmans Ltd* v *Freeman Matthews Treasure Ltd* [1985] 3 WLR 1016.

iii) surplus funds once the purpose of a trust has been fulfilled.

If the purpose is charitable and the donor is unascertainable, the funds will be applied cy-pres following s14 of the Charities Act 1960. If the donor is ascertainable, then his contribution will be held on resulting trust for him unless he waives his right to it under s14. (See also chapter 7).

If the purpose is not charitable and the donor is ascertainable, his contribution will similarly be held on resulting trust for him - *Re Abbott* [1900] 2 Ch 326 - unless the donations were in the form of subscriptions under a contract. In the latter situation, it seems that the subscriptions would go to the Crown bona vacantia following *Re West Sussex Constabulary's Widows, Children and Benevolent (1930) Fund Trusts* [1971] Ch 1. More problematic is when the donors are unascertainable. It was held in *Re Gillingham Bus Disaster Fund* [1958] Ch 300 that the donations would nevertheless be held on resulting trusts for the donors. However, a different conclusion was reached in the *Re West Sussex* case, in which it was held that the donors should be considered as parting with the money outright and thus it would go to the Crown bona vacantia.

iv) dissolution of unincorporated association

The courts avoid the application of resulting trusts as far as possible, and instead treat the matter as one of contract. In *Re Sick and Funeral Society, Golcar* [1973] Ch 51 it was said that equal division would be ordered in the absence of rules to the contrary. However, in *Re Buckinghamshire Constabulary Widows' and Orphans' Fund Friendly Society (No 2)* [1979] 1 All ER 623 it was held that the destination of the surplus funds would be governed exclusively by the contract between the members and this was reiterated in *Re GKN Bolts and Nuts Ltd* [1982] 2 All ER 855. A further possibility is to follow the cases concerning failure of purpose above so that a resulting trust would exist in favour of each member to the extent of his contribution or subscription.

10.3 Analysis of questions

Problems may be set on any aspect of this topic and will often be combined with other topics. In particular, a question on the dissolution of an unincorporated association may also require consideration of whether the gift to the association was in fact valid anyway (chapter 5); a problem involving jointly-owned property addresses the topics of both resulting and constructive trusts (chapter 12). Essay questions may also be set on any aspect of the topic although these are less likely. For an example of a question in which the student is required to address several topics in addition to resulting trusts, see chapter 22.

10.4 Question

Joe organised holidays for schoolchildren. In 1982 he employed Harry, who was a travel agent, to book hotel accommodation for Joe's Tours. In the course of doing this work, Harry contracted as principal with the various hotels, and paid accounts submitted by them for the bookings made for Joe. Each month Joe paid Harry a fee for his services and also a sum equal to that which Harry owed the hotels for the accommodation booked for Joe's Tours.

By 1964, Harry was in financial dificulties and Joe, who was worried about the danger to his business if Harry's business collapsed, proposed that he, Joe, pay a monthly sum into a special bank account at Harry's bank on which Harry could draw for the sole purpose of settling the invoices submitted by the hotels. Harry agreed to the arrangement and in May this year, Joe paid £50,000 into the special account to cover the hotel expenses incurred from January to April.

Harry has recently been declared bankrupt. Joe claims that the money in the special account ought to be applied to paying the debts owing to the hotels.

Advise Joe.

University of London LLB Examination
(for External Students) Law of Trusts June 1985 Q4

Skeleton solution and comment

This question requires consideration and interpretation of the cases of *Barclays Bank* v *Quistclose Investments Ltd* [1970] AC 567 and *Carreras Rothmans Ltd* v *Freeman Matthews Treasure Ltd* [1985] 1 All ER 155 and the conclusions drawn must be applied to the facts given.

• Introduction - general rule that no fiduciary relationship exists between debtor and creditor.

• Facts of the *Carreras Rothmans* case and the decision in that case.

• and in the *Barclays Bank* case.

• Application to the present facts and conclusion.

Suggested solution

The issue involved in this question is whether a fiduciary relationship has arisen in respect of the £50,000 paid by Joe into a special bank account at Harry's bank so that this money is held upon trust to meet hotel expenses. The original arrangement between Joe and Harry was one of debtor/creditor and this in itself does not give rise to any fiduciary relationship. See *Rowlands* v *National Westminster Bank* (1978). But such a relationship may be altered as between a debtor and creditor so that a fiduciary relationship arises. Where this is so there are dangers of coming into conflict with the statutory rules ordering the payment of debts on bankruptcy.

The present facts are not dissimilar to those which arose in the recent decisions of Peter Gibson J in *Carreras Rothmans Ltd* v *Freeman Matthews Treasure Ltd* (1985). In that case Carreras Rothmans employed Freeman to do its advertising for cigarette brands and paid Freeman a monthly fee for its work and a sum to cover the expenses Freeman incurred in placing advertisements in newspapers, journals etc. In 1983 Freeman was in financial difficulties and Carreras Rothmans worried about damage to its business interests, proposed that it would pay money into a special bank account in order to meet expenses incurred by Freeman in placing advertisements for Carreras Rothmans. Unfortunately, Freeman went into liquidation a short time after almost £600,000 had been placed in the special bank account and at the time of liquidation most of the money remained in this special bank account. Carreras Rothmans claimed that there was a trust impressed upon the monies. This claim was upheld.

The decision in the *Carreras Rothmans* case rests on several grounds which equally apply to the facts of the present problem. In the *Carreras Rothmans* case Freeman were never free to deal with the monies put into the special account as they pleased; they were not paid to Freeman beneficially.

Instead, the monies were paid in for the specific purpose of meeting the claims of third parties and the account was nothing more than a conduit pipe to ensure that payment would be made to these third parties. Many steps were taken to ensure that the money would be protected from the dangers of being used to meet Freeman's creditors should Freeman go into liquidation. Any balance left after the third parties had been paid was to be paid to Carreras Rothmans and not to be kept by Freeman. The bank at which the special account was opened was informed of the conditions involved and the purpose of the account in order to prevent it exercising any rights of set-off it might have against monies in the account. All these factors pointed to the conclusion that a trust was intended of the monies in the account even if the word trust was not used. Reference was also made to the House of Lords decision in *Barclays Bank Ltd* v *Quistclose Investments* (1970) where it was recognised that arrangements for the payment of a person's creditors by a third person could give rise to a trust, primarily for the creditors, and secondarily, if the primary trust fails, for the third person.

If the above decisions are applied to the facts of the present case it would seem that the same result ought to follow and that the £50,000 should be regarded as being held upon trust to pay the hoteliers for accommodation booked by Harry on Joe's behalf.

A special bank account was opened into which the £50,000 was paid and it is stated that Harry was only entitled to draw on this for the sole purpose of settling the invoices submitted by the hotels. These factors alone suggest that Harry was not entitled to deal with the funds in the account as if he were beneficial owner but instead, could only apply them for the limited purposes for which they had been placed in the account, viz, paying hotel bills. Now that Harry is bankrupt his trustees in bankruptcy cannot stand in any better position than Harry, he must consider himself as holding the funds in the account for the purpose of paying the hotel bills. There are, however, some weaknesses in Joe's case. He does not seem to have informed the bank of the purpose for the special account and conditions attaching thereto. Hence, it is possible that if the bank has a claim as a creditor, it may well be able to exercise its rights of set-off against the account leaving nothing or insufficient funds for payment of the hoteliers. But, if there is a surplus in the account after the hoteliers have been paid it would seem that under *Barclays Bank Ltd* v *Quistclose Investments* the surplus would have to be returned to Joe under the trust.

11 CONSTRUCTIVE TRUSTS

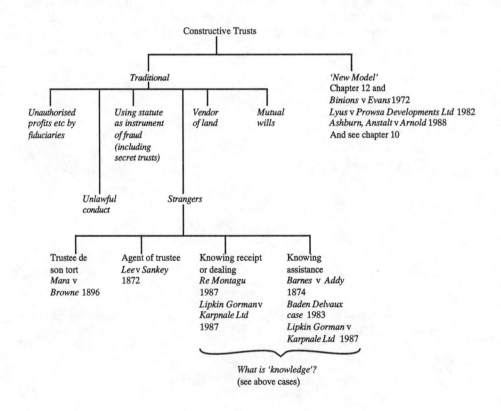

11.1 Introduction

Constructive trusts arise in various situations. The relevance of the concept in 'matrimonial' property is considered in chapter 12, and the rules relating to when a constructive trust will arise as a result of a breach by the trustees of their fiduciary duty is dealt with in chapter 14. Whether secret trusts are a breed of constructive trust is addressed in chapter 8. The degree of difficulty to be found varies between the different aspects of the topic. Undoubtedly, the area which creates the most problems is that of 'new model' constructive trusts as it is still developing rapidly. The student must, therefore, ensure that his knowledge is up-to-date.

11.2 Key points

Until the 1970s it was accepted that the operation of the constructive trust in English law was limited to defined situations, in contrast to the far more flexible approach employed by American courts. Recently, however, the distinction has narrowed; whilst the traditional categories remain 'new model' constructive trusts now operate in other areas too as and when equity requires.

Traditional categories:

a) *Unauthorised profits, etc by fiduciaries*

If a fiduciary benefits from his position, he will hold such benefits as constructive trustee for the person(s) in relation to who he is fiduciary. Trustees are clearly fiduciaries - their duties as such are examined in chapter 14. In addition, a director is in a fiduciary relationship to his company - *Regal (Hastings) Ltd* v *Gulliver* [1942] 1 All ER 378 -, an agent to his principal and partners to each other. Indeed, a fiduciary relationship can exist in any situation if circumstances suggest that it should.

b) *Using statute as an instrument of fraud (including secret trusts)*

If this is attempted, equity will intervene to impose a constructive trust as in *Bannister* v *Bannister* [1948] 2 All ER 133 and, arguably, in the case of secret trusts (see chapter 8).

c) *Mutual wills*

If a party to a mutual will alters it after the other party's death, the executors under the will will hold the estate on a constructive trust on the terms originally agreed.

d) *Unlawful conduct*

If a person benefits as a result of unlawful conduct, a constructive trust will be imposed on him of the benefit as in *Re Giles* [1972] Ch 544.

e) *Vendor of land*

Between exchange of contracts and completion, the vendor holds land on constructive trust for the purchaser in 'a modified sense' - per Kekewich J in *Royal Bristol Permanent Building Society* v *Bomash* (1887) 35 Ch 390.

f) *Strangers*

A stranger will only be liable as a constructive trustee of trust property in three circumstances:

 i) trustee de son tort

 If a person who is not a trustee and who has no authority from a trustee intermeddles with trust matters or acts as trustee - *Mara* v *Browne* [1896] 1 Ch 199.

 ii) knowing receipt or dealing

 If a person:

 • receives trust property with either actual or constructive knowledge that the transfer to him was in breach of trust; or

 • receives trust property and deals with it in a manner which he knows to be inconsistent with the trusts.

 Re Montagu [1987] Ch 264; *Lipkin Gorman* v *Karpnale Ltd* [1987] 1 WLR 987.

 iii) knowing assistance

 If a person has knowingly assisted in a dishonest and fraudulent design on the part of trustees - *Barnes* v *Addy* (1874) 9 Ch App 244 - whether or not the stranger in fact receives the trust property - *Baden Delvaux* v *Société General* [1983] BCLC 325.

 'Knowledge' in (ii) and (iii) has been the subject of much discussion. In the *Baden Delvaux* case, five types of knowledge were identified from actual knowledge to knowledge of circumstances which would put an honest and reasonable man on inquiry. In *Re Montagu* (1987) it was suggested that the latter type of negligence would not be sufficient and this was reiterated in *Lipkin Gorman* v *Karpnale Ltd* (1987) and more recently in *AGIP (Africa)* v *Jackson* (1991) The Times 9 January.

 iv) possession by an agent of the trustee

 The agent is a stranger who, if he deals with the trust property 'in a manner inconsistent with the performance of trusts of which he is cognisant, is personally liable for the consequences which may ensue upon his so dealing' - per Bacon VC in *Lee* v *Sankey* (1872) LR 15 Eq 204.

'New model' constructive trusts:

Chapter 12 deals with the 'matrimonial' aspects of this species of trust. However, the key to these trusts is their flexible nature and thus their operation has not been limited to 'matrimonial' property.

In *Binions* v *Evans* [1972] 2 All ER 70, vendors sold a house expressly subject to an agreement with the defendant that she could live there rent free for the rest of her life, at an accordingly reduced price. The plaintiffs brought proceedings for possession and it was held that they could not. Lord Denning thought that the defendant had a licence conferring an equitable interest. It was held in *Ashburn, Anstalt* v *Arnold* [1988] 2 All ER 147 that this is incorrect and that in fact the nature of her interest was that of a beneficiary under a constructive trust, a principle which had already been applied in *Lyus* v *Prowsa Developments Ltd* [1982] 2 All ER 953, on the basis that the plaintiffs' behaviour meant that it would be inequitable to deny the defendant an interest.

11.3 Recent cases

Re Montagu [1987] Ch 264
Lipkin Gorman v *Karpnale Ltd* [1987] 1 WLR 987
Ashburn, Anstalt v *Arnold* [1988] 2 All ER 147

11.4 Analysis of questions

General essay questions requiring discussion of recent developments are common and a good answer will present the relevant cases in a logical way and will offer an opinion on the state of the law at present. Questions on other areas which do not stand as topics in their own right are less common.

11.5 Questions

Question 1

Under a written contract for sale entered into in March 1983, A agreed to sell his house, Greytiles, to B for £70,000, completion to take place on June 10th 1983. On May 1st, C offered £90,000 for Greytiles and A accepted on terms that C would complete the purchase on June 1st. C knew of the contract between A and B but was advised that as it was not registered as a land charge under the Land Charges Act 1972, he could disregard it with impunity. On June 1, C paid the £90,000 to A's solicitors and A conveyed Greytiles to C.

B has now become aware of the sale to C and seeks your advice:

i) whether he has any proprietary claim against C;

ii) alternatively, whether he can claim that the £90,000 (which is still in the hands of A's solicitors) be paid to him.

University of London LLB Examination
(for External Students) Law of Trusts June 1983 Q3(b)

Skeleton solution and comment

This question addresses the topic of the vendor as a constructive trustee and, in particular, the decision in *Lake* v *Bayliss* [1974] 2 All ER 1114.

*   Effect of written contract; potential remedy against C.

*   Claim against A under *Lake* v *Bayliss* (1974).

Suggested solution

When A entered into a written contract with B in March 1983 to sell Greytiles to B for £70,000, he became a constructive trustee of the property for B from that time forth. See *Lysaght* v *Edwards* (1876). However, in breach of the contract of sale and the constructive trust A sold the property to C for £90,000. As B had failed to protect his interest in Greytiles by registering it as an estate contract under the Land Charges Act 1972 C is entitled to take free from B's interest. This is despite C's actual knowledge of the contract between A and B because a purchaser for value is now only affected by notice on the land charges register, not actual notice. See *Coventry Permanent Economic Building Society* v *Jones* (1951). Therefore it appears that B has no proprietary remedy against C.

B does, however, have a claim against A for damages for breach of contract but this would only enable B to recover for loss of bargain. As an alternative to this B may claim the proceeds of sale of Greytiles from A. Since Greytiles formed the subject matter of a trust B will be able to trace the property into its product, ie, the purchase money. In *Lake* v *Bayliss* (1974) such a claim succeeded. The result would be that B obtains the £90,000 which C paid to A under the contract and he could then complete his obligations under his contract with A by paying him the £70,000 or balance thereof which he owes. B could then keep the £20,000 profit for himself. As the £90,000 is still in the hands of A's solicitor B should obtain an injunction to prevent them paying it to A. There is a possibility that he could make the solicitors constructive trustees should they pay the money to A before he can get an injunction if they knew of all the facts, because as strangers to the trust between A and C they would have knowingly dealt with the property in a manner inconsistent with that trust.

Question 2

'Recent developments in the field of constructive trusts demonstrate beyond peradventure that Equity is by no means beyond the age of child-bearing.' Discuss.

University of London LLB Examination
(for External Students) Law of Trusts June 1986 Q5

Skeleton solution and comment

This is a common type of question which requires a detailed knowledge of recent developments and discussion of recent cases.

- Introduction - the traditional approach of English law compared to that of American law.

- Summary of recent developments and introduction of 'new model' constructive trusts by the courts.

- Consideration of the cases and developments in detail

- Development of the law since Lord Denning's retirement.

- Conclusion.

Suggested solution

The traditional approach of English law to the constructive trust is that it is a substantive institution only imposed in certain well-defined situations, for example, breach of fiduciary duty. Thus provided the facts of a case came within the bounds of one of these well-defined situations, a constructive trust could be imposed. See *English* v *Dedham Vale Properties* (1978); *Re Sharpe* (1980). This approach should be contrasted with the American approach to constructive trusts, where they are treated as a remedial institution. No clearly defined principles are laid down for the imposition of such trusts, instead they are imposed to prevent unjust enrichment, ie cases where the holder of the legal title may not in good conscience retain the beneficial interest. See *Beatty* v *Guggenheim Exploration Co* (1919).

The American concept of the constructive trust has been creeping into English law in recent years, particularly in the area concerned with informal family arrangements as to the ownership of property. Many cases in this area, if and when decided on the lines of resulting trusts, produced what were considered to be unjust results. Accordingly, recourse was made to 'new model constructive trusts' as a means of providing a plaintiff with a remedy where established principles would not provide him with one and it was considered that he ought to win. Lord Denning MR was, before his retirement, prominent in adopting this approach as many of his decisions illustrate. Since his departure from the Court of Appeal, this approach would appear to have been adopted in some more recent decisions.

The idea of the new model constructive trust is traced back to Lord Diplock in *Gissing* v *Gissing* (1971) by Lord Denning MR in *Eves* v *Eves* (1975), where he said 'Equity is not past the age of child-bearing. One of her latest progeny is a constructive trust of a new model. Lord Diplock brought it into the world and we have nourished it.' Previously, in 1972 Lord Denning MR had shown enthusiasm for this new-found concept by applying it in three cases. In *Cooke* v *Head* (1972) he overturned a decision of Plowman J that a mistress was entitled to one twelfth of the proceeds of sale of a bungalow she had helped to build and awarded her one third. He added that in cases where two parties by their joint efforts acquired property for their joint benefit a constructive or resulting trust would be imposed whereby the legal owner holds the property on trust for both. Some attention appears to have been paid in this case to what the mistress might have been entitled if she had been a spouse claiming benefits under matrimonial legislation. In *Hussey* v *Palmer* (1972) he seems to have imposed a constructive trust in favour of the plaintiff who gave her son-in-law £607 to build an extra bedroom to her house for her use. The plaintiff fell out with the son-in-law, hence the claim. The decisions of the other judges in this case are based on the idea that there was a loan or resulting trust. Lord Denning MR did not make his classification very clear but he did make clear the basis upon which he was imposing the trust, namely on the grounds of justice and good conscience where the defendant cannot conscientiously keep the property for himself alone. In *Binions* v *Evans* (1972), the new model constructive trust was imposed on a purchaser of a cottage in favour of the occupant by reason of an agreement between the vendor and occupant that the occupant could reside there rent free for the rest of her life. The price paid by the purchaser was reduced to take this matter into account. Lord Denning MR considered that the occupant had a licence giving an equitable interest but added if he were wrong on this a constructive trust would nevertheless be imposed on the purchaser as it would be wrong to allow him to remove the occupant contrary to the basis on which he took the property.

In *Lyus* v *Prowsa Developments* (1982) a constructive trust was imposed on purchasers of a building plot who purchased it from a company who had agreed to build a house thereon for the plaintiff. The company went into liquidation and the plot was sold subject to the plaintiff's agreement. The Court of Appeal headed by Lord Denning MR concluded that the sale 'subject to' the agreement imposed a constructive trust. In the recent case of *Ashburn Anstalt* v *Arnold* (1988), it was held that Lord Denning's licence explanation in *Binions* v *Evans* (1972) was incorrect and that, in fact, the correct interpretation of a similar situation was that employed by the court in *Lyus* v *Prowsa Developments* (1982). It was underlined, however, that a prerequisite for a constructive trust to be imposed was that the plaintiff's behaviour must be such that it would be inequitable to deny the defendant an interest in the property; a slightly, stricter approach than that preferred by Lord Denning.

In *Eves* v *Eves* (1975), a constructive trust was imposed by Lord Denning MR but not by the other members of the Court of Appeal. This case concerned an unmarried couple living together, the man purchased a house in his name and told the plaintiff it was their house but would have to be in his name alone as she was under 21. This was merely an excuse by the man to avoid a conveyance into joint names. The woman did not contribute to the purchase of the house but she brought up two children she had to the man and did much work in the house and garden. Lord Denning MR imposed a constructive trust in these circumstances on the ground that it would be inequitable to deny the woman a share in the house. But it is notable that the other two judges in the case found in favour of the woman on the basis that there was an enforceable agreement between the parties that the woman shall have a share in the house by reason of her labour in repairing and improving it.

Since Lord Denning MR's departure from the Court of Appeal, decisions have both supported and ignored his approach. In support is the recent decision in *Grant* v *Edwards* (1986), this case concerned an unmarried couple. A house was purchased and conveyed into the name of the defendant and his brother. The plaintiff was told that she could not be on the title because this might affect her claims against her husband in divorce proceedings. In fact this was an excuse to keep her name off the title, the defendant did not intend her name to be on the title at all. The plaintiff made substantial indirect contributions to repaying the mortgage, to the housekeeping and to household expenses and bringing up the children. A constructive trust was imposed on the defendant on the ground that it would be inequitable for him to claim sole beneficial ownership because he had led her to believe she had an interest in the property. On the faith of this the plaintiff had made her contributions. Sir Nicholas Browne-Wilkinson VC added that in cases such as this guidance might in future be obtained from the principles underlying the law of proprietary estoppel. The concept of new model constructive trusts was, however, not applied in *Burns* v *Burns* (1984).

In this case the plaintiff made no contributions to the purchase of the house which was in the defendant's sole name. The parties were unmarried. These were no misleading statements from the defendant as to ownership. The Court of Appeal refused to give the plaintiff any share in the property on the basis only that she looked after their children and the home. It might be added that as there were no grounds for imposing a constructive trust a resulting trust only could benefit the plaintiff and she was unable to prove an interest in the property for herself.

More recently, in *Lloyds Bank* v *Rosset* (1990), the House of Lords has attempted to restrict the circumstances in which a constructive trust will be imposed. If there was an agreement between the parties that the property is to be shared beneficially, it would only be necessary for the non-legal owner to show that he had acted to his detriment or significantly altered his position in reliance. But if there was no agreement reached between the parties, a common intention to share will be readily inferred if the non-legal owner has made direct contributions to the acquisition, but it is doutful if anything less will do. The court will not impose a trust merely because it would be reasonable that the beneficial interest be shared and Lord Bridge doubted that the conduct of the female partner in *Eves* v *Eves* and *Grant* v *Edwards* would have been sufficient to justify the imposition of a trust hat there not been an express agreement to share the beneficial interest.

From all the cases discussed it would appear that there is further development of the constructive trust to bridge the gap between resulting and constructive trusts and provide a solution in those cases which do not, on their facts, fall neatly into either camp.

12 MATRIMONIAL PROPERTY (INCLUDING THAT OWNED BY CO-HABITEES)

12.1 Introduction

12.2 Key points

12.3 Analysis of questions

12.4 Recent cases

12.5 Question

12.1 Introduction

It has been established at least since *Pettitt* v *Pettitt* [1970] AC 777 that beneficial interests in property owned by one or both parties to a marriage or other similar relationship will be determined by the law of trusts. The judges in the relevant cases, however, seem confused as to the nature of such trusts - resulting and/or constructive? In addition, it is generally accepted that the concept of proprietary estoppel may come to the aid of a party who cannot establish a beneficial interest in the form of a resulting or constructive trust.

Due to the resulting complexity of the topic and the fact that the topic encompasses several rather than a single area of the law of trusts, it seemed appropriate to devote a separate chapter to the problem.

The topic has been the subject of dramatic developments in recent years; indeed, the idea that constructive trusts are of any relevance in this area is a new one introduced by Lord Denning within the last twenty years. As a result the student must ensure that he has an up-to-date knowledge of the important case law and should not rely on out-of-date textbooks.

12.2 Key points

It has been established since *Pettitt* v *Pettitt* [1970] AC 777 that the question as to whether a party has a beneficial interest in property is to be determined by the law of trusts.

If the parties are married, many of the questions can be answered by reference to the matrimonial statutes which deal with declaration of beneficial interests and adjustment of such interests. In addition the presumption of advancement from husband to wife may be relevant. The law of trusts is also important.

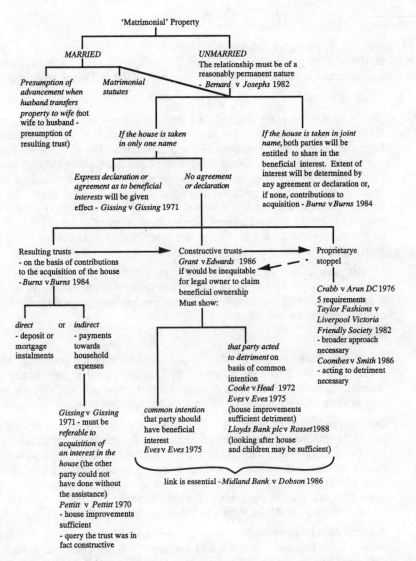

If the parties are unmarried then, provided the relationship is of a sufficiently permanent nature - *Bernard* v *Josephs* [1982] Ch 391 - the question of beneficial interests will be determined by the law of trusts:

a) *If the house is taken in joint names*

Prima facie, both parties will be entitled to a share in the beneficial interest. The extent of that interest will be decided in the same way that the question of whether a party has a beneficial interest at all, in the case of a house taken in one name only, is decided (see below) - *Burns* v *Burns* [1984] Ch 317.

b) *If the house is taken in only one name*

If there is an express declaration or agreement by the parties as to beneficial interests, this will be given effect - *Gissing* v *Gissing* [1971] AC 886. If there is no such agreement, the question will be determined by the following principles:

i)   resulting trusts

The 'non-owning' party will have a beneficial interest under a resulting trust if (s)he has contributed to the acquisition of the house, and the extent of such interest will be the amount of the contribution - *Burns* v *Burns* (1984). The contribution may be direct - payment of purchase price, deposit and/or mortgage instalments - or indirect - payments towards household expenses. Indirect contributions must be financial and must be 'referable to the acquisition of an interest in the house' - *Gissing* v *Gissing* (1971) and more recently in *Winkworth* v *Edward Baron Development Co Ltd* [1988] 1 FLR 237. In other words, it must be that the other party would not have met the mortgage payments without such assistance.

It was suggested in *Pettitt* v *Pettitt* [1970] AC 777 that home improvements would constitute a sufficient indirect contribution. However, it is submitted that 'contributions' such as this are now properly covered by constructive trusts.

ii) constructive trusts

It is a new idea that constructive trusts should cover the area of jointly-owned property. It is now, however, well established that they do and if a claimant fails to establish a beneficial interest under a resulting trust they may nevertheless be able to do so under a constructive trust.

In *Grant* v *Edwards* [1986] Ch 638 it was held that a constructive trust would be imposed if it would be unequitable for the legal owner to claim beneficial ownership. This will be the case if the claimant ('non-owning' party) can show that there existed a common intention that (s)he should have a beneficial interest and that (s)he acted to (her)his detriment on the basis of that common intention. The link between the two aspects of the test is essential - *Midland Bank Ltd* v *Dobson* [1986] 1 FLR 171.

A common intention will exist in a situation like *Eves* v *Eves* [1975] 1 WLR 1338. Examples of what will and what will not constitute sufficient detriment can be found in *Cooke* v *Head* [1972] 1 WLR 518, *Eves* v *Eves* (1975) and *Lloyds Bank plc* v *Rosset* [1988] 3 All ER 915. The concept of 'detriment' in constructive trusts is wider than the concept of 'indirect contribution' in resulting trusts.

iii) proprietary estoppel

As a last resort, it is possible that a 'non-owning' party could establish a beneficial interest under the doctrine of proprietary estoppel. However, in view of the very wide nature of constructive trusts it is unlikely that proprietary estoppel will help where constructive trusts have failed.

The case of *Crabb* v *Arun District Council* [1976] Ch 179 laid down five requirements which must be fulfilled in order to establish a case of proprietary estoppel. It was suggested in *Taylors Fashions* v *Liverpool Victoria Friendly Society* [1982] QB 133 that the approach should in fact be more flexible than this. However, it is clear from subsequent cases including *Coombes* v *Smith* [1986] 1 WLR 808 that detrimental conduct is still a requirement.

12.3 Analysis of questions

Consideration of the various rules relating to beneficial interests in 'matrimonial' property may be necessary either in a problem which addresses the question directly or in an essay question requiring the student to discuss the development of constructive trusts in recent years (an example is given in chapter 11). Problem questions require a structured approach as shown in the problem checklist and in the model answer below.

12.4 Recent cases

Thomas v *Fuller Brown* [1988] 1 FLR 237
Winkworth v *Edward Baron Development Co Ltd* [1987] 1 All ER 114
Lloyds Bank plc v *Rosset* [1988] 3 All ER 915

12.5 Question

Problem checklist

a) Will the principles of resulting trust create a beneficial interest in the property? Has the party made a contribution:

   i) direct - purchase price, deposit or mortgage instalments; or

   ii) indirect - must be referable to the acquisition of an interest in the property?

   If so, then a resulting trust exists in their favour to the extent of the contribution. If not;

b) Will the principles of constructive trust create a beneficial interest?

   i) is there a common intention that the party should have an interest; and

   ii) has the party acted to their detriment on the basis of that common intention?

If so, then a constructive trust exists in their favour. The extent of the interest will depend on what the parties intended. If not;

c) Does a remedy exist under the doctrine of proprietary estoppel?

Question

In 1965 Jane, who was divorced, went to live with Peter, who had left his wife. A year later a house was bought in Peter's name, the purchase money coming from his savings and by way of mortgage. At this time Jane gave up her job when a child was born to them, and in addition to looking after their child, Jane performed all the usual domestic duties in the house. In 1977, Jane went back to work and used her earnings to contribute towards the housekeeping expenses, and to pay for decorations to the house. In 1978 Peter built an extension to the rear of the house and he told his neighbour, Ned, that if it had not been for the fact that both he and Jane were working he would not have been able to afford to build the extension.

Last year Jane, taking the child with her, left Peter and she now wishes to claim a beneficial interest in the house. Peter and Jane have never been married.

Advise Jane.

University of London LLB Examination
(for External Students) Law of Trusts June 1984 Q2(b)

Skeleton solution and comment

The structure follows that in the problem checklist above. The length and depth of the answer presuppose that this is a whole, rather than half of a question. As half of a question in an examination, the answer would have to be modified (shortened) accordingly.

Suggested solution

This situation concerns an unmarried couple and thus the matrimonial statutes are of no assistance. Consequently, whether Jane has a beneficial interest in the house is to be determined by the law of trusts - *Pettitt* v *Pettitt* (1970). Although Peter is the sole legal owner of the house, he may nevertheless be trustee of part of the beneficial interest in the house for Jane, if it can be shown that she does in fact have such an interest under either a resulting or a constructive trust or, as a last resort, under the doctrine of proprietary estoppel.

For Jane to establish an interest in the house under a resulting trust, she must show that she made a contribution - either direct or indirect - to the acquisition of the house - *Burns* v *Burns* (1984). A direct contribution would be a contribution to the purchase money or the mortgage instalments, which Jane has not made. An indirect contribution must be financial and must be 'referable to the acquisition of an interest in the house' - *Gissing* v *Gissing* (1971), and more recently *Winkworth* v *Edward Baron Development Co Ltd* (1987). This means that the indirect contribution must have enabled the other party to meet the mortgage payments. The time Jane spent bringing up their child and performing domestic duties would not qualify as an indirect contribution as it is not financial (although it could be argued that it enabled Peter to work and, therefore, to pay the mortgage instalments and thus should, logically, so qualify). As regards the payments by her for decorations, although it was suggested in *Pettitt* v *Pettitt* (1970) that home improvements should qualify as indirect contributions, subsequent cases suggest that this is not the case and it is submitted that any interest created as a result is better explained in terms of constructive trusts (see below). Finally, Jane's contributions to household expenses will give rise to a resulting trust in her favour if Peter would not have continued to meet the mortgage instalments otherwise. Peter's comments to Ned suggest that although this is probably not the case (Peter had previously been paying the mortgage instalments and supporting himself Jane and the child), Jane's contribution did enable him to build the extension and thus a resulting trust will operate to give Jane a beneficial interest in the increase in the value of the house due to the extension, the value of which will be the value of her contributions to household expenses up until the extension was completed.

It is possible that Jane has a further interest in the house as a result of her other financial and non-financial contributions via the machinery of a constructive trust. The use of constructive trusts in this area is a recent idea. However, it now well established that a constructive trust will be imposed if Jane can show that a common intention existed that she would have a beneficial interest in the house and that she acted to her detriment on the basis of this common intention - *Grant* v *Edwards* (1986). Although the contribution to decoration would clearly constitute sufficient detriment, it is doubtful whether the time spent bringing up the child and carrying out domestic duties would. Lord Denning in *Hall* v *Hall* (1981) suggested that it would, and although his views have been strongly criticised in recent cases, in the recent decision of *Lloyds Bank plc* v *Rossett* (1988) it was held that it may constitute sufficient detriment. Browne-Wilkinson V-C's comments in *Grant* v *Edwards* (1986) were applied - that once a common intention had been established any act done by the party 'to her detriment relating to the joint lives of the parties is ... sufficient detriment to qualify'. However, on the facts there is no evidence of a common intention that Jane should have a beneficial interest in the house, and without this no constructive trust will arise. More information is needed from Jane as to whether the question of whether she was to have an interest in the house was ever discussed by Peter and herself.

A final possibility is that Jane has an interest of some description as a result of the application of proprietary estoppel. For this to be of assistance Jane must have believed that she had an interest in the house and must have acted to her detriment on the basis of this belief; Peter must have known of her belief - *Crabb* v *Arun District Council* (1976). Although, recently, the courts have employed a more flexible approach to proprietary estoppel - *Taylor Fashions Ltd* v *Liverpool Victoria Friendly Society* (1982) - it seems reasonable to presume that these requirements remain. If there is no common intention between the parties of Jane's beneficial interest, it is unlikely that a court would find that the requirements of belief concerning proprietary estoppel were present as the two ideas are similar, - as are, in fact, the concepts of constructive trusts and proprietary estoppel as a whole. As a result, if Jane fails to establish an interest via a constructive trust, she is unlikely to do so using proprietary estoppel.

**PART TWO
THE NATURE OF
TRUSTEESHIP**

13 BEGINNING AND TERMINATION OF TRUSTEESHIP

13.1   Introduction

13.2   Key points

13.3   Analysis of questions

13.4   Questions

13.1   Introduction

This chapter covers introductory points which relate to trusteeship, knowledge of which is vital before the more intricate aspects of trustees' powers and duties can be considered. Neither these introductory points nor the law concerning the appointment of trustees and the termination of trusteeship, present any difficult concepts. Instead, the topics are technical and require the student to familiarise himself fully with the relevant statutory provisions.

13.2   Key points

Introductory

a) *Types of trustees*

In addition to individuals (with capacity), various other types of trustees may be appointed and may act as trustee. These include, primarily, firms of solicitors; trust corporations (often banks and insurance companies); judicial trustees (appointed by the court under the Judicial Trustees Act 1896); the Public Trustee (who may be appointed by whoever is entitled to appoint under the Public Trustee Act 1906).

b) *Capacity*

Any person who has capacity to hold property has capacity to be a trustee. An infant, therefore, cannot validly be appointed a trustee of any property (LPA 1925 s20). However, if the situation arises, he can hold personal property on resulting or constructive trust. He cannot do so in the case of realty as he cannot validly hold the legal estate in land.

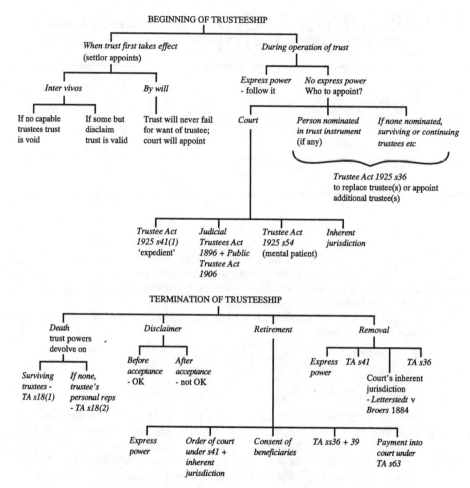

BEGINNING OF TRUSTEESHIP

When trust first takes effect
(settlor appoints)

During operation of trust

Inter vivos

By will

Express power
- follow it

No express power
Who to appoint?

If no capable
trustees trust
is void

If some but
disclaim
trust is valid

Trust will never fail
for want of trustee;
court will appoint

Court

*Person nominated
in trust instrument
(if any)*

*If none nominated,
surviving or continuing
trustees etc*

Trustee Act 1925 s36
to replace trustee(s) or appoint
additional trustee(s)

*Trustee Act
1925 s41(1)*
'expedient'

*Judicial
Trustees Act
1896 + Public
Trustee Act
1906*

*Trustee Act
1925 s54*
(mental patient)

*Inherent
jurisdiction*

TERMINATION OF TRUSTEESHIP

Death
trust powers
devolve on

Disclaimer

Retirement

Removal

*Surviving
trustees -
TA s18(1)*

*If none,
trustee's
personal reps
- TA s18(2)*

*Before
acceptance*
- OK

*After
acceptance*
- not OK

*Express
power*

TA s41

TA s36

Court's inherent
jurisdiction
- *Letterstedt* v
Broers 1884

*Express
power*

*Order of court
under s41 +
inherent
jurisdiction*

*Consent of
beneficiaries*

TA ss36 + 39

*Payment into
court under
TA s63*

NB Capacity; Number of trustees; Types of trustees; Vesting of trust property

c) *Number of trustees*

The only limitations are statutory:

i) maximum number

If the trust involves realty, the number of trustees shall not exceed, nor be increased beyond, four - Trustee Act 1925 (TA) s34(2). Section 34(3), however, identifies exceptions to this rule including trusts involving land held for charitable, ecclesiastical or public purposes.

ii) minimum number

- a sole trustee of land (not being a trust corporation) cannot act effectively as he cannot give a valid receipt for the proceeds of sale or other capital money under the LPA 1925 and the SLA 1925 as relevant.

- if more than one trustee was originally appointed, then a sole surviving trustee cannot retire from the trust and appoint a sole trustee (not being a trust corporation).

Appointment of trustees

a) *Initial appointment by the settlor*

   i) Inter vivos trust

The settlor will appoint the first trustee(s). If for some reason the appointment is invalid, the trust will fail. If, however, the appointment is valid, but the trustee(s) disclaim the trust, the trust is valid and the court will appoint new trustees provided that it is not, 'of the essence ... that the trustees selected by the settlor and no-one else shall act as the trustees of it' - *Re Lysaght* [1966] Ch 191 per Buckley J.

   ii) Trust created by will

The trust will never fail for want of a trustee even if none were appointed; if necessary, the court will appoint.

b) *Subsequent appointments*

If there exists an express power concerning appointment of new trustees, then this will determine who can appoint and in what circumstances. If no such provision exists, or if such provision addresses only the question of who can appoint, then resort must be had to statutory provisions and to the court's inherent jurisdiction.

   i) if the trust instrument states who is to exercise any power of appointment, and all such persons exist.

If this is the case, such person(s) will have a power of appointment under TA s36 (see (ii) below).

   ii) if no person(s) exist under (i) above but if there exist surviving or continuing trustee(s) or personal representatives of the last surviving or continuing trustee. (A trustee who is retiring as a result of the appointment below falls within this category. If all the trustees predecease the testator, the personal representatives of the last to die do not fall within this category).

If this is the case, such person(s) will have the power of appointment under s36.

Under TA s36, the power of appointment can be exercised by the relevant persons in eight situations:

- Where a trustee is dead (including a trustee who dies before the testator - s36(8)).

- Where a trustee remains outside the United Kingdom for more than twelve months (uninterrupted period - *Re Walker* [1901] 1 Ch 879).

- Where a trustee wants to retire from a part of or from all of the trusts.

- Where a trustee refuses to act (including a disclaimer).

- Where a trustee is unfit to act (including a trustee who is bankrupt).

- Where a trustee is incapable of acting (not including bankruptcy).

- Where a trustee is an infant.

- Where a trustee has been removed under a power contained in the trust instrument. (This does not confer a power to remove a trustee).

An appointment under s36 must be in writing but cannot be made by will.

Under s36(1) more than one trustee can be appointed to replace only one trustee, thus increasing the number of trustees. Trustees may also be appointed under s36(6) if no vacancy exists by the same persons and in the same way provided that no more than three trustees are already acting. The effect of an appointment under s36 is that the new trustee(s) are in the same position as if they had been appointed by the trust instrument - s36(7).

iii) the court

The court can appoint new trustee(s) under:

- TA s41(1) - whenever it is expedient to appoint and inexpedient, too difficult or impracticable to do so without the assistance of the court. The provision can be used to appoint new trustee(s) in substitution for or in addition to existing trustee(s), if any.

- Its inherent jurisdiction. In view of the width of s41, this is rarely used unless a dispute exists and the trustee is to be removed against his will.

- TA s54 - where a mental patient is a trustee.

- Judicial Trustees Act 1896 and Public Trustee Act 1906.

The effect of an appointment is the same as that under s36 above.

In exercising its power of appointment, the court will follow certain principles laid down in *Re Tempest* (1866) 1 Ch App 485 - it will have regard to the wishes of the settlor; it will not appoint someone who is likely to prefer certain of the beneficiaries over others; it will consider whether the appointment will promote the execution of the trust - and in *Re Parsons* [1940] Ch 973 - it will not appoint someone if there is a conflict between his duty and his interest.

The court will not use its powers to interfere with an appointment by a person in (i) or (ii) above.

iv) the beneficiaries

The beneficiaries under a trust have no power regarding appointment of trustees. In theory, the trustees have a duty to consult the beneficiaries before appointing a new trustee. However, if they do not do so, the court will not interfere with the appointment.

c) *Vesting of the trust property*

In general, a conveyance or transfer by the old trustee(s) is necessary. If, however, the appointment is by deed, s40(1) TA provides that the trust property will automatically vest in the new trustee unless the property is of a type listed under s40(4) which identifies exceptions to the rule (mortgages, leases and shares). If the court appoints or if for some reason there are problems concerning vesting, the court has wide powers to make vesting orders under the TA.

Termination of trusteeship

This may occur in four ways:

a) *Death*

The trust estate and the trust powers (under s18(1) and s18(2) TA) devolve on the surviving trustee(s) or if none, on the personal representatives of the last surviving trustee.

b) *Disclaimer*

A trustee can disclaim at any time before acceptance of the office, but not after - *Re Shannon* [1942] Ch 311. Partial disclaimer is impossible - *Re Lister* [1926] Ch 149. Acceptance may be express or implied, and whether it will be implied will depend on the circumstances. It is now clearly established that any suggestion that one of several trustees cannot disclaim is incorrect - *J W Broomhead (Vic) Pty Ltd* v *J W Broomhead Pty Ltd* [1985] VR 891.

c) *Retirement*

This is possible in five ways:

i) express power in trust instrument.

ii) under TA.

- s36 - a trustee can retire on appointment of a replacement.

- s39 - a trustee can retire, in any event, if the trustees who will continue (not being less than two in number or a trust corporation) by deed consent to his retirement.

iii) under an order of the court

The court can make such an order under s41 on the appointment of a new trustee, or under its inherent jurisdiction in an action to administer the trust.

iv) by consent of the beneficiaries

This is an application of the rule that it is a defence to an action for breach of trust that the beneficiaries (being sui juris) all consented to it.

v) payment into court

This amounts to retirement to an extent although he remains a trustee for certain purposes.

d) *Removal*

This is possible in four ways:

i) express power.

ii) under TA s36 - if trustee falls within one of the eight situations.

iii) under TA s41 - the court can do so when appointing a new trustee but will not do so if there is a dispute.

iv) under the court's inherent jurisdiction.

This was done in *Letterstedt* v *Broers* (1884) 9 App Cas 371 and in *Clarke* v *Heathfield (No 2)* [1985] ICR 606.

13.3 Analysis of questions

The student may well need to show knowledge of the introductory points in any question concerning trusteeship, although a question will not be set on any of these points alone. The appointment of trustees and the termination of trusteeship, however, commonly form the subject-matter of questions. Both problem questions and essay questions are possible as are a combination of the two. Essay questions are commonly divided into several short points; problem questions are often essay questions in disguise in that the question will direct the student to specific aspects which must be considered. When answering problem questions on this topic, the crucial first step is to identify who is being advised, as the emphasis of the answer may be very different depending on whether the answer must advise either the trustee(s) or the beneficiary(ies). As with all topics on trusteeship, a question may well require consideration of other such topics. See chapter 21 for an example of a question combining several such topics.

13.4 Questions

Question 1

By his will, a testator who died last year, appointed Tick and Tock to be his executors and trustees and left his residuary estate consisting of freeholds, leaseholds, shares in limited companies and bearer securities upon trust for his three sisters in equal shares absolutely. The three sisters are all of full age and desire the trust to continue.

Tock has been living in Spain for the last six weeks and although he intends to remain ordinarily resident in England, he has indicated that he intends to spend quite a bit of his time in Spain in the future. Tick wishes to appoint Little in place of Tock but the three sisters either want Tock to remain or Large to be appointed in his place. Advise Tick:

i) Who has the power to decide on the person to be appointed;

ii) By whom the appointment will be made;

iii) By what method the appointment will be made;

iv) How the trust property will be vested in the new trustee (jointly with Tick).

University of London LLB Examination
(for External Students) Law of Trusts June 1987 Q6(b)

Skeleton solution and comment

Whilst this looks like a problem question and the rules must be applied to the particular facts given, it is, in a way, an essay question in disguise as the examiner is clearly more concerned to see whether the student knows the rules regarding the points in (i) to (iv), rather than whether he can unravel a complex set of facts and apply the relevant rules. A problem question in this form usefully offers a perfectly adequate structure for the answer, thus avoiding the difficulties this aspect of answering a more general problem question presents.

i)   The answer first considers whether s36 can be used, and, if so, by whom. It then goes on to consider what influence the beneficiaries can have on such appointment, as a difference of opinion exists between Tick and them regarding an appointment.

ii)   This sub-question appears to be the same as (i) above. However, it is not. Instead, it requires the student to consider whether, in view of the dispute which exists, the court would make an appointment if desired.

iii) The answer considers the various formalities which are either necessary or advisable on appointment.

iv)   The rules regarding vesting of trust property must be considered; in particular, whether the provisions providing for automatic vesting would apply here in view of the nature of the trust property.

Suggested solution

i) If Tick wishes to appoint Little in place of Tock then he will have to use the provisions in s36 TA 1925. Under these the power to decide on the person to be appointed will be vested in the person given such power by the trust instrument. If there is no such person then the surviving or continuing trustees will have the power of appointment. As there are only two trustees in this trust and one is being removed the power will be vested in Tick in such circumstances as 'continuing' trustee means the trustee who will continue in office after the removal and appointment has been made. See *Travis* v *Illingworth* (1865). It would,

123

however, be prudent to get Tock's concurrence in the matters, if possible. Trustees must act jointly in the exercise of their powers. If a trustee is unfit or incapable of acting, he may be removed against his will and need not concur in his own removal. In this case there is no evidence that Tock is unfit or incapable, unless it could be said that his intention to spend time in Spain means that he would be incapable of discharging his duties as trustee. It seems likely that Tick cannot remove Tock against his will or appoint Little as an additional or replacement trustee unless Tock agrees. If Tock does agree, then Tock and Tick could jointly appoint Little as an additional trustee under Trustee Act 1925 s36(6) and Tock could then retire under Trustee Act 1925 s39. The beneficiaries do not have power to decide on the person appointed unless this was specifically given to them by the trust instrument. The trustees might consult them to ascertain their views and if it is a trust for sale of land they would be required to do so under s26(3) LPA 1925 and give effect to their wishes. Should the beneficiaries try to impose their views they would fail because as was pointed out in *Re Brockbank* (1948) the power to appoint is a discretionary power which will not be interfered with unless being used improperly.

ii) The appointment of the new trustee will be made by the person given such power by the trust instrument, if any, or by the continuing trustees if s36 is used. But, if there is a dispute as to whether the person proposed as new trustee is appropriate, it may be necessary to ask the court to make an appointment under s41. This should only be done when there are genuine difficulties in making the appointment outside court. In exercising its powers the court will consider the suitability of the proposed trustee with regard to the wishes of the settlor expressed in the trust instrument, whether the proposed trustee would be impartial and would promote the execution of the trust. See *Re Tempest* (1866).

iii) If the appointment is made under s36 TA 1926 then it must be in writing to comply with s36(1). No particular form is required, it is sufficient that the writing shows that an appointment is made. A deed of appointment is advisable in order to take advantage of the vesting provisions in s40 TA 1925.

iv) If the appointment is made in writing under s36, then it will be necessary to effect a transfer of the trust property into the names of Tick and the new trustee jointly. But, if a deed of appointment is used then there will be automatic vesting of the property in the new trustee jointly with Tick under s40(1)(b) TA 1925. The automatic vesting provisions do not cover all forms of trust property and under s40(4) land conveyed by way of mortgage to secure monies, leases under which the landlords consent or licence is needed for assignment and shares are excluded. In such cases there will have to be express vesting of the property in the new trustee. As the trust contains leaseholds and shares there will have to be express vesting in respect of them.

Question 2

In what circumstances and by whom may a trustee of a personalty settlement be removed from his trusteeship?

University of LLB Examination
(for External Students) Law of Trusts June 1987 Q6(a)

Skeleton solution and comment

This is a very general question requiring a structured and concise answer in view of the time constraints.

• Introduction; when and by whom an appointment can be made under s36.

• When the court will appoint under s41 and under its inherent jurisdiction.

Suggested solution

A new trustee of personalty may be removed under the provisions of s36 or s41 TA 1925 or under the court's inherent jurisdiction. Section 36 is primarily concerned with the appointment of new trustees outside court but this can only be done where at the same time an existing trustee is departing from the trusts. The circumstances in which this section may be used are set out therein and they include a number of circumstances which are tantamount to removal. These are where the trustee has remained outside the United Kingdom for a continuous period of 12 months, where he refuses to act in the trusts, where he is incapable of acting or unfit to act, is an infant or is being removed under an express power in the trust instrument. Removal of a trustee under s36 can only be on the grounds specified in the section and the power to remove thereunder is vested in any person appointed to carry out appointments and removals under the trust instrument or the surviving or continuing trustees of the trust for the time being. Continuing trustees means those who will still be in the trusts after the removal has been made. See *Travis* v *Illingworth* (1865). In all circumstances s36 will require a new trustee to be appointed in place of the trustee being removed.

Under s41 TA 1925 the court has power to appoint a new trustee or trustees where it is 'inexpedient, difficult or impracticable' to do so without its assistance. This provision is primarily concerned with appointment but it also extends to cases of removal of trustees. This might occur where a trustee is, for example, incapable of acting in the trust and refuses to retire, the use of s36 could lead to problems and the court's assistance can be sought in such circumstances to remove and replace him. See *Re Woodgate* (1857). The court also has power to remove a trustee under its inherent jurisdiction. This will be used in instances where s41 is inapplicable as where the beneficiaries do not want the trustees to continue acting in the trusts as they have lost confidence in them. The court will consider whether the best interests of the beneficiaries are served by a removal here and, if necessary, effect one. See *Letterstedt* v *Broers* (1884).

Question 3

a) Is it necessary or useful for a new trustee to be appointed by deed rather than by writing under hand?

b) Tug and Tow are trustees of a personalty settlement. Tug has been continuously abroad for the past 14 months. Advise Tow whether it is necessary or advisable for a new trustee to be appointed in place of Tug and if so in what manner this can be done.

c) Can a trustee who retires ever be made liable for breaches of trust which take place after his retirement and if so, in what circumstances?

University of London LLB Examination
(for External Students) Law of Trusts June 1984 Q8

Skeleton solution and comment

An essay question divided into three related areas, this question simply requires the student to state the relevant rules. Part (c) requires consideration of liability for breach of trust after retirement (chapter 20) and usefully illustrates how this topic may be introduced into a question primarily on appointment and retirement of trustees.

a) This question addresses the automatic vesting provisions under TA s40(1) whereby appointment by deed, although not necessary, is advisable unless the trust property is of a type listed in s40(4).

b) The problem posed relates specifically to the s36 ground that a trustee who has been outside the United Kingdom for a period greater than twelve months can be removed from office and another can be appointed in his place.

c) The student must consider the exceptions to the general rule that a trustee will not remain liable after retirement (see chapter 20).

Suggested solution

a) Under s36(1) of the Trustee Act 1925 the appointment of a new trustee need only be in writing, a deed is not necessary. However, if only writing is used then it will only amount to a bare appointment and further steps will have to be taken to vest the trust property in the new trustee. This is implicit in s36(7) which deals with the effect of a s36 appointment providing that he has the same powers, authorities and discretions as the original trustees 'as well as before as after all the trust property becomes ... vested in him'. To avoid the necessity of executing conveyances of property, etc to vest the trust property in the existing trustees and the new trustees an appointment of the trustees by deed is preferable. Under s40(1)(a) if a deed appointing a trustee contains a declaration that the trust property is to vest in him then it will vest in him on appointment together with the existing trustees without the need for any conveyance or assignments. Even if the deed of appointment contains no such declaration, then unless there is an express provision to the contrary, it will operate as if it did contain such a declaration. See s40(1)(b). However, these provisions are subject to s40(4) which requires an express conveyance where land belonging to the trust is mortgaged or is leasehold and the lease contains a covenant not to assign or let without licence or consent and where the company comprises stocks and shares. In these cases the automatic vesting by deed could have the effect of breaching covenants and other restrictions concerning the transfer of the property.

b) Under s36(1) of the Trustee Act 1925 a new trustee may be appointed in place of, inter alia, a trustee who has remained out of the United Kingdom for more than twelve months. As Tug has been continuously abroad it might be possible to remove him under this provision. But 'twelve months' here means an uninterrupted period of twelve months so in *Re Walker* (1901) the power did not apply where the trustee had been in London for one week in the relevant period. If this provision is to be used it must be clear that Tug has at no time returned to the United Kingdom in the last twelve months. This seems to be the case as the word 'continuously' is used. However, if events prove this not to be so then there would be no other ground on which he could be safely removed under s36(1), it may then be necessary to ask the court to substitute a new trustee in his place under s41(1) Trustee Act 1925 on the ground that it is 'inexpedient, difficult or impracticable' to make an appointment out of court. This assumes that there are no special powers in the trust instrument to remove a trustee in these circumstances.

It may well be more expedient for Tow not to bother trying to have Tug removed as a trustee at all. As this trust is one of personalty there is no limit (practical considerations aside) on the maximum number of trustees. Contrast trusts of land where the maximum number of trustees is four. See s34 Trustee Act 1925. It may be inconvenient for Tug to remain as trustee if his signature on documents will be required and it will not be possible to obtain this easily. It is dangerous for Tug to remain as trustee if he is not already involved in the trust, as if Tow commits a breach of trust Tug may well be liable for failing to keep an adequate check on Tow's actions.

If Tow decides on Tug's removal as a trustee then the person given the power to nominate new trustees under the trust will have to undertake the task of removal and replacement. If there is no such person nominated Tow will have to exercise this power. He must remember that a mere removal of a trustee without more cannot be carried out under s36(1), a replacement must be made at the same time. Thus, he must chose a suitable person to act with him in the trusts. Further, he might well consider if he cannot carry on in the trusts by himself alone but this really depends on the circumstances of the trust.

c) A trustee will remain liable for his own breaches of trust even after his retirement. See *Dixon* v *Dixon* (1878), but he will not be liable for breaches which take place after his retirement, as a general rule. There are, however, some circumstances where he may well be held liable for breaches after his retirement. This might arise where he retired knowing that his co-trustees would commit a breach of trust after his retirement or simply retired in order to facilitate a breach of trust. See *Head* v *Gould* (1898). Thus, if a trustee objected to a proposed course of action by his fellow trustees which amounted to a breach of trust he cannot escape the consequences of the breach by asking them to release him from the trust. He has a duty in such circumstances to seek an injunction to prevent the breach or if necessary, to seek their removal. See *Re Strahan* (1856).

However, the mere fact that a breach of trust ensues shortly after a trustee retires is not enough, in itself, to hold him liable for that breach. In *Head* v *Gould* Kekewich J said it would not suffice to show that the breach was rendered easy by reason of his retirement. It had to be shown that the breach which took place was contemplated by the trustees before his retirement. Further, if the trustee intended a breach of trust after his retirement, proof of this alone will not suffice to render him liable unless that particular breach actually took place. Should a trustee be sued for breach of trust in these circumstances then the usual defences such as in ss61 and 62 of the Trustee Act 1925 and the limitation periods will be available to him.

14 TRUSTEES' FIDUCIARY DUTIES

14.1   Introduction

14.2   Key points

14.3   Recent cases

14.4   Analysis of questions

14.5   Questions

14.1   Introduction

The student often finds that this topic is one of the more interesting aspects of the law concerning trusteeship. The law is based on common-law principles rather than on statutory provision and certain aspects of the rules have been and continue to be the subject of debate, and are criticised for being too harsh on the trustee. The topic presents no real conceptual difficulties except perhaps when distinguishing between the 'self-dealing' and 'fair-dealing' rules concerning the situation where a trustee purchases trust property. The reverse aspect of the duties not to profit is that if a trustee does so he will be a constructive trustee of such profits (see chapter 11).

14.2   Key points

a) *Duty not to profit from position as trustee*

This duty was expressly underlined by the court in *Bray* v *Ford* [1896] AC 44 by Lord Herschell:

'It is an inflexible rule of a Court of Equity that a person in a fiduciary position ... is not, unless otherwise expressly provided, entitled to make a profit; he is not allowed to put himself in a position where his interest and duty conflict.'

This general duty can be broken down into three main 'sub-duties'.

   i)   Duty not to receive remuneration

        A trustee is not entitled to receive remuneration for his services unless:

        • he is authorised to do so by the trust instrument.

            Any such clause will be strictly construed - *Re Chapple* (1884) 27 Ch D 584.

TRUSTEES' FIDUCIARY DUTIE

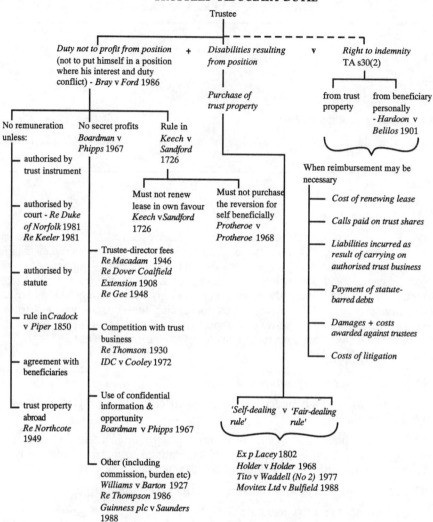

- he is authorised to do so by a court order under its inherent jurisdiction.

In deciding whether to exercise its jurisdiction, the court must balance two aspects of the beneficiaries' interests. Clearly, it is in the beneficiaries' interest that trust expenses should be kept to a minimum. However, it is also in their interest that the trust should be well administered and this may require remuneration to be paid to the trustee(s) - *Re Duke of Norfolk's ST* [1981] 3 All ER 220. It is clear from *Re Keeler's ST* [1981] 1 All ER 888 that the court can use its jurisdiction to authorise both future remuneration and the retention of past remuneration.

* he is authorised to do so by statute.

TA s42 authorises a trust corporation to charge remuneration; the Judicial Trustees Act 1896 gives similar authorisation to a judicial trustee; and the Public Trustee Act 1906 allows the Public Trustee to charge fixed fees.

* all the beneficiaries (who are all sui juris) authorise him to do so.

* trust property is situated abroad and the law of that country allows trustees to receive remuneration - *Re Northcote's WT* [1949] 1 All ER 442.

* the rule in *Cradock* v *Piper* (1850) 1 Mac & G 664 applies.

The rule is limited to allowing a solicitor/trustee to charge his usual professional costs for work done for himself and his co-trustees in a court matter provided that his activities have not increased the expense. The rule does not apply to non-court work. In that situation, the solicitor/trustee can employ any of his partners provided that it would be proper to employ a solicitor and that the solicitor/trustee receives no benefit.

ii) Duty not to receive secret profits

* trustee/director fees

If the trustee becomes director of a company in which the trust has a substantial shareholding, he will, in general, be liable to account as constructive trustee for any salary received (provided that the trust instrument does not authorise him to retain it) - *Re Macadam* [1946] Ch 73. The rule will not apply if the trustee/director became director before he became trustee - *Re Dover Coalfield Extension* [1908] 1 Ch 65 - or if the trustee became director by using his own personal shareholding. This is because the trustee must have received the fee as a result of his position as trustee.

* competition with the trust business

A trustee will be liable to account as constructive trustee for profits made by him from a business which competes with a business of the trust - *Industrial Development Comsultants Ltd* v *Cooley* [1972] 1 WLR 443 - provided that the businesses are in direct competition - *Re Thomson* [1930] 1 Ch 203.

- use of confidential information and opportunity derived from position as trustee

  The idea that confidential information constitutes trust property was introduced by *Boardman* v *Phipps* [1967] 2 AC 46 and has been criticised.

- other situations

  A trustee will be liable to account as constructive trustee for commission received by virtue of his office as in *Williams* v *Barton* [1927] 2 Ch 9. It appears from *Guinness plc* v *Saunders* [1988] NLJ Rep 142 and from *Re Thompson's Settlement* [1986] Ch 99 that if a trustee concurs in a transaction in which he has an interest which he fails to disclose, he will be liable for any profits thereby received.

iii) The rule in *Keech* v *Sandford* (1726) Sel Cas Ch 61

The rule is that if part of trust property comprises a lease, the trustee must not renew the lease for his own benefit even if the lessor has refused to renew it for the benefit of the trust. In *Protheroe* v *Protheroe* [1968] 1 All ER 1111 the rule was applied to the purchase of the reversion; it was held that, in the same way, the trustee could not purchase the reversion for his own benefit.

b) *Disabilities resulting from the trustee's position*

The main disability is to be found in the general rule that a trustee cannot purchase trust property. The rule, however, is not an absolute one. A distinction has been drawn between the situation where a trustee purchases trust property from himself - the 'self-dealing rule' - and where he in fact purchases trust property from the beneficiaries - the 'fair-dealing rule' - *Ex parte Lacey* (1802) 6 Ves 625; *Tito* v *Waddell* (No 2) [1977] Ch 106. If a trustee buys a beneficial interest in the trust from one of the beneficiaries, the onus is on the trustee to show that he did not exercise any undue influence; but if he can discharge this onus, the transaction is valid. If a trustee buys trust property, the transaction can always be set aside at the option of the beneficiaries even if the trustee paid the true market price. The trustee can seek the sanction of the court and in an exceptional case, as in *Holder* v *Holder* [1968] Ch 353, the court may ratify the transaction retrospectively. It was said in *Movitex Ltd* v *Bulfield* [1988] BCLC 104, that a trustee who does not satisfy the requirements of the 'fair-dealing' rule is guilty of a breach of his duty to the beneficiaries to act fairly but is not, strictly speaking, guilty of breach of trust.

c) *Right to indemnity*

TA s30(2) provides that a trustee can reimburse himself out of the trust for all expenses incurred in the execution of the trust (provided that they are properly incurred). The main situations in which reimbursement is necessary are listed on the flowchart.

The trustee also has, in certain circumstances, a right of indemnity from the beneficiaries personally, as shown in *Hardoon* v *Belilos* [1901] AC 118.

14.3   Recent cases

Movitex Ltd v *Bulfield* [1988] BCLC 104
Guinness plc v *Saunders* [1988] NLJ Rep 142

14.4   Analysis of questions

A question on this topic may be worded as such or, alternatively, worded as one on constructive trusts (see chapter 11). Many types of questions are possible; the topic is a wide one and lends itself equally well to essay and problem questions. Problem questions commonly combine this area with that of remedies for breach of fiduciary duty (see chapter 20). For an example of a 'combination' question of this nature, see chapter 21.

14.5   Questions

Question 1

See chapter 21 for a problem question.

Question 2

'A trustee must not profit from his trust'. Consider the application of this principle in the context of each of the following:

i) The retention by a trustee holding shares in a limited company, of remuneration received by the trustee as a director of the company;

ii) The renewal by a trustee in his private capacity of a lease where the expiring lease formed part of the trust property;

iii) Charges for acting in the trust made by (a) the Public Trustee as trustee and (b) a solicitor/trustee.

University of London LLB Examination
(for External Students) Law of Trusts June 1983 Q7

Skeleton solution and comment

This is a self-structuring essay question, usefully isolating specific issues for consideration from a very wide topic. Had the question asked for a discussion of the quote given without being more specific, the student would have had to give careful consideration to structure, and would have had to address more aspects of the topic concisely, in less depth than is done here.

i) Consideration of the law concerning trustee-director remuneration, beginning with the general rule in *Re Macadam* (1946) and moving on to the various exceptions to and limitations of the rule.

ii) This calls for discussion of the rule in *Keech* v *Sandford* (1726) as modified by more recent cases.

iii) a) The answer states the general rule that a trustee shall not receive remuneration for his services, and then explains how the Public Trustee constitutes an exception to this.

   b) The general rule is again stated, and then goes on to consider exceptions relating to a solicitor-trustee - in particular, the rule in *Cradock* v *Piper* (1850).

Suggested solution

i) Where a trustee is holding shares on behalf of a trust in a limited company and receives remuneration for acting as a director of that company then he will have to account for the remuneration under the rule that a trustee must not profit from his trust. See *Re Macadam* (1946). However, this general principal is subject to a number of exceptions. If the trust instrument expressly or impliedly authorises the trustee to keep director's fees he will not have to account for them. See *Re Llewellin's WT* (1949). The trustee will not have to account for the director's fees either if he was a director of the company before being appointed as a trustee. See *Re Dover Coalfield Extension* (1908). Nor will he have to account for them if he held shares in the company in a personal capacity and used those shares to procure the directorship, *Re Gee* (1948). For the exception in *Re Gee* to operate it is necessary for the trustee to show that he would have been appointed as a director even if he had used the trust shareholding to vote against himself. Apart from these exceptions the trustee may apply to the court under its inherent jurisdiction, for an order permitting him to retain the director's fees. Whether this jurisdiction is exercised will depend on whether the court considers that payment of the trustee outweighs the consideration that the trust be administered gratuitously by the trustee and free from unjustified claims. See *Re Duke of Norfolk's ST* (1981). In *Re Keeler's ST* (1981), the court exercised the inherent jurisdiction in favour of trustee directors who were performing vital work for the companies but not in favour of mere honorary directors.

ii) If a trustee renews a lease which formed part of the trust property for himself in his private capacity, then under *Keech* v *Sandford* (1726) he will hold the lease on a constructive trust for the beneficiaries of the trust. This rule is strict so that it does not matter where the lessor refused to renew the lease on behalf of the trust itself. This is because the trustee is expected to make his best effort on behalf of the trust and may not do so if there was a possibility that he could gain the lease for himself. In *Keech* v *Sandford* it was said that the trustee was the only person of all mankind who could not have the lease. Although the rule in *Keech* v *Sandford* is strict it may not be absolute. In *Holder* v *Holder* (1968) which was concerned with the purchase of trust property by the trustees the court held that such a transaction was permissible provided the trustee could show that he had not taken any advantage of his position. Therefore, it should follow if the trustee could show that the trust no longer needed or wanted the lease and he had not taken advantage of his office to procure it for himself, he should be allowed to retain it for himself beneficially. However, this would probably be difficult to establish.

iii) a) The general rule is that a trustee must give his services to the trust gratuitously no matter how onerous or difficult the administration of the trust happens to be. See *Barrett* v *Hartley* (1866). There are numerous exceptions to this rule one of which permits the Public Trustee to charge for his services as trustee. Under s2 Public Trustee Act 1956 the Public Trustee may act in the administration of small estates, act as custodian trustee, act as an ordinary trustee or be appointed to be a judicial trustee. By s9 of the same Act the services of the public trustee are to be paid for in accordance with such charges as the Treasury with the sanction of the Lord Chancellor may fix. The charges may be by way of a percentage or in such other way as may be fixed.

b) A solicitor/trustee is subject to the general rule that a trustee is not entitled to remuneration for his services. However, he is entitled to charge out-of-pocket expenses for any business he does in relation to the trust whether it is contentious or non-contentious. *Re Pooley* (1888). Under the rule in *Cradock* v *Piper* (1850) a solicitor/trustee is, however, entitled to receive his profit costs when he acts as a solicitor in an action or other legal proceedings on behalf of himself and a co-trustee jointly except so far as the costs have been increased by him being one of the parties. The rule applies to both hostile proceedings and friendly actions in chambers, for example, to obtain maintenance for an infant. See *Re Corsellis* (1887). However, it does not apply to the administration of estates out of court or to any proceedings which the solicitor/trustee brings on behalf of himself alone. See *Lyon* v *Baker* (1852).

In the majority of cases where a solicitor is requested to act as a trustee he will require that the trust instrument contain a clause permitting him to receive remuneration for his services. Such clauses are perfectly legitimate but they must be carefully drawn as the court construes them narrowly and against the solicitor/trustee. *Re Gee* (1948).

15 POWERS OF INVESTMENT

15.1   Introduction

15.2   Key points

15.3   Recent cases

15.4   Analysis of questions

15.5   Questions

15.1   Introduction

What a trustee's powers of investment are depends on whether an express power exists, and also on the nature of the trust property. An understanding of the relationship between the various powers is central to a grasp of the topic as a whole. Once this has been done, the topic presents no real difficulties. The student will, however, be expected to be aware of the wide criticism of the limited statutory powers and of the various proposals for reform, and to formulate an opinion of his own concerning this.

15.2   Key points

A trustee when investing trust property must limit himself to authorised investments (authorised either by an express power or by statute) and must have regard to general principles which have been formulated on such investment:

a) *General principles*

It was said in *Learoyd* v *Whiteley* (1887) 12 App Cas 727 that the trustee when investing trust property must not only act as a business man of ordinary prudence, but must also avoid all investments of a hazardous nature. And in *Bartlett* v *Barclays Bank Trust Co Ltd* [1980] Ch 515, a distinction was drawn between a prudent degree of risk and hazard; the former would be acceptable. In accordance with trustees' fiduciary duties (see chapter 14), a trustee will not be allowed to invest in anything in which he has a personal interest - *Re David Feldman Charitable Foundation* [1987] 58 OR (2d) 626.

In addition, under the Trustee Investments Act 1961 (TIA), a statutory duty to consider the suitability of particular investments, especially in the light of the need for diversification, is provided by s6.

b) *Non-fiduciary considerations*

The best interests of the beneficiaries are generally their financial interests. Thus, non-financial considerations must not be taken into account when deciding what to invest in, except in the exceptional situation when all the actual or potential beneficiaries are adults with very strict moral views on particular matters - *Cowan* v *Scargill* [1985] Ch 270.

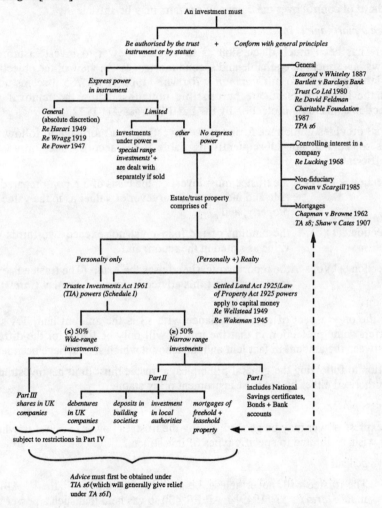

c) *When the trust property includes a controlling interest in a company*

The application of the general principles in (a) above to this particular situation was considered in *Re Lucking's WT* [1967] 3 All ER 726. It was said that the trustee should not simply consider the information he receives as shareholder, but should be, in some way, represented on the board. The extent of such representation will depend on the circumstances; he may be required to act as managing director or he may only need to ensure that he has a nominee on the board who can report back to him. This was interpreted more liberally in *Bartlett* v *Barclays Bank Trust Co Ltd* (1980) in which it was said that the trustee need not always be represented on the board if the circumstances did not require this; other methods of control over the company's affairs may be sufficient.

d) *When a mortgage is invested in*

There has been much discussion as to whether power to invest in mortgages allows investment in equitable and second mortgages. In view of the objections to the latter put forward in *Chapman* v *Browne* [1902] 1 Ch 785 it seems unlikely that the latter, at least, are permissible notwithstanding the removal of the objection concerning protection by the Land Charges Act 1972.

TA s8 provides guidelines for a trustee investing in a mortgage to follow. If he does so, he will not subsequently be liable if the security later proves to be insufficient:

Section 8(1)(a) - the trustee must invest on the basis of a report prepared by an able and independent surveyor or valuer as to the value of the property; and

Section 8(1)(b) - the amount of the loan must not exceed two-thirds of the value as stated in the report; and

Section 8(1)(c) - the report expressly advises the loan. (The trustee is entitled to presume that this advice is correct - *Shaw* v *Cates* [1909] 1 Ch 389).

If the only aspect of non-compliance with s8 is the amount lent, TA s9 still offers some protection in that the trustee will only be liable for the difference between the amount in fact lent and the amount which should have been lent.

In addition to following the general principles, a trustee must limit his investments to those authorised either by the trust instrument or by statute:

a) *Express power*

An express power may be general, giving the trustees power to invest in whatever they wish, or limited to specific types of investment.

i) general

The trustee will, nevertheless, be subject to certain limitations. Although in *Re Harari's ST* [1949] 1 All ER 430 it was held that such a power would not be interpreted restrictively, the case of *Re Power's WT* [1947] Ch 572 (distinguishing *Re Wragg* [1919] 2 Ch 58) established that the word 'invest' implied a yield of income and, thus, non-income-producing property would not be permissible as an investment.

ii) limited

The trustee will have powers of investment both under the express power and under the TIA. Property invested in under the express power will be dealt with entirely separately from the TIA as a 'special-range investment'(unless such property is also a 'narrow-range investment' under the TIA in which case it will in fact be dealt with under the provisions of the Act). If 'special-range investments' are sold and converted into other types of property, they must then be dealt with under the TIA.

b) *Trustee Investments Act 1961 (TIA)*

The powers of investment under the Act apply to all trustees to the extent that any express powers do not. Investments which are authorised are listed under the First Schedule to the Act:

i) Part I - 'narrow-range' investments, including National Savings certificates, bonds and bank accounts.

ii) Part II - 'narrow-range' investments including investments in local authorities and government bodies, deposits in building society accounts, debentures in UK companies (subject to restrictions in part IV) and mortgages of freehold and leasehold (of a term of at least sixty years) property.

iii) Part III - 'wide-range' investments including shares in UK companies (subject to restrictions in part IV).

Before investments are made under part II or part III, proper advice must be obtained by the trustee - TIA s6(2).

If a trustee wishes to invest in 'wide-range' investments under part III, he must first split all the trust property to be dealt with under the Act into two equal parts. Only one part can be invested in 'wide-range' investments; the other half, at least, must be invested in 'narrow-range' investments.

c) *Powers under Settled Land Act 1925 (SLA) and Law of Property Act 1925 (LPA)*

In addition to the powers above, if part of the trust property comprises of land held either under a settlement or on trust for sale, the powers of investment under the SLA and LPA, respectively, apply. These powers include the power to purchase land - freehold or leasehold - for a term of at least sixty years. The powers under the SLA apply notwithstanding that all the land originally held has been sold as the proceeds are capital money to which the provisions apply equally. However, it appears from *Re Wakeman* [1945] Ch 177 that if all the land held under a trust for sale is sold, then the LPA powers cease to apply, despite dicta to the contrary in *Re Wellsted's WT* [1949] Ch 296.

TA s57 gives the court power to vary the powers of investment under a trust. Although cases such as *Re Kolb's WT* [1962] Ch 531 suggested that this power should only be exercised in exceptional circumstances, it has since been recognised - *Trustees of the British Museum* v *Attorney-General* [1984] 1 All ER 337 - that this is no longer the case in the light of the inadequacy of the TIA.

15.3 Recent cases

Re David Feldman Charitable Foundation [1987] 58 OR (2d) 626

15.4 Analysis of questions

The topic lends itself equally well to essay questions (in particular those requiring criticism of the TIA) and to problem questions. The latter are commonly combined with a question on remedies for breach of trust (see chapter 20 for an example) and, indeed, with any of the other topics on trusteeship (see chapter 21 for an example). When answering a problem question on the powers of investment, a logical approach is essential in order to avoid any possible confusion resulting from the relationship between the different powers.

15.5 Questions

Problem checklist

a) Is there an express power under the trust instrument?

   If not, go to (d).

b) If so, is it full?

   If so, any investment is OK provided it produces income; if not, got to (c).

c) If it is limited, is the investment within the power?

   If not, got to (d). (If so, it is OK).

d) Is the investment within the TIA?

   i) Is it 'wide-range'? - If so, 50:50 split is necessary.

   ii) Is it 'narrow-range'? - If so, investment is OK.

   If not go to (e).

e) Is it the purchase of land?

   If not, the investment is unauthorised; if so, the investment is authorised provided part of the trust property already comprises of land.

f) If the investment is authorised under (a) to (e) above, did the trustee act in a way laid down by the general principles?

   If so, there is no breach of trust; if not, go to (g).

g) If the investment is unauthorised or if the answer to (f) is no, the trustee is guilty of breach of trust (see chapter 20 for remedies).

Question 1

Edgar and Frank are the trustees of a Trust Fund which is valued at £500,000. The trust funds are held on trust for Herbert for life, with remainder to his children in equal shares.

Edgar tells Frank that as Herbert is a confirmed teetotaller, does not smoke and is a pacifist, none of the trust funds should be invested in any company which is engaged in the alcohol or tobacco trade or the manufacture of armaments.

Advise Frank.

University of London LLB Examination
(for External Students) Law of Trusts June 1985 Q8(b)

Skeleton solution and comment

This question addresses the problem of whether trustees' personal views on particular investments can properly be taken into consideration, and requires an application of what was said in *Cowan* v *Scargill* (1985) to the facts.

- Introduction identifying the issue; statement of general rule in *Cowan* v *Scargill* (1985).

- Exception to the rule and whether it can apply to the facts in question. Conclusion.

Suggested solution

The main issue in this problem is whether Edgar and Frank, as trustees, can refrain from exercising their investment powers so as to ensure that the trust funds are not invested in a company which either they or the beneficiaries object to on moral or social grounds. This problem was considered in *Cowan* v *Scargill* (1984) where five trustees of a National Coal Board pension fund refused to assent to investments in, inter alia, any industry which competed with the coal industry in the provision of energy. Megarry V-C pointed out that trustees when making investments had a duty to put the interest of their beneficiaries first and the interests of the beneficiaries were normally their best financial interests. Thus, if a trustee failed to make an investment on moral or social grounds which was in the best financial interests of the beneficiaries his conduct would be open to criticism. Further, a trustee had to put his own personal views aside when making trustee investments. Edgar and Frank cannot allow their personal views to determine whether or not investments should be made in companies engaged in the alcohol or tobacco trades or the manufacture of armaments.

However, it may be that the beneficiaries would or do object to investments under the trust being made in certain types of industry. In *Cowan* v *Scargill* Megarry V-C pointed out that if the only actual or potential beneficiaries are all adults and they consider that, for example, investment in alcohol or tobacco trades is objectionable, then it could be concluded that such was not for their 'benefit'. 'Benefit' is construed widely and could include arrangements which worked to the financial disadvantage of a beneficiary where better financial returns could only be obtained from sources that the beneficiary considered evil. It is unlikely that this dicta could be applied here since the trust is for the benefit of Herbert and his children. The trustees could not consider Herbert's views alone when considering the matter of investment so that if his children had no particular objection to investment in alcohol or tobacco companies or armaments manufacture their duty would be to look to financial benefits. If Herbert's

141

children are infants the position would be no different because the dicta in *Cowan* v *Scargill* on this point were limited to trusts where all the beneficiaries are adults. It therefore seems that Edgar and Frank should consider their duty as being to obtain the best financial return on the trust fund even if this means investing in industries which Herbert regards as objectionable. However, if they can find investments which are as good as those Herbert might object to they could purchase these because it would be difficult to hold such investments to criticism.

Question 2

Consider, critically, the powers of investment which the Trustee Investment Act 1961 gives to trustees.

University of London LLB Examination
(for External Students) Law of Trusts June 1985 Q8(a)

Skeleton solution and comment

This is a common type of question requiring a critical examination of the provisions of the TIA. A good answer must include reference to the proposals of the Law Reform Committee in their 23rd Report.

- Introduction - background to TIA and present judicial feeling about the adequacy of its provisions.

- The Law Reform Committee's Report - proposals concerning investment in land and present situation on land.

- General operation of TIA and Committee's proposals for reform.

- Present provisions concerning advice and proposals for change.

- Proposed changes in provisions concerning mortgages and proposed reversal of principle in *Re Power* (1947).

Suggested solution

When the Trustee Investments Act 1961 was passed into law it was regarded at that time as a revolutionary step in trustee investment because prior to then a trust without express investment powers was limited to making investments in government securities under general law. This led to dicta in cases such as *Re Kolb's Will Trusts* (1961) that the courts would not widen trustee investment powers under an application made by reason of the Variation of Trusts Act 1958 to enable trustees to invest beyond the scope of the provisions in the 1961 Act. But with the passage of time, which has seen substantial changes in investment conditions and practices, it is now apparent that the provisions of the 1961 Act are out of date and in need of substantial amendment. See *British Museum Trustees* v *Attorney-General* (1984).

The Law Reform Committee in its 23rd Report on 'The Powers and Duties of Trustees' highlighted many of the problems with the provisions of the 1961 Act. These powers which apply to trusts of personalty with no investment powers, ie outside the scope of the Settled Land Act 1925 investment powers, do not permit trustees of such trusts to invest in the purchase of freehold or leasehold property. It has been widely recognised that such property has been a good investment in the last decade providing both a hedge against inflation together with satisfactory returns in the form of income. Consequently the Law Reform Committee recommended that all trustees should have power to purchase freehold or leasehold property under the general law provided appropriate advice is taken. In addition, the limitation on purchasing leaseholds of not less than 60 years unexpired term as investments as contained in s73 of the Settled Land Act 1925 was considered as no longer justifiable since many short leases were capable of retaining a high value and, in any event, the depreciation in the value of such assets could be offset in many cases by the creation of a sinking fund.

The Trustee Investments Act 1961 divides the investments trustees are permitted to make into three categories: Schedule 1 Part I, which do not require investment advice and Schedule 1, Parts II and III which do require investment advice. A trustee can invest all the trust fund in Schedule 1 Parts I and II but should he desire to invest in Schedule 1 Part III the trust fund must be divided into two equal parts, the 'narrower-range' and the 'wider-range' the former being the Schedule 1 Parts I and II investments and the latter the Schedule 1 Part III investments. Once this division is made it is irrevocable. The securities contained in Schedule 1 Parts I and II are mainly fixed interest securities and the original purpose of the 1961 Act was to set up a system to enable trustees to invest in equity stock and shares within Schedule 1 Part III. Because of changed financial conditions the scheme under the 1961 Act has proved to be over-cautious in its approach to investing in shares. This can be seen from the considerable restrictions in Schedule 1 Part IV on the type of company in which trustees may invest. In addition, the administration of the 1961 Act has been found 'to be tiresome, cumbrous and expensive in operation'. Consequently, the Law Reform Committee recommended revision of these powers so that the system referred to be abolished and replaced by a system with the trust fund investment powers divided into two categories. One category would cover all those investments now found in Schedule 1 Parts I and II and such investments could be made without advice. The second category would comprise investments which could only be made with advice and it was recommended that it should include any other investment quoted on the English Stock Exchange. Trustees should be free to invest the trust fund in such proportions as they choose in these categories.

The provisions on seeking investment advice were also considered by the Law Reform Committee but no change was recommended as provisions of s6 of the 1961 Act were considered adequate. However, it was recommended that a failure to seek advice should be regarded as an automatic breach of trust where the recommendations suggested it should be obtained. Emphasis on the need for trustees to keep a balance between income and capital in the trust fund was recommended by a new statutory provision to this effect.

Another area which the Law Reform Committee considered in relation to the 1961 Act was the present powers of trustees to invest in mortgages under Schedule 1 Part II and ss8 and 9 of the Trustee Act 1925. At present trustees may only invest in first mortgages and it was concluded that there was now a case to permit trustees to invest in second mortgages because of the possibility of protecting priority under the registration provisions of the Land Charges Act 1972. But second mortgages would be subject to the s8(1)(b) of the Trustee Act 1925 in that the total advance under the first and second mortgage should not exceed two-thirds of the value of the property. It was also recommended that the decisions in *Re Power's WT* (1947) should be statutorily reversed so that trustees have power to either purchase a house outright or buy a house on mortgage as a residence for a beneficiary. This would overcome the difficulty that use of trust property in this way was not an 'investment' for the purposes of the 1961 Act.

16 THE DUTY NOT TO
DELEGATE THE TRUST

16.1   Introduction

16.2   Key points

16.3   Analysis of questions

16.4   Questions

16.1   Introduction

The topic, although quite narrow, includes some areas of complexity and difficulty; notably, the provisions in the Trustee Act 1925 concerning the liability of trustees for the defaults of their agents. The courts have not, themselves, solved the problems and so the student can only hope to understand the issues and to be aware of the various interpretations which have been put forward.

16.2   Key points

The general rule is that trustees are under a duty not to delegate the trust. The main exception to this, prior to 1925, was that delegation was possible in cases of legal and moral necessity - *ex parte Belchier* (1754) Amb 218 and *Speight* v *Gaunt* (1883) 22 Ch D 727 - which was interpreted in *Fry* v *Tapson* (1884) 28 Ch D 268 as meaning that agents could be employed whenever a prudent man of business would do so.

The Trustee Act 1925 introduced far more extensive powers of delegation and, according to Maugham J in *Re Vickery* [1931] 1 Ch 572, 'revolutionises the position':

a) *Section 23(1)*

This provision allows trustees to delegate ministerial acts, but not discretions such as investment decisions.

b) *Section 23(2)*

This provision enables trustees to delegate ministerial acts and discretions but only as regards property situated outside the United Kingdom.

c) *Section 23(3)*

This provision authorises delegation to a solicitor of the act of receiving and giving a discharge for trust money or property and to a solicitor or banker of the act of receiving and giving a discharge for money payable to a trustee under an

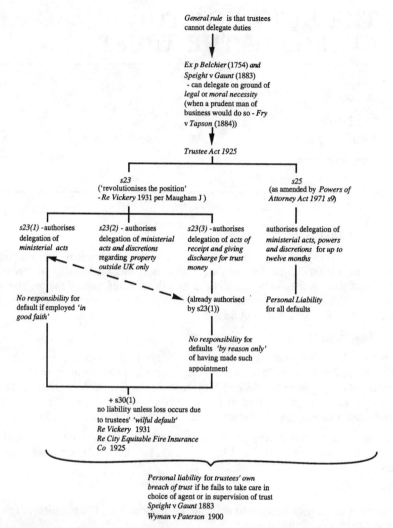

General rule is that trustees
cannot delegate duties

Ex p Belchier (1754) *and*
Speight v *Gaunt* (1883)
- can delegate on ground of
legal or *moral necessity*
(when a prudent man of
business would do so - *Fry*
v *Tapson* (1884))

Trustee Act 1925

s23
('revolutionises the position'
- *Re Vickery* 1931 per Maugham J)

s25
(as amended by *Powers of*
Attorney Act 1971 s9)

s23(1) -authorises
delegation of
ministerial acts

s23(2) - authorises
delegation of *ministerial*
acts and discretions
regarding *property*
outside UK only

s23(3) -authorises
delegation of *acts of*
receipt and giving
discharge for trust
money

authorises delegation of
ministerial acts, powers
and discretions for *up to*
twelve months

No responsibility for
default if employed *'in*
good faith'

(already authorised
by s23(1))

Personal Liability
for all defaults

No responsibility for
defaults *'by reason only'*
of having made such
appointment

+ s30(1)
no liability unless loss occurs due
to trustees' *'wilful default'*
Re Vickery 1931
Re City Equitable Fire Insurance
Co 1925

Personal liability for *trustees' own*
breach of trust if he fails to take care in
choice of agent or in supervision of trust
Speight v *Gaunt* 1883
Wyman v *Paterson* 1900

insurance policy. Such acts are already authorised as ministerial acts by s23(1) and thus s23(3) seems unnecessary.

The main distinction between the two provisions would seem to lie in the extra protection afforded to a purchaser under the Law of Property Act 1925 if he insists that delegation should take place under s23(3) rather than s23(1).

d) *Section 25*

This section enables a trustee to delegate powers and discretions as well as ministerial acts even if the trust property is not situated abroad. An important disadvantage of delegation under s25 is the continuing liability of the trustee (see below).

If a trustee properly delegates some aspect of the trust under the above provisions, he will not, in certain circumstances, be liable for the defaults of and any loss occasioned by his agent.

a) *Section 23*

    i) (1) - the trustee will not be held responsible if the agent was employed in good faith.

    ii) (2) and (3) - the trustee will not be liable for any such defaults 'by reason only' of having made the appointment.

In addition to the protection offered by the provisions themselves, s30(1) TA states that the trustee will not be liable unless the loss occurs due to his own 'wilful default'. The relationship between 'wilful default' in s30(1) and 'in good faith' in s23(1) has been the subject of much discussion and depends on the correct definition of the two phrases. In *Re City Equitable Fire Insurance Co* [1925] Ch 407 'wilful default' was defined as 'a consciousness of negligence, or breach of duty, or a recklessness in the performance of a duty', and this definition was adopted in *Re Vickery* [1931] 1 Ch 572.

It should be noted that the protection offered to the trustee by the above provisions in no way protects him against liability for his own breach of trust - if he fails to properly appoint an agent or to supervise the trust. This possibility of personal liability was underlined in both *Speight* v *Gaunt* (1883) 22 Ch D 727 and *Wyman* v *Paterson* [1900] AC 271.

b) *Section 25*

The trustee remains personally liable for all defaults of or loss occasioned by his agent.

16.3 Analysis of questions

The rule against delegation is generally examined as part of a problem question, combining both this topic and other topics on trusteeship. The key to a good answer is to identify what the trustee wishes to delegate or has delegated and to consider only the relevant provisions.

16.4 Questions

Problem checklist

a) What does the trustee want to delegate/has the trustee delegated?

If ministerial acts only, go to (b); if discretions too, go to (c).

b) If simply receipt for trust property, delegation is possible under s23(1) or s23(3) - latter offers less protection to trustee. If other acts too, delegation is possible under s23(1).

c) If the property is abroad delegation is possible under s23(2). If it is not, delegation is only possible under s25 which offers the trustee no protection.

Questions

See Chapter 21 (questions 5 and 6).

17 POWERS OF ADVANCEMENT AND MAINTENANCE

17.1   Introduction

17.2   Key points

17.3   Analysis of questions

17.4   Question

17.1   Introduction

The law on this topic is derived primarily from two sections of the Trustee Act 1925 which must be learnt. The aspect which students tend to have most difficulty with is the distinction between vested and contingent interests and the question of whether the latter carry intermediate income. The answer can be found by reference to a combination of common sense, statutory provisions and individual decisions and must be fully understood before s31 can be applied.

17.2   Key points

The Trustee Act 1925 ss31 and 32 give trustees wide powers to use income and capital for the maintenance of infant beneficiaries and for the advancement or benefit of all beneficiaries, provided that the trust instrument shows no contrary intention.

Income

In the absence of any express power, income under a trust can be used for the benefit of a beneficiary who is not in receipt of such income under TA s31 or under the court's inherent jurisdiction.

a) *TA s31*

The trustees can use the income for the 'maintenance, education or benefit' of an infant beneficiary under a trust whose interest carries 'intermediate income'. To the extent that it is not so used, the income must be accumulated and added to the capital under s31(2). If the infant dies before reaching the age of 18 or marrying, his estate will not be entitled to these accumulations even if his interest is vested - *Re Delamere's ST* [1984] 1 All ER 588. At the age of 18 or earlier marriage, the income (but not the accumulated income) will be paid to the beneficiary. The beneficiary becomes entitled to the accumulations when he becomes entitled to the capital.

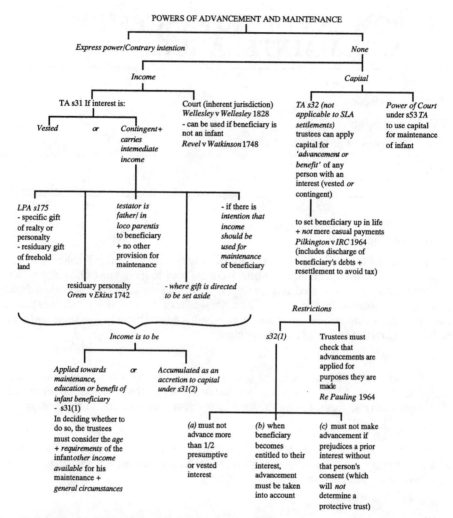

POWERS OF ADVANCEMENT AND MAINTENANCE

Express power/Contrary intention — *None*

Income — *Capital*

TA s31 If interest is:

Vested   *or*   *Contingent +*
                    carries
                    intemediate
                    income

Court (inherent jurisdiction)
Wellesley v *Wellesley* 1828
- can be used if beneficiary is
not an infant
Revel v *Watkinson* 1748

TA s32 (not
applicable to SLA
settlements)
trustees can apply
capital for
*'advancement or
benefit'* of any
person with an
interest (vested *or*
contingent)

Power of Court
under s53 *TA*
to use capital
for maintenance
of infant

LPA s175
- specific gift
of realty or
personalty
- residuary gift
of freehold
land

*testator is
father/ in
loco parentis*
to beneficiary
+ no other
provision for
maintenance

- if there is
*intention that
income
should be
used for
maintenance*
of beneficiary

to set beneficiary up in life
+ *not* mere casual payments
Pilkington v *IRC* 1964
(includes discharge of
beneficiary's debts +
resettlement to avoid tax)

residuary personality
Green v *Ekins* 1742

- *where gift is directed
to be set aside*

Restrictions

Income is to be   *s32(1)*   Trustees must
                                    check that
                                    advancements are
                                    applied for
                                    purposes they are
                                    made
                                    Re Pauling 1964

*Applied towards   or   Accumulated as an
maintenance,   accretion to capital
education or benefit of   under s31(2)*
infant beneficiary
- s31(1)*
In deciding whether to
do so, the trustees
must consider the *age
+ requirements* of the
infant*other income
available* for his
maintenance +
general circumstances

(a) must not
advance more
than 1/2
presumptive
or vested
interest

(b) when
beneficiary
becomes
entitled to their
interest,
advancement
must be taken
into account

(c) must not make
advancement if
prejudices a prior
interest without
that person's
consent (which
will *not*
determine a
protective trust)

i)   'maintenance, education or benefit'

When deciding whether to use the income for such purposes, the trustees
must consider the age and requirements of the infant, whether other income
is available for his maintenance and the general circumstances of the case.
If the discretion is exercised in good faith the court will not interfere -
Bryant v *Hickley* [1894] 1 Ch 324.

ii) 'intermediate income'

A vested gift (eg 'To X') will always carry intermediate income. A contingent gift, however (eg 'To X on attaining 21') will not. It will carry intermediate income, and thus s31 will apply, in the following circumstances:

- under LPA s175, a specific gift of realty or personalty or a residuary gift of freehold land will carry intermediate income.

- a gift of residuary personalty carries intermediate income - *Green* v *Ekins* (1742) 2 ALK 743.

- if the settlor is the father of or stands in loco parentis to the infant beneficiary and the contingency is attaining the age of 18 or earlier marriage, the gift will carry intermediate income.

- where the gift is directed in the instrument to be set aside.

- if the instrument shows an intention that the income should be used for the maintenance of an infant beneficiary - *Re Selby-Walker* [1949] 2 All ER 178.

b) *Court's inherent jurisdiction*

The court's inherent jurisdiction to allow income to be used for an infant's maintenance was underlined in *Wellesley* v *Wellesley* (1828) 2 Bli NS 124, and it was stated in *Revel* v *Watkinson* (1748) 1 Ves Sen 93 that the jurisdiction could also be used to grant maintenance when the beneficiary is not an infant.

Capital

In the absence of any express power, trust capital can be used for the benefit of a beneficiary who is not yet entitled to such capital under TA s32 and s53.

a) *TA s32*

The trustees can apply the capital for the 'advancement or benefit of any person with an interest in it (vested or contingent). Section 32 does not apply to SLA settlements.

i) 'advancement or benefit'

This means setting up the beneficiary in life - *Pilkington* v *IRC* [1964] AC 612 - and includes the discharge of the beneficiary's debts and a resettlement of capital to avoid tax (although NB the rules against perpetuities).

ii) restrictions of the power of advancement

- the trustees must ensure that the advancements are applied for the purposes for which they are made - *Re Pauling's ST* [1964] Ch 303.

- s32(1)(a) - the trustees must not advance more than half of the beneficiary's presumptive or vested share or interest.

- s32(1)(b) - when the beneficiary becomes absolutely entitled to their interest the advancement must be taken into account.

- s32(1)(c) - an advancement must not be made if it prejudices a prior interest unless the person with such an interest gives consent to the advancement. If the life tenant under a protective trust gives consent, the protective trust will not be determined under s33.

b) *TA s53*

The court has power to order the use of capital for an infant's maintenance.

17.3 Analysis of questions

The topic is commonly examined in problem questions - generally, either the whole or most of a question will be devoted to this area. Provided the student applies the relevant statutory provisions and principles to the facts, the question should present no real difficulties. As with all problem questions, a concise logical approach is essential. In chapter 21, there is an example of a combination question, which illustrates a combination of this topic with the subject of variation of trusts (chapter 18).

17.4 Question

Under the trusts of a settlement, a personalty fund worth £150,000 is held by the trustees upon trust for such of the settlor's grandchildren, Tom, Dick and Harriet, as attain the age of 25 in equal shares absolutely. Tom is now 25, Dick is 18 and Harriet is 13. Advise the trustees:

i) Whether they may now distribute one third of the capital of the trust fund to Tom;

ii) Whether they should distribute any, and if so what, trust income and to whom;

iii) Whether they may advance the sum of £25,000 out of capital to enable Dick to train for a commercial pilot's licence;

iv) Whether they may pay out of trust moneys the school fees of Harriet who is about to go to a boarding school.

University of London LLB Examination
(for External Students) Law of Trusts June 1987 Q3

Skeleton solution and comment

The main issues in this question are the provisions contained in ss31 and 32 of Trustee Act 1925, although a consideration of the rule in *Saunders* v *Vautier* (1841) is also necessary in the first part (see chapter 19).

i) Application of the rule in *Saunders* v *Vautier* (1841) to Tom and of the class-closing rules.

ii) Consideration of the trust income as applied in accordance with TA s31 distinguishing present income and past accumulated income and in each case, taking each beneficiary in turn.

iii) Whether the trustees can advance £25,000 to Dick depends on whether an application of TA s32 is possible.

iv) The school fees may be able to be paid under either s31 or s32 and both must be considered.

Suggested solution

i) The trustees may distribute one third of the capital to Tom, if he demands it, as he has now fulfilled the contingency of attaining 25 as imposed by the trust. Under the rule in *Saunders* v *Vautier* (1841) a beneficiary of full age who has an absolute, vested and indefeasible interest in property may at any time, notwithstanding any direction to accumulate, demand his share. Tom's interest became indefeasible in one-third of the fund when he attained 25 but not before then because it was liable to be defeated if he died before 25. See *Berry* v *Green* (1938). He may receive further capital in the future if other beneficiaries do not attain 25 as the gift is 'to such grandchildren as attain 25' in equal shares.

The distribution to Tom cannot be prevented by the fact that the other beneficiaries have not attained 25 as the gift is not contingent on all of them attaining that age. It will not be prevented by the nature of the property in the trust as this will have to be sold, if necessary, in order to pay him his share. Thus, for example, if the trust had control of a company which it would lose because Tom demanded his share, this could be used to stop him demanding that share. See *Re Weiner* (1956) and *Lloyd's Bank plc* v *Duker* (1987). The possibility of further grandchildren being born will not prevent distribution of one-third to Tom as the class of beneficiaries closed at the latest on Tom attaining 25.

ii) The trust income has to be considered in two parts, the accumulated income from past years, if any, and income arising in the current financial year. The former is held by the trustees as an accretion to the capital of the property from which it arose and as one fund with this capital for all purposes. See s31(2)(iii) TA 1925. Thus, when Tom attained 25 he should have been given the accumulated income on his share together with the capital, if he exercised the rule in *Saunders* v *Vautier*. The accumulations on the shares of Dick and Harriet may not, as a general rule, be paid to them until they fulfil the contingency under s31(2). However, this general rule is subject to one exception in that the trustees may use the accumulated income for the maintenance of infant beneficiaries under s31 and this would allow them to maintain Harriet but not, of course, Dick as he is now 18.

Income arising in the current financial year should be paid over to Tom, should he wish the trust to continue in respect of his share, and to Dick, as it arises. When a beneficiary attains 18 then under s31(1)(ii) TA 1925 all the income on his share must be paid to him as it arises. The income on Harriet's share will have to be accumulated under s31 as she is unable to give a valid receipt therefore. The trustees may, however, use the whole or such part of it, as they in their absolute discretion think fit, for Harriet's maintenance, education or benefit under s31(1) TA 1925.

iii) An advance of £25,000 to Dick to enable him to train for a commercial pilot's licence is possible under s32 TA 1925 provided the settlor has not excluded the power of advancement thereunder. The sum of £25,000 is however, the maximum advance that can be made to Dick as s32(1)(a) only permits total advancements of up to one-half of a beneficiary's presumptive share. If Dick has already received advancements from the trust for other purposes then these will have to be taken into account in deciding the maximum advance that can be made. When distribution of the fund eventually takes place the amount that is advanced to Dick will have to be brought into account as part of his share under s32(1)(b) TA 1925. In determining whether to advance the trustees will have a complete discretion but they are obliged to ensure that the purpose for which the advance is required is prudent and that the money is applied to it. See *Re Pauling's Settlement Trusts* (1964).

iv) Harriet's school fees may be paid by the trustees exercising their powers either under s31 or s32 TA 1925. As Harriet is still an infant the power of maintenance is available in her case and this allows the trustees to apply the income on her share for, inter alia, her education. The trustees could use both current and accumulated income for this purpose. Alternatively the trustees could use the power of advancement under s32 and apply the capital of Harriet's share to pay her school fees. This would be necessary if the total income was insufficient to do so, which would appear to be unlikely in this case.

The limitations under s32 in making advancements would apply and once the trustees had advanced more than one-half of her presumptive share they would have to seek the approval of the court to make further advancements. It would appear more prudent to use s31 in this case in view of the size of Harriet's share.

18 VARIATION OF TRUSTS

18.1   Introduction

18.2   Key points

18.3   Recent cases

18.4   Analysis of questions

18.5   Questions

18.1   Introduction

This topic is commonly considered by students to be a difficult one. Much of the difficulty stems from a misconception of the application of the most important statutory provision in this area - the Variation of Trusts Act 1958 - which, rather than giving the court a general power to authorise variations, is simply an aspect of the well established rule that variation is possible if all the beneficiaries consent. Once this idea is grasped, neither the Act itself, nor the other aspects of the topic should raise any serious problems.

18.2   Key points

The general rule is that variation of trusts is not possible due to the duty that trustees must not deviate from the terms of a trust - *Re New* [1901] 2 Ch 534. This rule is, however, subject to a number of important exceptions.

a) *Statutory provisions*

i) TA s53

Under this provision, the court can authorise variations which enable the transfer of trust property so that the capital or the income can be used for the maintenance, education or benefit of an infant beneficiary.

It was held in *Re Gower's Settlement* [1934] Ch 365 that the court could authorise a mortgage of trust property under s53, and in *Re Meux's Will Trusts* [1958] Ch 154 the sale of the whole of the beneficial interest was authorised where the proceeds were to be resettled on new trusts. It would not be so authorised if no resettlement was intended.

ii) TA s57(1)

This section, which is not applicable to Settled Land Act (SLA) 1925 settlements, enables the court to authorise an otherwise unauthorised act involved in the management and administration of the trust, if it is expedient for the trust as a whole. It is clear that this provision in no way

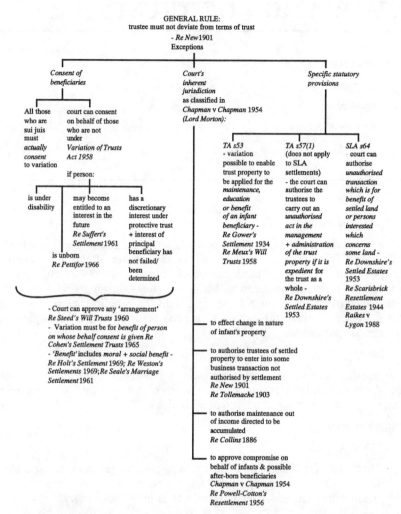

GENERAL RULE:
trustee must not deviate from terms of trust
- *Re New* 1901
Exceptions

Consent of beneficiaries

All those who are sui juis must *actually consent* to variation

court can consent on behalf of those who are not under *Variation of Trusts Act 1958*

if person:

is under disability

may become entitled to an interest in the future *Re Suffert's Settlement* 1961

is unborn *Re Pettifor* 1966

has a discretionary interest under protective trust + interest of principal beneficiary has not failed/ been determined

- Court can approve any 'arrangement' *Re Steed's Will Trusts* 1960
- Variation must be for *benefit of person on whose behalf consent is given Re Cohen's Settlement Trusts* 1965
- *'Benefit'* includes *moral + social benefit* - *Re Holt's Settlement* 1969; *Re Weston's Settlements* 1969; *Re Seale's Marriage Settlement* 1961

Court's inherent jurisdiction as classified in *Chapman v Chapman* 1954 *(Lord Morton):*

TA s53 - variation possible to enable trust property to be applied for the *maintenance, education or benefit of an infant beneficiary* - *Re Gower's Settlement* 1934 *Re Meux's Will Trusts* 1958

- to effect change in nature of infant's property

- to authorise trustees of settled property to enter into some business transaction not authorised by settlement *Re New* 1901 *Re Tollemache* 1903

- to authorise maintenance out of income directed to be accumulated *Re Collins* 1886

- to approve compromise on behalf of infants & possible after-born beneficiaries *Chapman v Chapman* 1954 *Re Powell-Cotton's Resettlement* 1956

TA s57(1) (does not apply to SLA settlements) - the court can authorise the trustees to carry out an *unauthorised act in the management + administration of the trust property if it is expedient* for the trust as a whole - *Re Downshire's Settled Estates* 1953

Specific statutory provisions

SLA s64 - court can authorise *unauthorised transaction which is for benefit of settled land or persons interested which concerns some land* - *Re Downshire's Settled Estates* 1953 *Re Scarisbrick Resettlement Estates* 1944 *Raikes v Lygon* 1988

enables the alteration of beneficial interests - *Re Downshire's Settled Estates* [1953] 1 All ER 103. An application under s57 could be made to authorise an investment outside the powers of the trustees.

iii)   SLA s64

This provision (which applies both to SLA settlements and to land held on trust for sale) allows the court to authorise any transaction affecting land which benefits either the settled land or the persons interested in it. Unlike the previous statutory provision in (ii) above this section does allow the alteration of beneficial interest - *Re Downshire's Settled Estates* (1953).

In *Re Scarisbrick Resettlement Estates* [1944] Ch 229, trustees were authorised to sell capital to enable the continued and necessary occupation of the land, and in *Raikes* v *Lygon* [1988] 1 All ER 884, the use of some settled property to maintain other settled property was allowed despite the difference in potential beneficiaries under the two settlements.

b) *The court's inherent jurisdiction*

The court will authorise variations of trusts under its inherent jurisdiction in limited circumstances, as classified by Lord Morton in *Chapman* v *Chapman* [1954] AC 429:

   i)   the court can authorise changes in the nature of an infant's property.

        This head was relevant in the light of pre-1926 law and is no longer of importance.

   ii) the court can authorise transactions which are unauthorised by the settlement.

        This head was previously underlined in *Re New* [1901] 2 Ch 534 in which it was said that authority would be given when such a transaction is desirable for the benefit of the estate and of all the beneficiaries. This flexible approach as applied in *Re New* (1901) was considered in *Re Tollemache* [1903] 1 Ch 955 in which *Re New* was described as the 'high-water mark' of the court's inherent jurisdiction to vary trusts. This head does not enable the court to authorise the alteration of beneficial interests.

   iii) the court can authorise maintenance out of income which was directed to be accumulated.

        This was done in *Re Collins* (1886) 32 Ch D 229.

   iv) the court can approve a compromise on behalf of infants and of possible after-born beneficiaries.

        This is possible only where dispute existed as to beneficial interests - *Chapman* v *Chapman* (1954) and *Re Powell-Cotton's Resettlement* [1956] 1 All ER 60 and such a variation would clearly involve the alteration of beneficial interests.

c) *Consent of the beneficiaries*

It is generally accepted that consent of all beneficiaries (provided they are sui juris) is a defence to any breach of trust, including a breach of the duty not to deviate from the terms of the trust. A problem arises when the beneficiaries are not, for some reason, in a position to consent. In this situation, the court may be able to consent on those beneficiaries' behalf under the Variation of Trusts Act 1958. (Those beneficiaries who are in a position to consent must still do so).

Under the Variation of Trusts Act 1958 s1, the court can approve any 'arrangement' varying the trust on behalf of, and provided that it is for the 'benefit' of, any of the following persons:

i)   persons under a disability - in particular, infants (s1(1)(a)).

ii) persons who may become entitled to an interest in the future (s1(1)(b)).

If a person already has an interest, albeit contingent, s1(1)(b) will not apply - *Re Suffert's Settlement* [1961] Ch 1 - and the beneficiary in question must themselves actually consent.

iii) persons unborn (s1(1)(c))

If there is no possibility of a person ever being born - for example, if the class of beneficiaries is children of a woman who is beyond child-bearing age as in *Re Pettifor's WT* [1966] Ch 257 - an application under s1(1)(c) is inappropriate and unnecessary.

iv) persons with a discretionary interest under a protective trust which has not been determined (s1(1)(d)). In this case the variation need not be for the benefit of the person concerned.

The word 'arrangement' was intended to be a wide and flexible one, and thus a proposal will qualify as an 'arrangement' unless it studies at the root of the settlor's intention - *Re Steed's WT* [1960] Ch 407.

The proposed variation must be for the benefit of the person on whose behalf the court's approval is sought - *Re Cohen's ST* [1965] 3 All ER 139.

The term 'benefit' includes moral and social benefit - *Re Holt's Settlement* [1969] 1 Ch 100. Whether tax advantages will qualify as a 'benefit' depends on whether they are the primary reason for the proposed variation. If they are, they will not so qualify and the variation will not be allowed - *Re Weston's Settlements* [1969] 1 Ch 223; if the advantages are simply incidental to the primary purpose of the trust, the variation will be allowed: *Re Seale's Marriage Settlement* [1961] Ch 574.

18.3   Recent cases

Raikes v *Lygon* [1988] 1 All ER 884

18.4   Analysis of questions

Both essay and problem questions on variation of trusts are common, as are a combination of the two in mixed questions. As a matter of style, it is advisable with a problem question to begin by considering the possibility of a variation under the Variation of Trusts Act 1958 and only to go on to consider other powers of variation if the Act does not provide a solution. This is because the Act was intended to rationalise much of the pre-existing law and thus provides far more extensive powers than any of the individual aspects of the previous law. It must be remembered, however, that the Act will be of no help if some of the beneficiaries are in a position to consent but refuse to do so.

18.5   Questions

Question 1

a) In what circumstances may the terms of a trust be varied?

b) Under a settlement of personalty, Tick and Tock hold investments worth £250,000 upon trust to pay the income to Adrian for life upon protective trusts with remainder to such of Adrian's children as attain the age of 21, if more than one in equal shares. Adrian is married and has two children only, Ada and Betty aged 22 and 24.

Advise Adrian, Ada and Betty on their chances of being able to determine the trust and divide the investments amongst themselves.

University of London LLB Examination
(for External Students) Law of Trusts June 1983 Q6

Skeleton solution and comment

This question is a fairly typical mixed question requiring a précis of the principles of the variation of trusts and then an application of those principles to a particular set of facts, which also requires brief consideration of TA s33 and of trustees' power of advancement under s32. The student should ensure that he allocates his time equally between each part in a question of this nature.

a) • Introduction - statement of the general rule and its erosion.

• Consideration of TA s57.

• Summary of SLA s64.

• Explanation of the provisions under the Variation of Trusts Act 1958 and their effect - in particular, the classes of persons on whose behalf the court can approve a variation and the meaning of the word 'benefit'.

• Reference to other powers to vary trusts.

b) • Possibility of application of principle in *Re Smith* (1928) - not available here.

• Application to court under Variation of Trusts Act 1958 s1(1)(d) - provisions of the Act and relevant general principles.

• Last resort of an advancement under TA s32 (see chapter 17) provided that Adrian consents in writing.

Suggested solution

a) The general rule is that the court has no power to sanction a departure from the terms of a trust no matter how advantageous it may be to the beneficiaries. See *Chapman* v *Chapman* (1954). However, this general rule has been considerably eroded since 1925 by statutory powers given to the courts to vary trust instruments. These are in addition to the limited powers the court has always had under its inherent jurisdiction.

Under s57 Trustee Act 1925 the court can confer the power on trustees to effect any transaction which is expedient in the management or administration of the trust but which the trustees have no power to do under the trust instrument. The aim of this provision is to ensure that the trust is managed as advantageously as

159

possible in the interests of the beneficiaries and it has therefore been used to authorise the sale of chattels, land and a reversionary interest. See *Re Hope* (1929); *Re Beale's ST* (1932); and *Re Cockerill's ST* (1956) and to permit the trustees to buy a house for the tenant for life (*Re Power's WT* (1947)). However, s57 does not give the court power to alter beneficial interests under a trust.

By s64(1) SLA 1925 the court can authorise any transaction for the benefit of settled land or land held on trust for sale or for the beneficiaries thereunder if such a transaction could have been effected by an absolute owner. 'Transaction' is widely defined as it appears to allow variation of beneficial interests as well as permitting trustees to exercise powers they do not have under the trust instrument.

The Variation of Trusts Act 1958 gives the court extensive powers to approve variation of trusts. Under s1(1) of the Act the court can approve an arrangement on behalf of (a) infants and others incapable of consenting (b) persons who are more than one contingency away from attaining an interest in the trust, (c) persons unborn, and (d) persons with an interest under a protective trust where the interest of the principal beneficiary has not failed or determined. Under the 1958 Act the court will only approve an arrangement on behalf of those in (a) - (c) above if it is for their 'benefit'. Benefit for these purposes includes financial benefit. See *Re T's ST* (1964) and moral and cultural benefit also. See *Re Weston's Settlements* (1969). Thus, it has been held to be a benefit to remove restrictions on religion in a trust to improve family relations. *Re Remnant's ST* (1970) and to give property to the children of a mental patient who would, if of sound mind, probably release her life interest in their favour. See *Re CL* (1969). The powers under the 1958 Act permit the court to vary or revoke trusts or enlarge the powers of the trustees in the management or administration of the trust. However, these powers are only exercisable on behalf of those mentioned in (a) - (d) above. The 1958 Act does not permit the court to give consent to a variation on behalf of any other persons, if such persons refuse to consent then the variation cannot be made. But, with such consents the court can redraw administration and investment clauses and change beneficial interests to mitigate tax liability.

The above statutory provisions set out the main powers available to vary trusts. The court also has power to vary trusts in a limited way under its inherent jurisdiction so as to permit maintenance of an infant beneficiary out of capital, see *Re Collins* (1886) and to approve a compromise or arrangement over disputes as to interests in a trust. See *Chapman* v *Chapman* (1954). There is also some power, under divorce legislation, to vary trusts after breakdown of marriage.

b) If this protective trust was for the benefit of Adrian with remainder to Ada and Betty only then it might be possible for them to end the trust and demand the transfer of the property to themselves provided they and any persons entitled in the event of a discretionary trust arising under s33 Trustee Act were all sui juris and consented. See *Re Smith, Public Trustee* v *Aspinall* (1928). However, this is not the case as the remainder is for all of Adrian's children who attain 21.

It appears that an application would have to be made to the court under s1(1)(d) of the Variation of Trusts Act 1958 to revoke the trusts if Adrian, Ada and Betty are to get rid of the protective trust, and divide the investments amongst themselves. The court's consent would be required to approve this revocation on behalf of persons (whether or not unborn or unascertained) who would be entitled to a discretionary interest in the trust if the protective trust failed or determined. The proviso to s1(1) of the 1958 Act that the variation must be for the benefit of such persons does not apply to s1(1)(d). If it is clear that Adrian is unlikely to father more children the court will probably approve the revocation of these trusts. Regard will be had to the proposal as a whole and approval will be given so long as the proposal is fair and proper in the light of the purposes of the trust as appears from the trust instrument and from the evidence before the court. See *Re Steed's WT* (1960). Tax mitigation considerations will not bar the application either. In some cases it is unnecessary to apply to the court under the 1958 Act if it is clear that a contingency is not capable of happening. Thus, in *Re Pettifor's WT* (1966) it was held that no application need be made in respect of a contingency covering the birth of a child to a woman where she was past child-bearing age. Unfortunately, this principle is not applicable to Adrian.

Should the court refuse to approve the revocation of these trusts the only thing which Adrian, Ada and Betty can do is convince the trustee that they ought to exercise the power of advancement under s32 Trustee Act 1925 in favour of either Ada or Betty. In this way up to half the presumptive shares of these beneficiaries could be advanced to them under s32(1)(a) with the written consent of Adrian under s32(1)(c). Adrian's written consent to such advancements would not determine the protective trust under s33. It would not be possible for the trustees to advance capital to Adrian who, as the life tenant, is only entitled to the income of the trust.

Question 2

'In general, the Court has no power to sanction a departure from the terms of a trust even though such a departure might well be advantageous to the beneficiaries.'

Consider how far this statement remains true to-day having regard to (i) statutory provisions, and (ii) general equitable jurisdiction.

University of London LLB Examination
(for External Students) Law of Trusts June 1986 Q7

Skeleton solution and comment

This is a general question about the various ways in which a trustee may be able to depart from the terms of the trust. A structure is essential and, as with problem questions, as the most important provision in this area is the Variation of Trusts Act 1958, this is a good starting point.

- Introduction - the general rule as stated in the question, the fact that it has been eroded and a brief explanation of the provisions of the Variation of Trusts Act 1958.

161

- The limitations of the 1958 Act - the classes of persons in s1(1) and the meaning of the word 'benefit'.

- Provisions of TA ss53 and 57.

- SLA s64 - summary of the section.

- Court's inherent jurisdiction as classified in *Chapman* v *Chapman* (1954).

Suggested solution

The statement quoted: viz that the Court has no power to sanction a departure from the terms of a trust even though it may be advantageous to the beneficiaries, has been considerably eroded by statutory provisions but has been little affected by general equitable jurisdiction. The most important provision affecting departure from the terms of a trust is the Variation of Trusts Act 1958. This Act gives the Court wide powers to approve variations of trusts on behalf of infants, unborn persons who are are several contingencies away from attaining an interest, and others. The powers, which are discretionary, permit the Court to approve on behalf of the classes of persons specified, any arrangements for varying or revoking all or any of the trusts or enlarging the powers of the trustees in managing or administering the trust property. The most notable aspect of the 1958 Act is that it permits the Court to vary beneficial interests under a trust.

There are, however, some limitations on the operation of the 1958 Act. It only enables the Court to approve variations on behalf of the classes of persons set out in s1(1)(a)-(d), no variation can be approved on behalf of any other person so that the agreement of beneficiaries who are outside these classes must be obtained to any variation. In respect of the classes on whose behalf variations may be approved the Court may only approve a variation on behalf of those within s(1)(a)-(c) if it is for their benefit. Benefit for these purposes is not limited to financial benefit, it includes moral and social benefits and maintaining good family relations. See *Re Weston's Settlements* (1969); *Re Remnant's ST* (1970). In deciding whether or not it will approve a variation the Court must also consider the purpose of the settlor, thus it will not approve a variation which cuts at the root of the settlor's intentions. In *Re Steed's WT* (1960) approval was refused to a variation which was aimed at eliminating a protective trust giving an absolute interest to the beneficiary as the avowed purpose of the trust was to protect the beneficiary from her own financial folly.

Apart from the Variation of Trusts Act 1958 the provisions in s53 and s57 of the Trustee Act 1925 and s64 of the Settled Land Act 1925 permit the Court to sanction a departure from the terms of a trust. Under s53 of the Trustee Act the Court may order the sale of property held upon trust for an infant beneficiary so that the proceeds of sale may be used for his maintenance, education or benefit. Section 57 of the Trustee Act gives the Court power to sanction extra powers of management and administration to trustees to enable the trust to be managed as advantageously as possible in the interests of the beneficiaries. This section does not enable the Court to approve variations in beneficial interests. Its original purpose was to enable the

Court to sanction transactions it might have otherwise have considered were not within its inherent jurisdiction. Thus, the section refers to specific transactions but it is sufficiently wide to enable most matters pertaining to management or administration of a trust to be dealt with by the Court. See *Re Downshire's SE* (1953). It should be noted that s57(4) provides that the section does not apply to Settled Land Act settlements.

Under s64 of the Settled Land Act 1925, which applies to both SLA settlements and trusts for sale of land, the Court has power to approve 'any transaction' concerning the land which is for the benefit of the land or the beneficiaries and which could have been affected by an absolute owner. The term 'transaction' is widely defined and it enables the Court to alter not only powers of management or administration but also beneficial interests. See *Re Simmons* (1956).

The Court's general equitable jurisdiction or inherent jurisdiction to sanction a departure from the terms of a trust is limited and in many instances has been overtaken by the statutory provisions already considered. In *Chapman v Chapman* (1954) Lord Morton classified the cases where the Court had power to sanction a departure from the terms of a trust. First, he referred to cases in which the Court effected changes in the nature of an infant's property. This case is really of little importance today as it was intended primarily to deal with cases where under the pre-1926 Law the trustees had no power to convert realty into personalty and vice versa. Second, he referred to cases in which the Court allowed trustees of settled property to enter into some transaction which was not authorised by the settlement. This aspect of the inherent jurisdiction was confined to cases of 'emergency' ie where circumstances had arisen which could not have been foreseen or anticipated by the settlor. There was no power to approve transactions merely because they were in the interests of the beneficiaries. See *Re New* (1901). This part of the inherent jurisdiction is now eclipsed by s57 of the Trustee Act which was intended to supplement its shortcomings. Third, he referred to cases where the Court allowed maintenance out of income which the settlor had directed to be accumulated. This power enabled the Court to order maintenance out of accumulations or to break an accumulation when there were no other funds available to maintain the infant. See *Re Collins* (1886). This inherent jurisdiction is often resorted to today, and it can bring about a variation of beneficial interests. Fourth, he referred to cases in which the Court approved a compromise on behalf of infants and possible after-born beneficiaries. This jurisdiction is confined to cases where there is a genuine dispute as to interests therein. Accordingly, it is arguable that the compromise does not alter the trusts but only settles doubts as to the extent of beneficial rights therein. Prior to the passing of the 1958 Act it was considered in *Chapman v Chapman* (1954) that this provision could not be used as a means of varying beneficial interests by concocting artificial disputes. It was this decision that prompted the passing of the Variation of Trusts Act 1958, referred to above.

19 MISCELLANEOUS POWERS AND DUTIES OF TRUSTEES

19.1   Introduction

19.2   Key points

19.3   Recent cases

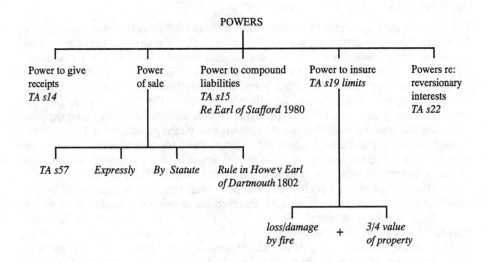

POWERS

| Power to give receipts
TA s14 | Power of sale | Power to compound liabilities
TA s15
Re Earl of Stafford 1980 | Power to insure
TA s19 limits | Powers re: reversionary interests
TA s22 |

TA s57   *Expressly*   *By Statute*   *Rule in Howe v Earl of Dartmouth* 1802

loss/damage by fire   +   *3/4 value of property*

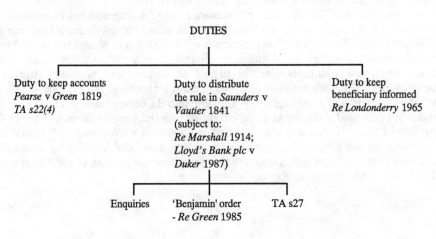

DUTIES

| Duty to keep accounts
Pearse v Green 1819
TA s22(4) | Duty to distribute the rule in *Saunders* v *Vautier* 1841 (subject to: *Re Marshall* 1914; *Lloyd's Bank plc* v *Duker* 1987) | Duty to keep beneficiary informed
Re Londonderry 1965 |

Enquiries   *'Benjamin' order - Re Green* 1985   *TA s27*

19.1 Introduction

This chapter groups together those powers and duties of trustees which the student must be aware of, but which do not justify chapters of their own, nor fit neatly into chapters concerning other topics. None of the individual areas raises serious difficulties, nor will any of them alone form the subject-matter of a question; instead, the student may be required to consider one or more of the areas as a side-issue in a question (generally a problem) concerning primarily another topic. For this reason, there is not a 'question' section in this chapter; questions involving these miscellaneous duties can be found in several other chapters in the second half of this book, including chapter 21 of various 'combination' questions.

19.2 Key points

Powers

In addition to the powers which have already been considered in previous chapters, trustees have several more minor powers as follows:

a) *Power of sale*

Specific powers of sale can be found in various statutory provisions including the SLA, the LPA, the TA and the Trustee Investments Act 1961. In addition, the trust instrument may itself empower the trustees to sell trust property and where the property in question is residuary personalty, a power may arise under the rule in *Howe* v *Earl of Dartmouth* (1802) 7 Ves 137. If a power of sale is not available in one of these ways, the trustees can, as a last resort, apply to the court for an order for sale under TA s57.

b) *Power to give receipts*

Under TA s14 trustees are empowered to give receipts even if the trust instrument shows a contrary intention. If the receipt is for proceeds of sale of land, at least two trustees or a trust corporation are required to give a good receipt.

c) *Power to insure*

TA s19 gives trustees power to insure trust property against loss or damage by fire only up to three-quarters of the value of the trust property.

d) *Power to compound liabilities*

The Trustees have power to compound liabilities in respect of external disputes under TA s15. In exercising this power, the trustees must take into account all relevant circumstances and, in particular, the interests of the beneficiaries - *Re Earl of Stafford* [1980] Ch 28.

e) *Powers concerning reversionary interests*

These are dealt with under TA s22.

Duties

a) *Duty to distribute*

Trustees are under a duty to distribute the trust property to those who are rightfully entitled to it. Under the rule in *Saunders* v *Vautier* (1841) Beav 115, if all the beneficiaries are of full age and have between them an absolute vested interest in the trust property, they can call on the trustees to hand it over to them, and individual beneficiaries who satisfy the requirements can also do so to the extent of their share - *Berry* v *Green* [1938] AC 575. It was shown in the case of *Re Smith* [1928] Ch 915 that the rule applies equally to discretionary trusts. Indeed, the only limitation on the rule is found in the nature of the trust property. Although in *Re Marshall* [1914] 1 Ch 192 it was underlined that the beneficiary has a right to have his share handed over to him, in *Lloyd's Bank plc* v *Duker* [1987] 3 All ER 193, a beneficiary was not allowed to take his share of the trust property (a majority shareholding in a private company) in specie as to do so would unduly prejudice the other beneficiaries.

In order to distribute according to their duty, trustees should make enquiries, fulfil the requirements of TA s27 and, if a known beneficiary cannot be found, obtain a 'Benjamin' order from the court as was done in *Re Green's Will Trusts* [1985] 3 All ER 455.

b) *Duty to keep accounts*

This duty is imposed on trustees with a related duty to produce the accounts to the beneficiaries when asked to do so - *Pearse* v *Green* (1819) 1 Jac & W 135. TA s22(4) allows the trustees to have the accounts audited should the circumstances require this.

c) *Duty to keep the beneficiaries informed*

It was held in *Re Londonderry's Settlement* [1965] Ch 918 that beneficiaries were entitled to inspect all trust documents containing information which they were entitled to know, although beneficiaries under a discretionary trust were not so entitled as far as confidential information concerning the exercise of the discretion was concerned.

19.3 Recent cases

Lloyd's Bank plc v *Duker* [1987] 3 All ER 193

20 REMEDIES FOR BREACH OF TRUST

20.1   Introduction

20.2   Key points

20.3   Recent cases

20.4   Analysis of questions

20.5   Questions

20.1   Introduction

Whenever a breach of trust occurs, the question of remedies must be addressed and so the topic is relevant to almost every aspect of trusteeship covered in the last half of this book. A personal remedy against the trustee does not raise any difficult concepts. The proprietary remedy of tracing is, however, one which students often have problems with - in many cases, this is due to a fear of the mathematical nature of the rules, concerning tracing into a mixed fund. Such a fear is easily overcome by a step-by-step approach to and practice of problems on the subject.

20.2   Key points

If a beneficiary is seeking a remedy for breach of trust, he must first sue the trustee(s) personally, and only to the extent that this remedy is unavailable or is insufficient will the proprietary remedy of tracing be possible - *Re Diplock* [1948] Ch 465. In cases concerning the administration of estates a personal remedy against the recipient of the trust property may be available as a last resort - *Ministry of Health* v *Simpson* [1951] AC 251.

Personal remedy against trustee

a) *Position of beneficiary vis-a-vis the trustees*

The trustees are jointly and severally liable and so the beneficiary can sue any or all of them - *Attorney-General* v *Wilson* (1840) Cr & Phil 1.

If a trustee is liable and is also a beneficiary, he will not be able to claim any beneficial interest until he has made good his breach.

There are several important defences available to a trustee against an action for breach of trust:

BENEFICIARY'S REMEDIES FOR BREACH OF TRUST

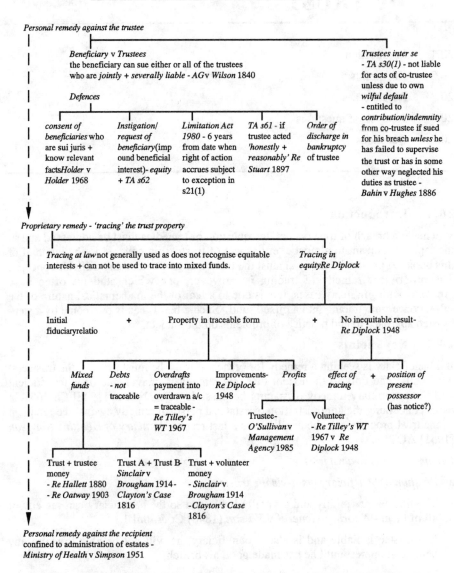

Personal remedy against the trustee

Beneficiary v Trustees
the beneficiary can sue either or all of the trustees
who are *jointly + severally liable - AGv Wilson* 1840

Defences

| *consent of beneficiaries* who are sui juris + know relevant facts*Holder* v *Holder* 1968 | *Instigation/ request of beneficiary*(imp ound beneficial interest)- *equity + TA s62* | *Limitation Act 1980* - 6 years from date when right of action accrues subject to exception in s21(1) | *TA s61* - if trustee acted *'honestly + reasonably' Re Stuart* 1897 | *Order of discharge in bankruptcy* of trustee |

Trustees inter se
- *TA s30(1)* - not liable
for acts of co-trustee
unless due to own
wilful default
- entitled to
contribution/indemnity
from co-trustee if sued
for his breach *unless* he
has failed to supervise
the trust or has in some
other way neglected his
duties as trustee -
Bahin v *Hughes* 1886

Proprietary remedy - 'tracing' the trust property

Tracing at law not generally used as does not recognise equitable
interests + can not be used to trace into mixed funds.

Tracing in equityRe Diplock

Initial
fiduciaryrelatio

+

Property in traceable form

+

No inequitable result-
Re Diplock 1948

| *Mixed funds* | *Debts* - not traceable | *Overdrafts* payment into overdrawn a/c = traceable - *Re Tilley's WT* 1967 | *Improvements- Re Diplock* 1948 | *Profits* | *effect of tracing* | + | *position of present possessor* (has notice?) |

Trustee-
O'Sullivan v
*Management
Agency* 1985

Volunteer
- *Re Tilley's WT*
1967 v *Re
Diplock* 1948

| Trust + trustee money - *Re Hallett* 1880 - *Re Oatway* 1903 | Trust A + Trust B- *Sinclair* v *Brougham* 1914 - *Clayton's Case* 1816 | Trust + volunteer money - *Sinclair* v *Brougham* 1914 - *Clayton's Case* 1816 |

Personal remedy against the recipient
confined to administration of estates -
Ministry of Health v *Simpson* 1951

i) consent of the beneficiaries

Whether a beneficiary has consented is a question of fact which will depend on the circumstances. In order to consent a beneficiary must be sui juris and must have known of all the relevant facts although he need not know that he is, in fact, consenting to a breach of trust - *Holder* v *Holder* [1968] Ch 353.

ii) instigation or request or consent in writing of a beneficiary

It is established both as an equitable principle and under TA s62 that if a beneficiary instigates or requests a breach of trust, his beneficial interest may be impounded - he will have to indemnify the trustee out of his beneficial interest. To rely on the equitable principle, the trustee must show that the beneficiary benefited in some way from the breach. This is not necessary under s62, although the section does require consent to be in writing, and knowledge of the relevant facts by the beneficiary - *Re Somerset* [1894] 1 Ch 231.

iii) the Limitation Act 1980.

The Act provides that no action can be brought against a trustee more than six years after the right of action accrued. This is subject to two important exceptions in s21(1) - there is no period of limitation if the breach of trust was fraudulent or if the trustee is still in possession of either the trust property itself or its proceeds. In the case of a beneficiary who is an infant, the six year period does not begin to run until he attains majority. Similarly, in the case of a reversionary interest under a settlement, the period does not begin to run against the remainderman until the interest falls into possession.

iv) TA s61

Under s61 it is a defence that the trustee acted 'honestly and reasonably' and 'ought fairly to be excused'. Whether he did so will depend on all the circumstances including adherence to any relevant statutory guidelines such as those concerning advice in the sphere of investments (see chapter 15). The importance of the 'reasonably' requirement was underlined in *Re Stuart* [1897] 2 Ch 583 in which it was said that it would be relevant to consider whether the trustee would have acted similarly had he been dealing with his own property.

v) discharge in bankruptcy

Once an order of discharge has been made in respect of the trustee, he is no longer liable unless the breach was fraudulent.

b) *Position of the trustees inter se*

TA s30(1) provides that a trustee is not liable for breaches of trust committed by his co-trustees unless the breach somehow occurred through his own 'wilful default' as defined in, amongst others, *Re Vickery* [1931] 1 Ch 572. The practical effect of this is that if an innocent co-trustee is sued for a breach for which his co-trustee was wholly liable, he will not be liable provided that he was in no way guilty of a breach of trust himself - for example, in the supervision of the trust as in *Bahin* v *Hughes* (1886) 31 Ch D 390. In practice it is likely that if one trustee has been active in committing the breach, his co-trustee will be liable for failure to check his actions.

In addition to the s30 protection, a retired trustee will not be liable for breaches committed by his successors unless he knew that a breach of trust would follow his retirement - *Head* v *Gould* [1898] 2 Ch 250. Similarly, a new trustee will not be liable for breaches committed by his predecessors unless he discovers such a breach and fails to remedy it.

c) *Measure of liability*

The amount for which the trustee will be held liable is generally the amount of loss caused to the estate. In the sphere of unauthorised investments:

i) if breach of duty to sell unauthorised investments, is liable for the difference between what he would have received if he had sold at the correct time and the amount received when it was in fact sold.

ii) if breach is that a proper investment was improperly sold, the liability is the difference between the amount received and the value at the commencement of proceedings or at the date of judgment (it is unsettled which is the correct date), plus any income which would have been received from the proper investment.

iii) if breach is that the trustee made an unauthorised investment.

Any profit made as a result of the breach must be held on trust. In addition to liability for loss, the trustee will be liable to pay interest at a fixed rate if the income received on the property is lower. If it is higher, the trustee is liable to account for the actual income. If the income which should have been received is higher, then the trustee will be liable for this amount.

If the trustee has committed more than one breach, the loss made on one cannot be set off against a profit made on another except in the limited situation when the breaches stem from a single investment policy - *Bartlett* v *Barclays Bank Trust Co Ltd* [1980] Ch 515.

Proprietary remedy - tracing

Tracing trust property is possible both at law and in equity. It is, however, generally done in equity as the legal remedy does not recognise a beneficiary's equitable interest (and so a beneficiary cannot trace against a trustee and would have to join the trustee as a party when tracing against anyone else). Nor does the legal remedy allow tracing into a mixed fund.

To be able to trace trust property in equity, the beneficiary must show three things:

a) *Initial fiduciary relationship*

The emphasis in this requirement is on 'initial', as once an initial fiduciary relationship such as trustee - beneficiary is established it does not matter that the person who is in possession of the trust property is in no such relationship to the beneficiary.

The number and variety of situations in which a fiduciary relationship may exist is limitless - *Re Hallett's Estate* (1880) 13 Ch D 696.

b) *The trust property must be in a traceable form*

It need not be in the same form as it was when it left the trust but it will not be traceable if it has been consumed or dissipated - *Re Diplock* [1948] Ch 465.

i) Payment of debts

If trust property or its proceeds are used to discharge a specific debt, the trust property will not be traceable - *Re Diplock* (1948). However, if the property is rather paid into an overdrawn account, this will not be the case and the property will continue to be traceable - *Re Tilley's Will Trusts* [1967] Ch 1179.

ii) Improvements to property

The property will only be traceable if the improvements result in an increase in the value of the property - *Re Diplock* [1948] Ch 465. Even then, the court may not allow the beneficiary to trace if it would be inequitable to do so (see (c) below).

iii) Profits

If the person in possession of the trust property makes a profit on it, whether he will be liable to account for such profits will depend on his relationship to the beneficiary.

• If he is the trustee and is, therefore, in a fiduciary position to the beneficiary, he will be liable for any profits made on the trust property (see chapter 14). If he mixes trust property with his own, the same should be true if he acted in breach of trust. It was suggested in *O'Sullivan* v *Management Agency* [1985] 3 All ER 351, however, that if a trustee acts with complete honesty he may be allowed to retain a share of the profits.

• If he is an innocent volunteer and the fund is unmixed, *Re Diplock* (1948) would suggest that he is entitled to keep any profit made on the trust property. Dicta in *Re Tilley's Will Trusts* (1967) suggest though, that he should in fact account to the trust for such profits, and thus, that he should account for a proportion of the profits if made on a combination of trust property and his own.

iv) Mixed funds

- If a trustee mixes trust property with his own property the trust is entitled to the value of the trust property used and if any doubt exists as to quantity, it is to be resolved in favour of the trust - *Indian Oil Corporation* v *Greenstone Shipping SA* [1988] QB 345.

  If the trust property is mixed with the trustee's own money in his bank account and amounts are withdrawn from the account then the first rule to apply is that the trustee is deemed to withdraw his own money first - *Re Hallett's Estate* (1880) 13 Ch D 696 - although if this results in an inequitable result, the rule was modified in *Re Oatway* [1903] 2 Ch 356 and, in fact, the trust will have a charge over both the funds in the bank account and over any traceable property purchased with money withdrawn from the account.

  It is important to note that if a trustee pays more of his own money into the account after the original mixing and withdrawals, the trust will not be able to trace against this subsequent payment in unless it was intended to repay money spent - *Roscoe* v *Winder* [1915] 1 Ch 62 - sometimes called the 'lowest intermediate balance' rule.

- If money from two or more trusts are mixed, their claims rank pari passu to each other - *Sinclair* v *Brougham* [1914] AC 398. If there are insufficient funds in the account to satisfy both claims, the rule of convenience in *Clayton's Case* (1816) 1 Mer 572 will apply - the withdrawals are deemed to be made in the order of the payments in, using the first trust money paid in first, if the mixing takes place in an active continuing bank account, eg a current account.

- If the trust money is paid into a bank account of an innocent volunteer, the same rules apply as between the volunteer and the trust as between two or more trusts above.

c) *No inequitable results*

Even if a tracing remedy is available above, the court will not grant relief if it would be inequitable to do so. As a result, tracing is not available against a legal purchaser without notice, of the trust property. Similarly, if trust property has been used by a volunteer to improve his house, the court will not enforce a sale of the house so that the trust could realise the trust property if this would cause the volunteer undue hardship.

Personal remedy against recipient

This remedy is used as a last resort and its application is limited to the administration of estates and is, thus, of limited value. See *Ministry of Health* v *Simpson* [1951] AC 251.

20.3 Recent cases

Indian Oil Corporation v *Greenstone Shipping SA* [1988] QB 345

20.4   Analysis of questions

Questions generally concentrate on either a personal or a proprietary remedy, although even in the latter case, the possibility of a personal remedy must at least be considered even if dismissed immediately following *Re Diplock* [1948] Ch 465. Problem questions are the more common method of examination; essays, when set, are more likely to address personal remedies - in particular, the defences available to a trustee - than proprietary remedies. In any problem question, the initial stage is to identify the breach of trust - if there is none, no remedy exists. As a rule of thumb, where the breach of trust in question involves the trustee gaining possession of trust property (breach of fiduciary duty - chapter 14) and mixing with other property, the examiner requires the emphasis of the answer to rest with consideration of tracing. In a question of this nature, it will often be stated in the facts that the trustee is insolvent so that a personal remedy is not available. If, on the other hand, the breach of trust involves some unauthorised investment and a resulting loss, the question will generally require the bulk of the answer to look at personal liability - measure of damage, defences etc. As can be seen, therefore, questions on breach of trust necessarily require consideration of at least one other topic on trusteeship - commonly, breach of fiduciary duty (chapter 14) or trustees' powers of investment (chapter 15).

20.5   Questions

Question 1

By his will, Uncle Croesus, who died in 1983, after appointing Tug and Tow to be his executors and trustees, left his country mansion to his trustees upon trust to sell the same and to hold the net proceeds of sale upon trust for his nephews and nieces in equal shares. After making enquiries, Tug and Tow discovered the existence of three nephews, Tom, Dick and Harry, and after selling the country mansion last year for £600,000, divided the £600,000 amongst these nephews in equal shares.

In fact, Uncle Croesus was also survived by a niece of whom Tug and Tow knew nothing and who died in January of this year leaving all her real estate to her son, Jack, and all her personal estate to her daughter, Jill.

Tom paid his £200,000 into his bank account which was then already in credit to the sum of £25,000. Shortly afterwards, he drew out £200,000 and invested it in a venture which failed. He still has £25,000 in his bank account.

Dick spent £100,000 of his £200,000 on a house which he still owns and spent the rest on gambling.

Soon after receiving his £200,000, Harry married Sarah and in consideration of the marriage, settled his £200,000 on trust for Sarah for life remainder to the children of the marriage.

Advise Jack and Jill whether they or either of them has any and if so what claims arising out of the foregoing facts.

University of London LLB Examination
(for External Students) Law of Trusts June 1985 Q9

Skeleton solution and comment

This is a question concerning breach of trust in distribution of the trust property. Whilst a personal remedy against Tug and Tow must first be considered, the bulk of the answer should address the possibility of the proprietary remedy of tracing - the fact that third parties are in receipt of the trust property and have used it in various ways, including payment into a bank account containing their own funds, indicates this.

- Identification of nature of breach of trust; possibility of a personal remedy against Tug and Tow - defences available to Tug and Tow under TA s27, TA s61 and if they obtained a 'Benjamin' order.

- Introduction to remedy of tracing in equity; three requirements for tracing to be available; consideration of first requirement of an initial fiduciary relationship.

- Possibility of tracing against Tom's share of trust property; application of principles governing mixing of funds by innocent volunteer - in particular, *Clayton's Case* (1816).

- Whether tracing is available in respect of Dick's share of money; property not traceable if dissipated; problem of inequitable results if allowed to trace against money spent on house.

- Tracing against Harry; property is traceable but tracing may result in inequitable results if situation is considered analogous to that of a bona fide legal purchaser without notice.

- Last resort of a personal remedy against Tom, Dick, and Harry under the principle in *Ministry of Health* v *Simpson* (1951).

Suggested solution

In this case Tug and Tow, the trustees of the Will of Uncle Croesus, committed a breach of trust by failing to distribute the property to those properly entitled thereto, namely, all the nephews and nieces of Croesus. On the death of Croesus' niece her share in the estate would have passed to Jill, as it would be regarded as personal property since the house was held on a binding trust for sale and the doctrine of conversion would apply. The first steps that Jill, who is now entitled to the share of Croesus' niece who was overlooked in the distribution, should take are to bring proceedings against Tug and Tow to recover from them the £150,000 that should have passed to her mother, ie Croesus' niece. See *Re Diplock* (1948). Such a claim is open to defeat by at least three possible defences on which there is no evidence at present. If Tug and Tow made all reasonable enquiries as to who Croesus' nephews and nieces were and advertised for claimants to his estate in accordance with the direction of the court under s27 of the Trustee Act 1925 then they would not be personally liable. Here the only option would be to trace for the monies they had lost. See s27(2) Trustee Act 1925. Another possibility is that Tug and Tow had evidence of the existence of Jack and Jill's mother but could not find her. They may have obtained a 'Benjamin' order to protect themselves from personal liability in distribution. If so, then having acted under the order of the court they will not be personally liable. See *Re Benjamin* (1902). If neither of these options are open to Tug and Tow then they may be able to rely on s61 of the Trustee Act 1925 in that, in the circumstances, they acted honestly and reasonably and ought to be excused the breach either in full or in part. As there is no evidence to indicate how they went about distribution of the trust fund it is impossible to decide if this or the other defences mentioned would actually succeed here.

If it turns out that Tug and Tow cannot be sued personally for the loss suffered by Jill, then she will have to consider tracing the monies they are now rightly entitled to into the hands of those who have been overpaid, ie Tom, Dick and Harry. As the distribution was made under the terms of the trust in the will the tracing action could take effect in equity only. See *Re Diplock* (1948). For such an action to succeed three elements have to be satisfied:

i)   that there is an initial fiduciary relationship;

ii)   the property being traced is in a traceable form and;

iii) that it is not inequitable to permit a tracing action in the circumstances.

There is clearly an initial fiduciary relationship in the present case since Tug and Tow were also trustees for the mother of Jack and Jill. It is the other two requirements which present more difficulty. Prima facie, Tom, Dick and Harry each received an overpayment of £50,000 and such sum has got to be identified in assets now in their hands.

Tom paid the £200,000 he received into his bank account which was at the time in credit in the sum of £25,000. But he then withdrew £200,000 from the account and invested it in a venture which failed. The balance of £25,000 is in the account. The account seems to be an active banking account and as such would be covered by the rule in *Clayton's Case* (1816). This rule provides that sums in the account are deemed to be withdrawn first and, if applied here would result in the £25,000 now in the account being regarded as part of the £200,000 Tom received under Croesus' will. Jack and Jill could make a claim to this £25,000 but this would be subject to whether it would be equitable to permit such a claim. Tom is an innocent volunteer and thus he ranks pari passu with Jack and Jill. It is strongly arguable that as he is an innocent volunteer that this result should flow here. See *Re Diplock* (1948). But the more probable result is that the balance of £25,000 would pass to Jill as there is no evidence to suggest that this would bring inequitable results to Tom.

As regards Dick, he spent £100,000 of the money he received on a house and the other £100,000 was spent on gambling. The latter sum has been entirely dissipated and therefore cannot be traced, there is nothing to trace into. See *Borden (UK) Ltd* v *Scottish Timber Products Ltd* (1981). The £100,000 spent on the house is traceable but here the issue arises as to whether it would be equitable to permit tracing into this property since Dick seems to have been an innocent volunteer throughout. I doubt if the court would take such a view in the present case in the absence of some very special circumstances which have not been indicated in the problem. In *Re Diplock* (1948) the Court of Appeal indicated that a tracing party would normally be given a charge on property purchased by a volunteer with a mixture of his own and the tracing party's money. Such cases were distinguished from those where the money had been used by the volunteer to alter or improve his land or buildings. In the latter the imposition of a charge would result in the volunteer having to exchange his land for money and, in any event, there might be problems in determining which part of his land the charge ought to attach to. But in the former case the sale under the charge would give both the volunteer and the tracing party what they had contributed, namely money.

As regards Harry, shortly after receipt of his £200,000 he made a marriage settlement and settled the sum on the trusts of his settlement. The property is in a traceable form if it is held on the trusts of the settlement. However, it is doubtful if it would be equitable to permit tracing in the circumstances. The settlement is a marriage settlement and, as such, is made for good consideration so that the position of those who are entitled thereunder is not dissimilar to that of bona fide purchasers for value. But it is also arguable that since valuable consideration has not passed the position of the beneficiaries under the marriage settlement should be treated in much the same way as that of mere volunteers. If this were to be the case it is likely that tracing would be permitted unless some special circumstances could be pointed to. See *Re Diplock* (1948).

Should tracing prove fruitless against some of the parties concerned or, as is likely in the case of Tom, only partly successful, then Jack and Jill may well consider the possibility of a claim in personam against those whom they have not been able to make full recovery by way of a tracing action. Such a claim was recognised by the House of Lords in *Ministry of Health* v *Simpson* (1951) but expressly limited to the administration of estates. It arises where, as here, there has been a wrong payment by personal representatives and all remedies against them have been exhausted. The underlying principle of such a claim was explained by Viscount Simonds, in *Ministry of Health* v *Simpson* (1951), as to avoid the evil of allowing one man to retain money legally payable to another.

Question 2

Robin is a trustee of two separate family trust funds, the Pink Fund and the Yellow Fund.

In September 1985, Robin's personal account at his bank was £5,000 in credit.

In October 1985, Robin withdrew £10,000 from the Yellow Fund and paid it into his own account.

In November 1985, he withdrew £15,000 from the Pink Fund and paid it into his own account.

In December 1985, he withdrew £25,000 from his own account and invested it in Post Office Savings Premium Bonds.

In April of this year, he won £50,000 on the Premium Bonds and paid it into his account.

In May, he withdrew £50,000 and invested it in further Premium Bonds.

Robin has recently had judgment given against him in a libel action and as a result has now been adjudicated a bankrupt. New trustees have been appointed of the Yellow Fund and the Pink Fund.

Advise the trustees of the Yellow Fund and the trustees of the Pink Fund as to their respective positions concerning the recovery of the misappropriated trust funds.

University of London LLB Examination
(for External Students) Law of Trusts June 1986 Q9

Skeleton solution and comment

This question also concentrates on the remedy of tracing. Its scope is, however, more limited than the previous question and a detailed consideration of the rules concerning mixed bank accounts is necessary.

- Consideration of personal remedy against trustee - not available as he is bankrupt.

- Introduction to tracing as a remedy; the three requirements.

- Entitlement to balance in bank account - application of rules in *Re Hallett's Estate* (1880); *Re Oatway* (1903); *Clayton's Case* (1816).

- Entitlement to charge over assets purchased from the mixed account and of the profits on the Premium Bonds - *Re Hallett's Estate* (1880) and *Re Tilley's WT* (1967).

Suggested solution

The normal remedy against a trustee who misappropriates trust property in breach of trust is to sue him personally for the lost funds together with interest thereon. See *Re Diplock* (1948). This remedy is of little value where, as in the present case, the trustee has been adjudicated a bankrupt, the only appropriate remedy is to follow the trust funds and recover them in the form that they now stand.

In order to trace funds three requirements must be satisfied: First, there must be an initial fiduciary relationship. This requirement was fulfilled in the present case as Robin was an express trustee of both the Pink Fund and the Yellow Fund. See *Chase Manhattan Bank* v *Israel-British Bank* (1981). Second, the property must be in a traceable form, ie it must not have been dissipated. This requirement is satisfied here also, there is £5,000 left in the bank account and the monies withdrawn from it were used to purchase premium bonds which, it would appear, are still held by Robin. See *Re Diplock* (1948). Third, there must be no inequitable results which would arise if tracing were allowed. As the tracing claim in this case must necessarily be in equity since it involves a trust, general equitable principles apply. But these are unlikely to bar a tracing claim in the present case because Robin, as trustee, must have been aware that his actions were in breach of trust. See *Re Diplock* (1948).

Robin mixed the funds of the Pink Fund and the Yellow Fund with his own monies in an active banking account. Two cases will be relevant in determining the respective claims of these funds, namely, *Clayton's Case* (1816) and *Re Hallett's*

177

Estate (1880). Under *Clayton's Case* (1816) payment of funds out of an active banking account are deemed to be appropriated to debts in the order that those payments were made into the account. This is sometimes called the 'first in, first out' rule, it is applied in the absence of express appropriation. *Clayton's Case* (1816) is unlikely to give the trustees of either the Pink or Yellow Funds any satisfaction here. This is because the first withdrawal was of £25,000 from a total of £30,000 in the fund as at December 1985. At that moment the £5,000 left would have been regarded as the balance of the £15,000 of the Pink Fund paid in in November 1985. However, there was £50,000 paid into the account in April 1986 as the winnings on the premium bonds, and in May £50,000 was withdrawn from the account to purchase more premium bonds. Therefore, under *Clayton's Case* (1816) the £5,000 balance of the Pink Fund was withdrawn to purchase the £50,000 worth of premium bonds. The £5,000 left in the account is winnings on the premium bond. However, Robin's trustee in bankruptcy will not be able to claim that the £5,000 left in the account is recoverable by him as a trustee cannot claim the benefit of *Clayton's Case* (1816) and his trustee in bankruptcy cannot be in a better position. See *Re Oatway* (1903). Accordingly, the position of the £5,000 left in the account is that the Pink Fund and the Yellow Fund are entitled to a joint charge over it, this charge will be proportionate to the extent of their respective claims. See *Re Hallett's Estate* (1880); *Roscoe* v *Winder* (1915).

The trustees of the Pink and Yellow Funds will also be entitled to a joint charge over those assets purchased by Robin out of the mixed account, namely, the premium bonds. See *Re Hallett's Estate* (1880). This is a joint first charge for the amounts owed to them after they have divided the £5,000 left in the account between them. As the premium bonds do not appear to have been disposed of there should not be any difficulty in either fund recovering its full entitlement to capital. But substantial profits were made by Robin because of his winning on the premium bonds. An issue which arises here is whether the funds may recover a proportion of these profits or even all of them. There is no clear answer to this point. Some dicta of Jessel MR in *Re Hallett's Estate* (1880) suggest that all the trusts may recover is the amount of trust money laid out in the purchase. But, in *Re Tilley's WT* (1967), Ungoed-Thomas J appeared to recognise the right of the trusts to share in the profits. Any other result might allow the trustee to profit from the breach and to obtain a profit in breach of his fiduciary duty. There are also some dicta in *O'Sullivan* v *Management Agency* (1985) which would appear to lend weight to a claim for profits by the trusts. They should try to pursue this aspect of their claim.

Question 3

a) In what circumstances, if any, will (i) the absence of intent to commit a breach of trust and (ii) the lapse of more than six years since the date of the breach, be a defence to an action for breach of trust?

b) It is provided by the terms of a settlement that trustees shall not be liable for acting bona fide on the advice of counsel as to what their duties are. The investment clause in the settlement authorises them to invest trust money 'in such manner as they shall think fit'. Two years ago, acting on the advice of counsel as to their powers, the trustees invested £100,000 of trust money in the purchase of shares in a private company; this company is now insolvent and in liquidation.

The beneficiaries are claiming damages of £100,000 from the trustees for breach of trust. Advise the trustees whether they have any defence to this claim.

University of London LLB Examination
(for External Students) Law of Trusts June 1983 Q9

Skeleton solution and comment

This is a mixed question requiring the student to address the area of personal remedies against trustees and, in particular, possible remedies, which may be available to trustees who are sued personally.

a) • General rule that liability for breach of trust is strict; possibility of a defence, though, under TA s61, which will depend on all the circumstances.

Effect of TA s30(1) that a trustee is not liable for breaches of co-trustees unless breach was due to his own wilful default.

  • General rule under the Limitation Act 1980 and the exceptions; delayed start of the limitation period if beneficiary is under a disability or if his interest is reversionary.

b) • General rule of trustees' liability vis-a-vis the beneficiaries.

  • Possible defence under s61 - in particular, whether acting on the advice of counsel was acting 'reasonably' applying the principles stated in the relevant cases.

Suggested solution

a) i) A trustee may commit a breach of trust through ignorance or because he has been wrongly advised by the agents he has employed to assist him. In such circumstances the breach may have resulted despite the trustee making every effort to do what was right. The trustee is, however, still liable to the beneficiaries to replace the loss which the breach caused; it is not an excuse to plead that he did not intend to commit the breach of trust. The more appropriate defence in such circumstances is s61 Trustee Act 1925. This provides that a trustee who has acted honestly and reasonably and ought fairly to be excused for the breach of trust may be wholly or partly excused the breach at the discretion of the court. It is up to the trustee to show that he acted honestly and reasonably if a s61 defence is to succeed. In *Re Turner* (1897) it was said that he must at least show that he was as prudent as he would have been in relation to his own affairs. Thus, in *Re Lord De Clifford's Estate* (1900) the trustees were excused where they relied on solicitor's advice in paying large sums to the solicitors for administration of an estate. Section 61 can therefore excuse a trustee who did not intend to commit a breach of trust. But a trustee may not obtain the benefit of the section even if he had no intention to commit a breach. Thus, in *Re Stuart*

(1897) trustees were not excused where they did not follow the proper statutory regulations as to investments on mortgage.

The provisions of s30(1) Trustee Act may also excuse a trustee who did not intend to commit a breach of trust. If his co-trustees caused the breach he will be excused if it did not arise through his own wilful default. The court also has a power to award contributions between trustees or a complete indemnity to a trustee where his co-trustees have committed a breach of trusts. These provisions are really to determine liability between the trustees inter se rather than vis-a-vis the beneficiaries.

ii) The general rule, as laid down by s21(3) Limitation Act 1980, is that no action can be brought by a beneficiary to recover trust property or in respect of a breach of trust after six years from the date on which the right of action accrued. This general rule is subject to a number of exceptions. Under s21(1)(a) there is no limitation period where there has been a fraudulent breach of trust to which the trustee was a party or privy. See *Thorne* v *Heard* (1895) and under s21(1)(b) there is no limitation period where the trust property of the proceeds thereof are in the possession of the trustee or were previously received by the trustee and converted to his use. The provisions of s21(1)(b) should be read subject to s21(2) where the trustee is also a beneficiary under the trust and gave himself and the other beneficiaries more than they were entitled to on distribution. This subsection provides that the trustee will only be liable for the excess over his proper share provided he had acted honestly and reasonably.

The lapse of six years or more from the date of the breach is a good defence even though the beneficiaries were not aware of the breach. See *Re Somerset* (1894). However, the running of time does not apply to a beneficiary whose interest is still in reversion; here time runs from the date the interest falls into possession, which may be more than six years after the date on which the breach occurred see s21(3), nor does it apply to beneficiaries under a disability, for example, a minor. See s28 Limitation Act, or where the right of action was concealed by fraud. See s32 Limitation Act.

b) Trustees are liable for a breach of trust even though it is caused by the negligent advice of counsel. The beneficiaries are not expected to do detective work to find out the real culprit. See *Attorney-General* v *Wilson* (1840). However, they must prove that the trustees actually committed the breach. See *Re Brier* (1884).

In the present case the trustees ought to plead s61 Trustee Act in defence. There is no other defence which is available. The action is clearly within the limitation period, s62 is not appropriate nor is acquiescence on the facts. Under s61 the trustees will have to show that they acted honestly and reasonably in the circumstances and therefore ought to be excused. In *Re Lord De Clifford's Estate* (1900) the trustees were relieved from liability where they paid money over to a solicitor on his advice; the trustees were able to show that what they had done was both honest and reasonable. It is unlikely that the trustees would be able to satisfy s61 in the present case. They may have acted honestly but I doubt if they acted reasonably. The trust stated that they would not be liable if they acted on the advice of counsel as to what their duties were. Although advice from counsel as to their duties on investment would have been covered by this provision, and probably s61 as well, the provision does not cover investment decisions. It is unreasonable to expect counsel to have expertise on investment matters and even the wide investment power given here could not excuse the trustees in this respect. It could hardly be said that they would have acted in the same way in dealing with their own property. See *Re Stuart* (1897). Further, when one considers the dicta of the House of Lords in *Learoyd* v *Whiteley* (1887) it could hardly be said that this was the manner in which a prudent man of business investing on behalf of others would have acted. The trustees should have sought advice on the investments from a suitably qualified investment manager or stockbroker. They are liable for the loss.

21 MISCELLANEOUS QUESTIONS

21.1   Introduction

21.2   Questions

21.1   Introduction

This chapter introduces no new information. Instead it contains both skeleton and full solutions and comments on a variety of 'combination' questions - those which require the student to address more than one of the topics considered in previous chapters.

21.2   Questions

Question 1

Under the trusts of the will of his father, John was entitled to a life interest in the income of a trust fund consisting of company shares. In 1984, on the occasion of the marriage of his brother, Kevin, John orally directed the trustees of the will to hold his beneficial interest under the will on trust for Kevin and the income has since been paid to Kevin.

In the autumn of 1985, John met Janet and they decided to set up house together. They decided to purchase a house for £60,000 of which £50,000 was provided by John and £10,000 by Janet. They had intended to purchase the house in their joint names, but, because of oversight, only Janet was named in the conveyance.

Last year John agreed to guarantee a debt of £100,000 owed by a friend and having been called upon to meet the guarantee and being unable to do so, John has now been adjudicated a bankrupt.

Advise John's trustee in bankruptcy whether he can have recourse to the income under John's father's will and as to the interest, if any, in the house to which he can lay claim.

University of London LLB Examination
(for External Students) Law of Trusts June 1987 Q4

Skeleton solution and comment

This question requires consideration of three topics - s53(1)(c) LPA, resulting trusts and the Insolvency Act 1986.

- Introduction; failure to comply with s53(1)(c) which is applicable here - *Grey* v *IRC* (1960).

- Nature of John's interest - fixed, discretionary or protective - which determines whether the trustee in bankruptcy can demand the income arising under it.

- Income received by Kevin - either belongs to John's estate or can be recovered under Insolvency Act 1986.

- John's interest in the house - operation of resulting trusts or application under Insolvency Act 1986 if express declaration that Janet owns the whole beneficial interest.

- Possibility of the operation of constructive trusts with regard to the improvements to the house.

Suggested solution

John's trustee in bankrutpcy would appear to have good prospects of having recourse to the income under John's father's Will. The oral direction given by John in 1984 to the trustees to hold his beneficial interest for Kevin was ineffective. As the beneficial interest is equitable in nature it may only be disposed of in writing signed by John under s53(1)(c) LPA 1925. A similar situation to this arose in *Grey* v *IRC* (1960) where the House of Lords held that a mere oral direction was incapable of being a valid disposition under s53(1)(c). The present case is distinguishable from *Vandervell* v *IRC* (1967) as that case involved a direction by a beneficiary to transfer the trust property itself to a third party, rather than the beneficial interest alone. This is something which John could not do as he was only given a life interest.

The trustee in bankruptcy could, therefore, demand that the trustees of John's father's Will pay to him the income in future. However, this will depend on the nature of the interest which John was given, a matter which is unclear. If it is a fixed interest the trustees are obliged to pay John all the income as it arises and the trustee in bankrutpcy could demand this. But, if John's interest is subject to a discretion in the trustees or arises under a protective trust the matter is otherwise. Under a discretionary trust the trustees could in their discretion decide not to pay anything to John whilst he was bankrupt in which case the trustee in bankruptcy could claim nothing. See *Gartside* v *IRC* (1968). Alternatively the trustees could decide to pay for benefits for John which were not capable of being intercepted by the trustee in bankruptcy, for example, rent or a dinner. See *Re Allen-Meyrick's WT* (1966) Under a protective trust the interest of John would terminate thereunder on his bankruptcy and he would have no further right to income but only a right to be considered for benefits under the discretionary trust arising thereafter. See s33 TA 1925.

As regards the income received by Kevin since 1984, it would be possible for the trustee in bankruptcy to recover this from him because John failed to divest himself of this properly. It therefore belongs to John's estate and could be recovered by tracing, if necessary. If Kevin successfully argued that each receipt of income from the trust was a valid gift from John then recovery of this money could be made under the provisions of ss339-341 of the Insolvency Act 1986. Gifts of income received within the two years of insolvency would be recoverable without more but income given to Kevin more than two years before then could only be recovered if it was shown that John was insolvent then, a matter which does not appear to be satisfied.

As regards John's interest in the house which is in Janet's name, it would appear that the trustee in bankrutpcy could recover five-sixths of the proceeds of sale on the ground that John paid £50,000 out of the £60,000 purchase price. This is because a resulting trust would operate here in the absence of any specific indications as to John's intentions in having the conveyance made into the sole name of Janet. In *Dyer* v *Dyer* (1788) it was clearly established that when property is purchased in the name of another without reasons as to the purpose it results to those who advanced the purchase money. It will be important to look at the conveyance to see if it makes any declaration as to the beneficial interests of Janet and John in the property. If it does then it will be conclusive and the court will not go behind it to ascertain the interest of the parties on the basis of contributions. See *Goodman* v *Gallant* (1986). If the conveyance declares that the whole beneficial interest in the house belongs to Janet then it would be possible for the trustee in bankruptcy to recover John's contribution thereto on the ground that this was a gift to Janet which was caught by ss339-341 of the Insolvency Act 1986. This would require the trustee in bankruptcy showing that the interest was given to Janet for no consideration or at an undervalue and as the conveyance took place less than two years ago, the transaction could be set aside as being within two years of John's bankruptcy.

If the conveyance does not contain any declarations as to the interests of John and Janet in the house then the court will assess their interests on the basis of their contributions. See *Gissing* v *Gissing* (1971). The initial contributions of £50,000 and £10,000 will be very important here but it may be that repairs and improvements to the house will increase the extent of the interests of either of them. See *Grant* v *Edwards* (1986). Should Janet make such a claim it will be for her to prove her expenditure while if John paid for improvements, the trustee in bankruptcy will have to prove the extent of this.

Question 2

Advise the potential beneficiaries in each of the following cases whether a valid and enforceable gift or trust has been created in their favour:

i) A, who had carried on a mail order business but who has now ceased trading and has been adjudicated a bankrupt, had had an oral arrangement with his bank, Banco plc, under which all moneys received by A from customers, were, pending despatch of the goods, paid into a 'Customers' pending orders Account' at the bank. When A ceased trading, money received from 500 customers remained in this account;

ii) On returning from their honeymoon to a furnished house owned by B, B said to his wife, Mrs B, 'My darling, this house and its entire contents are now your sole property';

iii) C sent to his son, S, a cheque for £50,000 payable to S, together with a letter stating that 'I am sending this money to you so that when your three children (now aged 10, 12 and 14 years) attain full age you can distribute it amongst them in such shares as you consider appropriate';

iv) D sent to his niece, N, a cheque for £10,000 payable to N and in an accompanying letter said: 'It is my wish that you use this money to further your non-nuclear campaign at Greenham Common'.

University of London LLB Examination
(for External Students) Law of Trusts June 1987 Q1

Skeleton solution and comment

This question covers three main topics - parts (i) and (iii) address two aspects of the requirement of certainty of intention, part (ii) looks at the formal requirements necessary for a valid gift of land and of chattels and part (iv) considers the validity of purpose trusts.

• The facts are very similar to *Re Kayford* (1975) and so this case must be considered in detail and applied to the present facts.

• Gift of house and contents - gift of house must satisfy the formal requirements in the LPA; gift of chattels simply requires clear intention to convey and delivery.

• Whether the words used are sufficiently imperative to create a trust.

• This raises two issues - whether the words are sufficiently certain to create a trust and, if so, the effect of the trust being for a purpose.

Suggested solution

i) If a valid and enforceable trust has been created in this case, then the customers of A who did not have their orders for goods fulfilled will be able to recover their money in full from the 'Customers' pending orders Account'. If there is no trust in their favour then the money they sent will form part of the general assets of the company and they will have to make a claim as ordinary creditors. The chances of the customers making a full recovery in the latter instance are likely to be small. A similar situation to that raised occurred in *Re Kayford* (1975) where it was held that there could be a trust provided all the requisites of a valid trust were present and a clear intention to create a trust was manifested. Matters such a paying customers' money into a separate bank account and only withdrawing it when orders had been fulfilled was regarded as strong, but not necessarily conclusive, evidence that a trust was intended. Whether a trust has been created here will depend on the purpose of A in paying the money into the 'Customers' pending orders Account'. If it was to ensure that the beneficial interest in the money remained in those who sent it until their orders were despatched there is a trust. See *Re Kayford* (1975). But, if it was for nothing more than the administrative convenience of A's business, it would be difficult to conclude that a trust was intended. If there is no clear evidence on these matters then A's payment of money into a separate bank account and his not removing it therefrom until goods were despatched is strong evidence in itself that he intended to create a trust. There are no difficulties with the other requirements to create a valid trust here. The subject matter is certain as are the objects and being a trust of money no formal requirements are necessary.

ii) The issue in this problem is whether B made an effective gift of the house and its contents to his wife by stating 'My darling, this house and its entire contents are now your sole property.' This cannot be an effective gift of the house because the formal requirements in s53(1)(a) of the Law of Property Act 1925 have not been satisfied. This provides that no interest in land may be created or disposed of except by writing signed by the person creating or conveying the same. Furthermore, it would be necessary for B to make a conveyance of the house to his wife by deed in order to satisfy s52 of the Law of Property Act 1925 and there is no indication that this was done. See *Richards* v *Delbridge* (1874). Thus, these words lack the necessary formality and the gift is also incompletely constituted. As regards the contents, no formal requirements need be satisfied in making a gift of chattels, so long as there is a clearly expressed intention and an appropriate act of delivery or equivalent of the chattels. See *Re Cole* (1964). It is doubtful if B's words would be acceptable as showing an intention to make a gift as the circumstances in which they were uttered, namely on return from his honeymoon, indicated that they may not have been intended to have a serious dispositive effect. In *Re Cole* a claim that a husband had given the contents of his house to his wife by saying 'It's all yours' was rejected taking into account the circumstances in which this was said and his subsequent dealings in the chattels. Much will depend on how and why B uttered these words.

iii) The problem here is whether C intended to create a trust with his son, S, as trustee or whether he made an outright gift of the £50,000 to the son subject to a moral obligation to use it for the benefit of his, S's, three children. In deciding if a trust was intended the context must be looked at as well as the words used. See *Re Adams and the Kensington Vestry* (1884). If the words are imperative in nature a trust will be held even though the word 'trust' itself is not used. The words used by C do not appear to be imperative in nature but show an absolute gift to S. This is because S is not required to distribute the money but informed that he 'can' distribute it as 'he considers most appropriate'. It seems that the reasonable inference to draw here is that S is given the money absolutely subject to a moral obligation that he should apply it for the benefit of his children as he considers appropriate. If he kept all the money for himself the court would not intervene because as was stated in *McCormick* v *Grogan* (1869) if a moral obligation is imposed the only sanction is that of the conscience of the donee should he fail to carry out the obligation. See also *Re Conolly* (1910).

iv) The issue here is whether N takes the £10,000 upon trust for a non-nuclear campaign at Greenham Common or whether this is an outright gift to him subject to a moral obligation that he so apply it. If the gift is construed as the former it would be void since it would be a trust for a purpose rather than a human object. As a general rule purpose trusts are void. See *Morice* v *Bishop of Durham* (1805) and there are no exceptional categories under which purpose trusts are upheld into which this gift falls and even if there were it would still fail as it is not limited in perpetuity. See *Re Astor's Settlement Trust* (1952). If the gift is construed as the latter then it would be valid as an absolute gift to N. It would appear that the words used by D are nothing more than a moral obligation as it would be impossible to construe 'It is my wish that ...' as indicating a trust. In *Re Hamilton* (1895) 'I wish them' was held not to create a trust and in *Re Diggles* (1888) no trust was created by the words 'It is my desire that ...' Therefore N takes the £10,000 absolutely.

Question 3

By his will, Smith who died last year, left £300,000 to his trustees to be applied and held upon the following trusts:

i) As to £100,000, upon trust to apply the annual income in awarding scholarships to such of the children of the directors and employees of Smith Ltd as qualify for admission to Eton College;

ii) As to another £100,000 upon trust to apply the annual income for such charitable and benevolent objects as his trustees should select;

iii) As to £50,000, upon trust to distribute the entire sum amongst the relatives of lifeboatmen who had died whilst on duty during the period of five years prior to Smith's death, and in such shares as his trustees should think fit;

iv) As to the remaining £50,000, upon trust for a period of twenty years from Smith's death, to apply the income for the provision of fresh flowers for and the maintenance of a memorial to the members of HM Forces killed in the Falklands War.

Advise the trustees as to the validity of each of the foregoing trusts.

University of London LLB Examination
(for External Students) Law of Trusts June 1983 Q4

Skeleton solution and comment

This question combines the topics of certainty of objects, purpose trusts and charitable trusts. Parts (i) - (iii) require consideration, firstly, of whether the trust qualifies as a valid charitable trust and, secondly, whether, if not, it can be upheld as an express private trust. Part (iv) addresses the exceptions to the rule against purpose trusts.

i) Possible charitable trust for the advancement of education; no satisfaction of the public benefit requirement; possibly valid as express private trust if satisfies relevant test for certainty of objects.

ii) Possible valid charitable trust if it is wholly and exclusively charitable - *Blair* v *Duncan* (1902).

iii) Possible valid charitable trust as for the relief of poverty; possibly valid as express private trust if it satisfies the *McPhail* v *Doulton* (1971) test for certainty of objects in discretionary trusts.

iv) The gift is not charitable but may be valid as an exception to the rule against purpose trusts under one of the classifications in *Re Endacott* (1960). Question of the rule against perpetual trusts.

187

Suggested solution

i) A gift to provide scholarships at a particular school is a good charitable trust for the advancement of education. Scholarships of this nature have been upheld for centuries at public schools and in colleges at Oxford and Cambridge. See *German v Chapman* (1877). However, a trust for the advancement of education must also satisfy the requirement of being for the public benefit if it is to obtain charitable status. See *Oppenheim v Tobacco Securities* (1951). The gift in this case does not satisfy that requirement as it is not intended to benefit the community at large or a section of the community. There is a nexus in this case, namely that the beneficiaries must be the children of employers or directors of Smith Co. The gift cannot obtain charitable status and it can be distinguished from the cases where scholarships provided at a school are charitable in that these are cases where any person at the school is entitled to compete or be considered for the scholarship and entrance to the school is not restricted to a particular group of individuals.

The gift in this case will, however, stand as a good private trust as it can satisfy the three certainties viz of words, of subject-matter and of objects. The objects would be ascertainable in this case as their identity is easily discoverable through Smith Co. Thus, whether the test is that laid down in *McPhail v Doulton* (1971) or otherwise the trust will stand. However this appears to be an attempt to create a perpetual trust as the direction is to apply the annual income for the stated purpose. If the trust is not a charitable one it will fail for infringing the perpetuity rules.

ii) A trust, in order to be charitable, must be for a purpose which is recognised in law as charitable and, except where it is for the relief of poverty, satisfy the public benefit requirement. In addition to these the trust must be wholly and exclusively charitable so that the funds or assets cannot be applied for non-charitable purposes. Further, there is no need to set out specific charitable objects in a charitable gift, so long as it is charitable in broad terms the charity commissioners or, if necessary, the court will devise a scheme for its application.

The gift of £100,000 for 'charitable and benevolent' objects is a good charitable gift. It is wholly and exclusively charitable even though all benevolent objects are not necessarily charitable. This is because the word 'and' between the words 'charitable', 'benevolent' indicates that 'benevolent' is to be read in conjunction with charitable so that the gift is limited to benevolent objects of a charitable nature. See *Blair v Duncan* (1902). However, if the gift had been 'charitable or benevolent' it would not have been a valid charitable gift since the word 'or' would allow the trustees to apply it in the alternative to either charitable objects or benevolent object whether charitable or otherwise. See *Chichester Diocesan Fund and Board of Finance v Simpson* (1944).

The trustees are therefore advised to apply the money for charitable objects as it is a valid charitable gift.

iii) This gift may be upheld as charitable if the court can find in it an intention on the part of the testator to relieve poverty or distress. It is not necessary to use the word poverty in order to have a good charitable trust for the relief of poverty; the court will look at the whole gift to see if it was meant. See *Re Dudgeon* (1896). It is difficult to see what other purpose the testator could have had in mind except the relief of poverty or distress among those relatives of lifeboatmen who died on duty. In *Powell* v *Attorney-General* (1817) a gift for the widows and orphans of seamen at a particular port was held to be charitable as it was for the relief of distress. Although the present case provides for the 'relatives' of lifeboatmen there appears to be no reason for any distinction. See also *Re Sahal's WT* (1958).

If the court felt unable to uphold this gift as charitable then it is unlikely that it would be upheld as a valid private trust. As it is a discretionary trust in nature the test of certainty of objects laid down in *McPhail* v *Doulton* (1971) would apply and there should be no difficulty in deciding whether a person is or is not a member of the class of objects.

iv) The gift of £50,000 for twenty years to provide fresh flowers for and the maintenance of a tomb for members of HM Forces killed in the Falklands War is not a charitable trust. Bequests for the erection of tombs, monuments and memorials outside a church or churchyard generally are not charitable. See *Re Vaughan* (1886). It appears to be quite irrelevant whether the tomb, monument or memorial is for ordinary individuals or for war heroes. However, this trust may be upheld as a good non-charitable purpose trust. Although such trusts are, as a general rule, void the courts have upheld them as valid in a few anomalous cases and new non-charitable purpose trusts will be upheld if they are exactly like those which have been previously upheld. See *Re Endacott* (1960). In *Pirbright* v *Sawley* (1896) a gift to maintain a grave and decorate it with flowers was upheld as valid and on this authority the gift could be upheld. A non-charitable purpose trust should also be limited in perpetuity, so that it will not last longer than twenty-one years. See *Re Astor's ST* (1952). The present gift satisfies this requirement so that if the trustees wish to perform the trust they can do so.

Question 4

Under the trusts of a settlement of personalty executed ten years ago, investments worth £500,000 are held by the trustees upon trust to pay the income to Albert for life upon protective trusts with remainder to such of Albert's children as Albert shall by deed or will appoint and in default of appointment in trust for such of his children as attain the age of 18 and if more than one in equal shares absolutely.

Albert is married and has three children, Betty, Clare and Donald aged 23, 21 and 2 respectively. Advise the trustees:

i) As to their duties in relation to the application of trust income in the event of Albert's bankruptcy;

ii) As to the distribution of the capital of the trust fund in the event of Albert's death in the near future;

iii) Whether if Albert, Betty and Clare were agreed, it would be possible to determine the trust and distribute the investments.

University of London LLB Examination
(for External Students) Law of Trusts June 1987 Q7

Skeleton solution and comment

This question requires the student to consider TA s33 concerning protective trusts, the application of the rule in *Saunders* v *Vautier* (1841) to protective trusts and, briefly, an application of the Variation of Trusts 1958.

i) Application of s33 TA to the facts in question.

ii) Effect of Albert's death.

iii) Application of rule in *Saunders* v *Vautier* (1841) to a protective trust - *Re Smith* (1928); possibility of an application to vary the trusts under the Variation of Trusts Act 1958 s1(1)(d).

Suggested solution

i) Albert has a protected life interest under the trust and in the absence of specific protective trusts being set out in the trust instrument, the provisions in s33 TA 1925 will apply. Under s33 Albert is known as the 'principal beneficiary' and he is entitled to all the income from the trust until he does or attempts to do any act or thing or until any event happens which would deprive him of the right to receive the income. If he was declared bankrupt then his trustee in bankruptcy would be entitled to intercept the income and deprive him of it. This would be an event which would end the protective trust in his favour. A discretionary trust would arise thereafter and under s33(1)(ii) this would be for the benefit of the principal beneficiary and his spouse and children, if any, or, if none, for the benefit of the principal beneficiary and those who would take the trust property if he were actually dead. Thus, the discretionary trust will be for the benefit of Albert, his wife and three children. The trustees will have a discretion to decide how much, if anything, they should receive from the trust.

ii) In the event of Albert's death the capital would have to be distributed in accordance with any appointment that Albert made to his children either by will or by deed since the trust gives him a power of appointment. If there are appointments to persons other than the children these can be ignored as the holder of a special power of appointment must appoint within the terms of the power. See *Re Ogden* (1933). If no appointment is made by Albert, the gifts over in default of appointment would operate so that the capital would be divided equally between such of his children as attained 18 in equal shares. In these circumstances Betty and Clare would be entitled to receive their shares immediately as they have fulfilled the contingency being 23 and 21 respectively. But as Donald is only 2, the trustees would have to hold one-third of the capital for him until he fulfilled the contingency and if he died before doing so they would have to distribute the remaining money between Betty and Clare equally.

iii) Albert, Betty and Clare would not be able to determine the trust and have the funds distributed because this can only be done under the rule in *Saunders* v *Vautier* (1841) if all the beneficiaries are of full age and absolutely entitled and agree to do so. This rule also applies to protective and discretionary trusts because, as was stated in *Re Smith, Public Trustee* v *Aspinall* (1928), where all the beneficiaries who are entitled to the whole trust between them get together and demand the trust fund then the fund must be handed to them. But, in the present case this dicta cannot apply because the agreement of Donald and possibly, Albert's wife would be necessary. Albert's wife would have the right to be considered for benefits if the trust became discretionary in nature and Donald cannot fulfill the requirements under *Saunders* v *Vautier* (1841) being only 2 years old. The only way in which it might be possible for Albert, Betty and Clare to get their wish is to apply to the Court under s1(1) of the Variation of Trusts Act 1958 seeking the court's approval on Donald's behalf under s1(1)(a) and under s1(1)(d) if Albert's wife did not consent. The court would have to be satisfied that any such variation was for the benefit of Donald before assenting thereto. See *Re Weston's Settlement* (1969).

Question 5

Roger and Stephen held certain investments upon trust for sale with power to postpone. Included in the trust estate are 50,000 shares in Zeno Ltd, a private company. By the terms of the trust, the trustees are directed to hold the net proceeds of sale and the net income until sale on trust for Harold for life with remainder to his children Alan and Bess, in equal shares absolutely.

In May 1984, Roger wished to retire from the trust and executed a deed declaring that Stephen was incapable of acting. Roger appointed Edward and Frances to be trustees in place of himself and Stephen. At that time Francis was on a world cruise which lasted for two months.

At a banquet in the City of London in July 1984, which Roger attended, Grant, a leading financial journalist, said to Roger, 'I know that your trust fund has shares in Zeno Ltd, the company is going to be taken over'. On the next day Roger purchased (from a third party) 150,000 shares in Zeno Ltd for £150,000. Edward and Francis were never given this information and in August 1984 they sold the 50,000 shares to Zeno Ltd at £2 each. The purchase price of £100,000 was paid to Charles, a stockbroker and has never been handed over to the trustees.

In April 1985 Zeno Ltd was taken over by Yentil plc, a public company, at a price of £4 per share. Roger made a profit of £450,000.

Recently, the beneficiaries of the trust learnt that Charles, the stockbroker, has gone to Spain and absconded with the proceeds of sale of the shares in Zeno Ltd.

Advise Harold, Alan and Bess.

University of London LLB Examination
(for External Students) Law of Trusts June 1985 Q6

Skeleton solution and comment

This is a complex question raising problems on the appointment and removal of trustees, trustees' fiduciary duties and powers of delegation.

- The retirement and removal of Roger and Stephen and the appointment of Edward and Francis - whether valid under TA s36(1). Consideration of Stephen's removal.

- Roger's retirement and the appointment of Edward and Francis; whether Edward has accepted the trust.

- Roger's potential liability to account for profits on the shares under the rule in *Boardman* v *Phipps* (1967).

- Liability of Edward and Francis for loss occassioned by their agent Charles; protection under TA ss23 and 30.

Suggested solution

The first matter in this problem is whether the retirement and the removal from the trust of Roger and Stephen respectively and the appointment of Edward and Francis as trustees are in order. It seems that Roger took the initiative to remove Stephen from the trusts and did so on the ground that he was 'incapable of acting therein'. This is one of the grounds for the removal of a trustee under s36(1) of the Trustee Act 1925 and is construed as including matters such as mental illness, age and infirmity. There is no evidence to indicate that this was an appropriate ground for Stephen's removal in this case. But it is worth noting that the grounds for removal under s36(1) are only exercisable where a replacement trustee is being appointed since the section is concerned primarily with the appointment of trustees rather than their removal. Thus, if Roger executed a deed to remove Stephen on the ground that he was incapable of acting and executed a separate deed, at a later date, to appoint Edward and Francis and to retire himself, then the position is likely to be that Stephen is still a trustee. Another matter which is not altogether clear is whether in fact Roger was the person who had the power under the trust instrument or the provisions of s36(1) to effect a removal and appointment.

Roger made an appointment of Edward and Francis as trustees in place of himself and Stephen which would tend to suggest that the appointments were made simultaneously with Roger and Stephen leaving the trusts. As for Roger's retirement this seems to be in order. A Trustee is not confined to retiring by deed under s39 of the Trustee Act, in which case he must ensure that at least two trustees or a trust corporation is left to act in the trusts. Instead a trustee who 'desires to be discharged from all or any of the trusts or powers reposed in or conferred on him' may do so under s36(1) if a replacement trustee is appointed at the same time. Thus, the distinction between these provisions, is that in the former a replacement trustee need not be appointed on retirement, whilst in the latter this is essential. But this leads on to the issue of whether the appointments of Edward and Francis were in order. There is nothing to suggest that Edward's appointment is irregular but in the case of Francis this is not so because he seems to have been on a world cruise at the relevant time. The question is whether a trustee can be appointed as such in his absence and without his consent. The case-law seems to draw a distinction between the appointment of a trustee and his acceptance of the trusteeship. A person appointed as a trustee cannot be compelled to accept the office and he may disclaim it. See *Re Tyron* (1844). Acceptance of trusteeship may be either express or implied. The latter will arise, for example, when the trustee appointed acts in the trusts. See *Mountford* v *Cadogan* (1810). But whether a trustee has acted in the trusts so as to be deemed to have accepted the appointment is a matter to be decided on the facts of each case. The conclusion that must follow is that the appointments of Edward and Francis are in order so that Roger and Stephen are discharged from the trusts since s36 only refers to 'appointment' and not to 'acceptance'. This assumes, of course, that Stephen's removal was proper.

The second matter in this question is whether Roger is liable to account to the trustees for the £450,000 profit he made on the purchase and resale of his shares in Zeno Ltd on the basis that he holds it as a constructive trustee for the trusts. Such a claim might be based on the principles laid down by the House of Lords in *Boardman* v *Phipps* (1967). In that case a trustee and solicitor to the trust were offered the opportunity to acquire shares in a company in which the trust already had a shareholding. The trustees rejected this opportunity for various reasons after the trustee and solicitor had made every effort to persuade them to accept it. Subsequently the trustee and solicitor purchased the shares for themselves. It seems that the majority of the House of Lords made them account for the profit they subsequently made on the shares because they had acted in the purchase of the shares as if they were acting for the trust or, at least, had not disabused anyone who might have thought so, of this fact. One immediate distinction that can be drawn between *Boardman* v *Phipps* (1967) and the present case is that at the time Roger made the purchase of the shares he was no longer a trustee. One of the defendants in *Boardman* v *Phipps* (1967) had never been a trustee but instead, as solicitor to the trusts was a fiduciary agent, whilst the other was a trustee. However, a fiduciary relationship may be said to continue where a trustee takes a benefit to himself obtained from knowledge or information acquired during his trusteeship.

This can be supported with reference to the decisions on the self-dealing rule where a trustee can be held liable to account for dealings in trust property after he has retired from the trust. See *Wright* v *Morgan* (1926). However, much emphasis was placed by the majority in the House of Lords in *Boardman* v *Phipps* (1967) on the confidential nature of the information the trustees obtained and used for their own benefit. It seems that a trustee given such information is not entitled to apply it for his own benefit. It is arguable that Roger did not receive confidential information here because the information came from a financial journalist and, in any event, concerned a public company and not a private company. In *Boardman* v *Phipps* (1967) the information was imparted by a member of the board and the company was private. But the mere fact that the information might become public knowledge at a later date should not matter if at the time it was given it was not publicly available. Thus, if it can be shown that Roger only obtained the information because the journalist believed he was still a trustee and would otherwise not have given it to him the necessary confidentiality may be established.

Whether Roger has a duty to account for the profit seems to be a border-line issue on the majority decision in *Boardman* v *Phipps* (1967). The fact that he did not communicate what he had been told might be regarded as indicating some sort of impropriety on his part but there is nothing in the form of concrete evidence to support this.

The third issue in this case is whether Edward and Francis are liable for the loss of £10,000 being the proceeds of sale of the trusts shareholding in Zeno Ltd with which Charles absconded. Charles was, as a stockbroker, the agent of Edward and Francis in this matter and therefore, under ss23 and 30 of the Trustee Act 1925 they will not be held liable for his acts or defaults unless they failed to ensure that he was a proper person to do this work, failed to supervise him or by their own wilful default permitted him the opportunity to abscond with the funds. See *Re Vickery* (1931). But if Edward and Francis had acted in accordance with the provisions of ss23 and 30 then they will not be held liable; for any other result would demand from them a greater degree of care in the affairs of the trust than they would exercise in their own affairs. Thus, in *Speight* v *Gaunt* (1883) trustees were absolved from any liability where a stockbroker acting for them in the purchase of shares absconded with a cheque they gave him to pay for the shares. The cheque had been given to the stockbroker in accordance with the usual business practice and the trustees had clearly acted as an ordinary prudent businessman would have acted. In the present case Edward and Francis seem to have acted as ordinary prudent businessmen and thus would not be held liable for the loss. It is likely to be very important to find out how long Charles had had the proceeds of sale before absconding. If he was allowed to retain the proceeds for a considerable time with no real enquiries being made by the trustees, they may be liable for the loss. The only recourse for the beneficiaries here is to seek Charles and recover the money from him, if he still has it, or something represented by it.

Question 6

Under a settlement of personalty, a fund worth £200,000 is held by Jack and Jill upon trust to pay the income to Amy for life upon protective trusts and subject thereto to hold the capital and income upon trust for Amy's three sons, Tom, aged 21, Dick, aged 18, and Harry, aged 13. The settlement provides that 'moneys requiring to be applied or invested hereunder may be applied or invested in any manner authorised by law'.

Advise Jack and Jill

i) Whether they are under any, and if so what, obligation to review their portfolio of investments from time to time;

ii) Whether they can lend Amy £40,000 out of the trust fund to enable her to purchase a house costing £60,000;

iii) Whether they can pay Harry's school fees (currently amounting to £4,000 a year) out of income or capital;

iv) Whether they can advance £10,000 to Dick out of capital to enable him to take a course leading to a flying instructor's rating (qualification);

v) Whether they can advance £10,000 out of capital to Tom to enable him to buy a fast food business franchise;

vi) Whether, if Jack wishes to go abroad for six months, he can delegate all or any of his powers, discretions and duties during the period of his absence and if so, to whom.

University of London LLB Examination
(for External Students) Law of Trusts June 1986 Q8

Skeleton solution and comment

This is a very wide question which covers several areas of the law - notably, trustees' powers of investment, powers of maintenance and advancement, TA s33 and protective trusts, and powers of delegation.

i) Investment powers - effect of the provision in the trust instrument; powers conferred by Trustee Investments Act 1961; duty to review investments and to obtain advice distinguishing between Part I and Parts II and III of the Schedule to the Act; possible protection under TA s4.

ii) Possibility of advancement under TA s32; investment in a mortgage under Trustee Investments Act 1961 and the guidelines contained in TA s8.

iii) Possible application of either s31 or s32 TA; requirement of consent under s32(1)(c) and effect on protective trust.

iv) Advancement under s32 TA subject to Amy's consent.

v) Possible advancement under s32 TA.

vi) Delegation under TA s25; lack of protection to Jack.

Suggested solution

i) The investment powers conferred upon Jack and Jill in this case, are the power of investment given by the Trustee Investments Act 1961. This is the only manner of applying or investing the funds in 'any manner authorised by law' in the absence of provisions to the contrary in the trust instrument or order of the court. The provisions of the 1961 Act clearly impose a liability to review investments in the trust portfolio. Under s6(3) it is provided that in respect of investments on which advice had to be obtained under s6(1) and (2) before being made, trustees must determine at what intervals the circumstances, and in particular the nature of the investments, make it desirable to obtain advice as to whether the investments continue to be satisfactory. The trustees must therefore obtain and consider such advice. Section 6(3) would appear to apply only to investments on which advice had to be sought under s6(1) and (2), this will include all investments in the Narrower-Range Part II and the Wider Range under the 1961 Act. But, as regards Narrower-Range Part I investments it would appear to be prudent to review such investments also from time to time otherwise it might be claimed, with justification, that such failure amounted to 'wilful default' and it is unlikely s4 of the Trustee Act 1925 could excuse him from liability.

ii) As Amy only has a protected life interest in the income there is no question of an advancement of capital to her being made under s32 of the Trustee Act 1925. But the trustees could lend her the £40,000 she requires to purchase the house provided that they follow the requirements of the Trustee Investments Act 1961 and the Trustee Act 1925 in making an investment by way of mortgage.

Under the 1961 Act trustees are authorised to invest trust funds in mortgage in freehold land in England, Wales or Northern Ireland or leaseholds in these jurisdictions if the lease has at least sixty years unexpired term and in mortgages on heritable security in Scotland. It would appear that such mortgages must be first legal mortgates although the 1961 Act and the 1925 Act are unclear on this point. See *Swaffield* v *Nelson* (1876); *Chapman* v *Browne* (1902).

If the house which Anne proposes to purchase comes within the investment provisions of the 1961 Act then the trustees must ensure that they follow the requirements of s8 of the Trustee Act 1925. Under this provision they must obtain a report as to the value of the property from an able practical surveyor or valuer who is independent of the owner. They must not advance more than two thirds of the valuation of the property by way of loan and they must ensure that the report required advises the loan as being suitable. On the facts, if the house is worth £60,000 there is no reason why the trustees should not loan £40,000 to Anne by way of mortgage provided the other provisions of s8 are satisfied.

iii) Harry is entitled in remainder to one third of the capital and income. At present all the income of the trust is being paid to Anne as the principal beneficiary under the protective trust. Thus there is no income available which might be applied for Harry's maintenance under s31 of the Trustee Act 1925. If this had been so it would have been in order to apply any available income in paying his school fees as the section refers to 'maintenance, education or benefit'. But under s32 of the Trustee Act it may be possible to make advancements out of Harry's share of the capital to pay his school fees, this section refers to 'advancement or benefit' and this will cover education also. See *Re Breed's Will* (1875). But there are some restrictions on advancement in s32 and under these it should be noted that the trustees may not advance to Harry more than half his presumptive share in total. Further, the written consent of Amy is required to any advancements under s32(1)(c), without this they cannot be made. This is because her entitlement to income would be affected by a reduction in the capital value of the fund through advancement. It might also be added that the protective trust in her favour will not be turned into a discretionary trust under s33 if she gives written consent to the advancement as this is specifically excepted by the section. Finally, should the protective trust be destroyed under s33, Harry would become one of the beneficiaries under the discretionary trust arising hereafter and the trustees could, at their discretion, use the income to pay his school fees.

iv) An advancement of £10,000 to Dick to take a course leading to a flying instructor's rating is feasible under s32 of the Trustee Act. Advancement or benefit includes any use of the trust money which will improve the material situation of the beneficiary (see *Pilkington* v *IRC* (1964)), so that a course giving Dick extra qualifications would be included. But the advancement can only be made if Amy gives her consent in writing to it under s32(1)(c), such consent will not destroy her protected life interest under s33 of the Trustee Act. If such consent is given in writing the advance may be made, it will be well within half of Dick's presumptive share but it will have to be brought into account under s32(1)(b) when further distribution of the capital is being made between Tom, Dick and Harry. The trustees will also have a duty to see that the money so advanced is going to be applied for the purpose for which it was advanced otherwise they may be personally liable to replace it. See *Re Pauling's Settlement* (1964).

v) An advancement which has as its object setting up a beneficiary in a Trade or business can be made under s32 of the Trustee Act 1925. See *Re Kershaw's Trusts* (1868). In the present case the trustees will have to observe the restrictions in s32(1)(a) and (b), already discussed as well as obtaining the written consent of Amy under s32(1)(c). Should they get consent to the advancement it will be incumbent upon them to ensure that in exercising their discretion to make an advancement that the purpose for which it is being made is a sound one. They must not advance if they feel the purpose is a waste of money. See *Pilkington* v *IRC* (1964).

vi) If Jack wishes to go abroad for six months then he may delegate any or all of his powers, discretions and duties under s25 of the Trustee Act 1925. To take advantage of it the trustee must execute a power of attorney, witnessed by one witness, under which the trusts, powers and discretions delegated are specified. The delegation may only be for a period not exceeding 12 months and delegation may be made to any person, including a trust corporation, other than a sole co-trustee. Thus delegation could not be made to Jill. Notice of the extent of the delegation, its commencement, duration and the reasons for it must be given to Jill and any person having power to appoint a new trustee.

Should Jack decide to delegate under s25 he should be warned that he remains liable for the acts and defaults of his delegate. Further, there are some powers and duties which he cannot delegate, notably the power to delegate and his own fiduciary duties.

Question 7

By a settlement made in 1970, the settlor, Sam, directed the Trustees, Tom and Terry, 'to hold the income of the Trust Funds during the life of the Settlor upon trust to pay or apply the same to or for the benefit of the Settlor and of any wife whom he may marry and the children of the Settlor ... or any of them as the Trustees shall in their absolute discretion think fit'.

'After the death of the Settlor the Trustees shall hold the income of the Trust Fund upon protective trusts for the benefit of any wife whom he may leave him surviving during her life'.

i) On the assumption that Sam is unmarried and aged 25, advise the Trustees whether they may advance the sum of £10,000 to Sam to enable him to purchase a house in which he wants to practise his profession of a doctor, and whether they should comply with Sam's demand that all the income from the Trust Fund be paid to him.

ii) Advise the Trustees as to the legal position on the assumption that Sam has died, having married Mavis, and that Mavis was adjudicated bankrupt after his death.

University of London LLB Examination
(for External Students) Law of Trusts June 1985 Q7

Skeleton solution and comment

The question raises three important issues - the question of advancement to Sam under TA s32, whether the trustees should pay the income to Sam and the operation of protective trusts under TA s33.

• Application of TA s32 to a life interest.

• Detailed examination of the limitation on the power of advancement under s32; meaning of 'advancement or benefit'.

• Nature of Sam's interest and whether he is entitled to all of the income under the trust.

• Operation of TA s33 and effect of Mavis' bankruptcy to the protective trusts.

Suggested solution

If Sam is unmarried and aged 25 and wishes to set up in practice as a doctor the trustees may only advance £10,000 from the trust fund for this purpose if there is either an express power of advancement in the trust instrument permitting this or if the statutory power of advancement under s32 of the Trustee Act 1925 applies. Whether an express power of advancement is available and if so applicable requires looking at the trust instrument. As for the statutory power of advancement under s32 this applies to all trusts of personalty unless it has been excluded by the trust instrument or perhaps, modified in some way. In the present case the trust is in the nature of a discretionary trust and Sam has a life interest under these discretionary trusts. There is nothing in s32 to suggest that it is inapplicable to discretionary trusts and it was applied in a discretionary trust in *Re Harris' Settlement* (1940). The fact that Sam only has a life interest will not affect the operation of s32 because in *Re Hastings-Bass* (1985) it was held that the section applied to a beneficiary who was only given a life interest in the income of the capital fund. Nor does it matter that there is a gift over on Sam's death because the terms of s32(1) deal with such points. Therefore, the statutory power of advancement is prima facie available in this case.

If the trustees wish to exercise the statutory power of advancement this will be 'in such manner as they may, in their absolute discretion, think fit'. However, the advancement must be by payment or application of the money for the 'advancement or benefit' of Sam. The words 'advancement or benefit' are construed as including the setting up of the beneficiary in life as by, for example, providing for his education, purchasing a house as a matrimonial home on the beneficiary's marriage or making a marriage settlement. There is no doubt that providing £10,000 to enable Sam to purchase a house from which he can practise as a doctor would be within s32. In *Re Williams' WT* (1953) it was specifically held that the purchase of a house for a beneficiary to practise from as a doctor was an 'advancement'. But even if the trustees are satisfied that the purpose for which the £10,000 is required is one within the terms 'advancement or benefit' in s32 they must ensure that the restrictions in s32(1)(a), (b) and (c) are not offended. Under s32(1)(a) trustees cannot advance to a beneficiary more than half his presumptive share under the trust. Sam is entitled to the capital of the trust fund on the death of his future wife. He has made no effective disposition on the remainder interest and thus there will be a resulting trust in his favour. However, no difficulties should arise in the present case because, on the facts, Sam is the only beneficiary under the trust and his presumptive share will be half the total fund. Under s32(1)(b) the trustees must take any advancement into account when Sam becomes absolutely entitled. This is not relevant in the present case as Sam is solely entitled. Section s32(1)(c) is not applicable either because there are no prior life interests to Sam's in the trust. Thus, the trustees may advance £10,000 to Sam if they consider it is appropriate to do so but they must ensure that the money is applied for the purpose specified otherwise they may find themselves liable for improper advancements as in *Re Pauling's Settlement Trusts* (1964).

The second issue is whether the trustees should pay all the income of the trust fund to Sam. As the trust is a discretionary trust in nature Sam's interest is in the nature of a right to be considered as a potential beneficiary and to take and enjoy whatever income the trustees decide to give him. See *Gartside* v *IRC* (1968). However, a discretionary trust may be either exhaustive or non-exhaustive, the former being one where the trustees are bound to distribute the whole income but have a discretion as to how distribution shall be made between the objects, the latter being where the trustees have a discretion as to the distribution and as to the amounts received by the beneficiaries. If the present trust were to be regarded as exhaustive Sam, as the only beneficiary should get all the income. However, whether the trust is in fact exhaustive is a matter of construction of the wording of the present trust. In my view it is not of the exhaustive variety because the trustees have a discretion to 'pay or apply' the income for the benefit of the settlor, any wife he might marry and his children, if any. The reference to 'apply' could include the accumulation of income for the beneficiaries if the trustees thought this desirable. Thus, Sam does not seem to have any right to all of the income but only a right to such income, if any, as the trustees choose to give him.

The third issue concerns the operation of protective trusts, under s33 of the Trustee Act 1925. If Sam has died having married Mavis then the provisions of the trust instrument creating a protective trust for the benefit of his surviving wife would have come into effect. In the absence of specific provisions in the trust instrument as to the operation of the protective trust the provisions of s33 of the Trustee Act 1925 will apply. Under s33 the 'principal beneficiary' under the protective trust, which is Mavis in this case, is entitled to all the income from the trust as it arises until she does or attempts to do any act or thing, or until any event happens which would deprive her of the right to receive the income or part thereof if she were a beneficiary entitled absolutely. On the happening of an event which would deprive her of the income or part thereof a discretionary trust would arise which in this case would be for the benefit of Mavis and the children of the marriage if any, but if no children, for Mavis and the persons who would be entitled to the trust property or income. As Mavis has been adjudicated bankrupt she has brought the provisions in s33 which bring the protective trust to an end, into operation and a discretionary trust now operates. This is because the effect of bankruptcy is to place the assets of the bankrupt in the hands of the trustee in bankruptcy so that any income paid to Mavis would go into the hands of the trustee in bankruptcy to meet the claims of her creditors. See *Re Evans* (1920).

Therefore, the trustees must consider themselves as holding the income on discretionary trusts for Mavis and the other persons entitled under such a trust under s33 of the Trustee Act 1925.

22 UNIVERSITY OF LONDON LLB (EXTERNAL) 1991 QUESTIONS AND SUGGESTED SOLUTIONS

UNIVERSITY OF LONDON

LLB EXAMINATION

PART I for External Students

LAW OF TRUSTS

Wednesday, 5 June 1991: 10 am to 1 pm

Answer four of the following eight questions

1. a) Distinguish between wholly secret and half-secret trusts. Is there any, and if so what, *rationale* for the different 'communication' rules?

   b) By his will, a testator left £50,000 to A and B and added 'it being my wish that they will give effect to the purposes set out in a separate letter which I have signed and handed to B'. Before the will was made, the testator revealed the contents of the letter to A alone, and then sealed it and handed it over to B saying that it was only to be opened after his death.

   Following the testator's death earlier this year, B opened the letter and found that it contained a direction to A and B to pay the £50,000 to the testator's former secretary, C who, one week before the testator's death, was killed in a car accident leaving an infant daughter, D.

   Advise A and B as to what they should do with the £50,000.

2. 'Purpose trusts are either charitable or non-charitable. If they are charitable, they are free from many constraints which apply to private trusts and, if they are non-charitable, they are subject to constraints from which other private trusts are free.'

   Develop and illustrate this proposition by reference to the relevant authorities.

3. a) 'Constructive trusts show the conscience of equity at work.'

   Discuss.

   b) Jack and Jill have for the last two years been living together in a flat. Jill had been the tenant of the flat for several years when, last year, the landlord offered to grant a 99-year lease to Jill at a nominal rent for £20,000, a price that was low by reason of the fact that Jill was a protected sitting tenant. Jill agreed but at her request the 99-year lease was granted to Jack who provided the whole of the £20,000. On the open market and with vacant possession, the leasehold flat would fetch £40,000 and Jack, having become disenchanted with Jill, is talking of selling and keeping the entire proceeds.

Advise Jill as to her interest, if any, in the flat or its future proceeds, on the assumption that her tenancy came to an end when Jack purchased.

4. By her will, Celia, after appointing Tug and Tow to be her executors and trustees, left her residuary estate to them upon trust to divide it into two equal parts and to hold such parts upon the following trusts:

   a) As to one part, upon trust to pay the income thereof to her husband, Henry, for life upon protective trusts and subject thereto upon trust for such of her children as should attain the age of 25;

   b) As to the other part, upon trust in equal shares for such of her children as should be living when her youngest child attains the age of 18.

Celia died last year leaving Henry and three children surviving, Tom, Dick, and Harriet, aged 3, 14 and 21.

Advise Tug and Tow:

   i) Whether they may have recourse to the trust income of either fund to pay school fees for Dick;

   ii) Whether they may apply trust capital from either fund to enable Harriet to purchase a fast food franchise (a business in which she has five years' experience);

   iii) Pending the attainment by Tom of the age of 18, what they should do with the income of fund b);

   iv) In the event of Henry's bankruptcy, what they should do with the income of fund a).

5. By a settlement made by Smith, the trustees, Dum and Dee, were directed to hold a trust fund consisting of shares and debentures in Alpha plc, a public limited company, and certain government stock, on trust to pay the income to Adam for life remainder to his children. The settlement contains no special investment clause except a provision that, before making any change of investment, the trustees should first obtain the consent in writing of Smith.

In 1987, Dum and Dee, with the consent in writing of Smith, sold the shares in Alpha to one of themselves, Dum, for £200,000 (their quoted value) and invested the proceeds in the purchase of shares in Beta plc, another public limited company.

In 1988, Dum and Dee, with the consent in writing of Smith, sold the government stock for £500,000 (its quoted value) and invested the proceeds in the purchase of freehold offices in Docklands.

In 1989, Dum and Dee, without the consent of Smith but with the encouragement of Adam, sold the debentures in Alpha plc for £100,000 (their market value) and invested the proceeds in shares in Delta plc, another public limited company.

The shares in Alpha plc are now worth £300,000; the shares in Beta plc are now worth £100,000; the shares in Delta plc are now worth £200,000 and the freehold offices are worth £250,000.

Advise a) Adam's children, b) Dum and Dee jointly as trustees, and c) Dum individually, as to their respective legal positions.

6. a) In what circumstances may a trustee be remunerated for his services to the trust?

    b) Consider the application of the maxim *delegatus non potest delegare* in the context of a trustee of a personalty settlement who wishes:

        i)   to go abroad for a period which may be between six to eighteen months;

        ii) to delegate to a stockbroker the power at his discretion to make changes of investment with a view to producing balanced gains in capital and income;

        iii) in exercise of an express power to revoke the trusts of the settlement and declare other trusts for the benefit of all or any of the same beneficiaries, to vest part of the trust fund in other trustees upon discretionary trusts for the beneficiaries.

7. Under the terms of the will of a testator who died in 1983, a fund of £3,000,000 was left to trustees upon trust to distribute the capital amongst such charitable or worthy causes and in such shares as the trustees should in their absolute discretion think fit and the residuary estate was left to the XY Charity. On various dates since the testator's death, the trustees dealt with the fund as follows:

    i)   £1m was paid to the AB hospital which spent £500,000 on dialysis machines and computer equipment and invested the balance in government stock which is now worth £550,000;

    ii) £1m was paid to the CD University which applied the money towards the cost of a new library building. The total cost of the building was £2m;

    iii) £1m was paid to the EF Foundation for the Relief of Poverty. It paid this sum into its bank account which at the time was £200,000 in credit. The following day, the EF Foundation drew out £500,000 and applied it in providing hotel accommodation for the homeless. One week later, it received a donation of £500,000 and paid this sum into its account. Since then, further sums have been drawn out and the present credit balance is £400,000.

Advise the XY Charity.

8.   a)   In what circumstances, if any, may the administration of an English trust be transferred abroad (in the sense of the trust fund being invested in overseas investments and the trustees being non-UK residents)?

     b)   Under the terms of a settlement, investments worth £500,000 are held upon trust to hold the income on protective trusts for Mary during her life and subject thereto for such of her children as attain the age of 21 in equal shares.

          Mary is a widow aged 50 and has three children aged 18, 20 and 23. Mary and her children are all agreed that they would like to terminate the trust and divide the investments amongst themselves in agreed shares.

          Consider whether this may be done i) without an application to the court, and ii) by making such an application.

Question 1

a) Distinguish between wholly secret and half-secret trusts. Is there any, and if so what, *rationale* for the different 'communication' rules?

b) By his will, a testator left £50,000 to A and B and added 'it being my wish that they will give effect to the purposes set out in a separate letter which I have signed and handed to B'. Before the will was made, the testator revealed the contents of the letter to A alone, and then sealed it and handed it over to B saying that it was only to be opened after his death.

Following the testator's death earlier this year, B opened the letter and found that it contained a direction to A and B to pay the £50,000 to the testator's former secretary, C who, one week before the testator's death, was killed in a car accident leaving an infant daughter, D.

Advise A and B as to what they should do with the £50,000.

University of London LLB Examination
(for External Students) Law of Trusts June 1991 Q1

General comment

This is a fairly standard question on the law relating to secret trusts. An explanation of the rationale for secret trusts will help explain the answers to the practical problems the examiner has devised in part b). A good question to answer as the law on secret trusts is usually self-contained.

Skeleton solution

Explain the difference between wholly secret and half-secret trusts - emphasise the communication rules - the 'evidence' theory - the 'incorporation' theory - Time of creation of secret trusts - possibility of revocation - *Re Gardner (No 2)*.

Suggested solution

a) According to Pennycuick J in *Re Tyler* (1891), the 'particular principles of law applicable to secret trusts are really concerned only with trusts created by will' and it is by construing the terms of a will that the most obvious difference between wholly and half secret trusts can be seen. Wholly secret trusts are those which according to the terms of the will are expressed as an absolute gift to a legatee, but where during the lifetime of the testator (before or after the making of his will) he has indicated to the legatee that the gift is to be held on trust for another person. Half secret trusts occur where the testator has left property by will 'on trust' to a legatee but where the will does not identify the terms of the trust or the intended beneficiary. In the case of half-secret trusts, the communication and acceptance of the trust and its terms must be made 'before or at the time of' the making of the will (*Re Keen* (1937)), and not afterwards. It also appears from *Re Keen* that in half secret trusts (but possibly not wholly secret), the communication to the trustee must not contradict the explicit terms of the will. Other differences are first, that wholly secret trusts of land do not need to comply with s53(1)(b) of the Law of Property Act 1925 (*Ottaway* v *Norman* (1972)), but half secret trusts of land do

205

(*Re Baillie* (1886)), although the latter case may well be wrong on the ground that 'equity will not permit a statute (s53) to be an instrument of fraud'; secondly, that in half-secret trusts, gifts to two or more trustees will be to them as joint tenants and therefore an acceptance by any one of them of the trust before the will is made will bind them all (*Re Stead* (1900)), but that in wholly secret trusts the gift *may* be to them as tenants in common so that only those who actually accept are bound; and thirdly, whereas a wholly secret trust can be revoked and replaced by a new wholly secret trust by the testator at any time up to his death, a half secret trust can only be revoked and the property held on resulting trust (because it is impossible to communicate a new trust after the will has been written).

The major difference is the communication rule, although there does not seem to be any satisfactory explanation for its existence. Indeed, in some common law jurisdictions (eg Australia) the distinction has been abolished and the wholly secret trust rule applied to both types. Two of the more cogent theories are: first, that the rule allowing acceptance after the will in wholly secret trusts was originally procedural viz, that evidence of events occurring after the will (ie acceptance) could be admitted by a court to prove a wholly secret trust so as to prevent fraud by the legatee/trustee. The fraud being that the legatee might otherwise keep property which he has promised to pass to someone else. But, in half-secret trusts, where the legatee is clearly stated to be a trustee, there is no possibility of fraud and therefore no need to examine the events occurring (ie acceptance) after the will was signed. Hence, acceptance after the will was not relevant. In other words, a rule of evidence has turned into a substantive rule of law; secondly, it may be that the half secret trust rule is a ghastly mistake because of confusion with the law of incorporation of documents. A will may be said to 'incorporate' another document if the will makes reference to that document *and* if that document was in existence at the time the will was made. It is easy to see how this rule could have been carried over to require acceptance of the trust at the time the will was made for half secret trusts. Of course, it is clear that neither of these theories (nor any other) is wholly satisfactory and the distinction should be abolished.

b) The immediate question to answer here is whether this is a wholly secret or fully secret trust. The crucial words are 'it being my wish'. If this imposes an obligation on A and B, it is half secret; if not, the words are to be ignored and we must consider the law of wholly secret trusts. These are precatory words and, following *Lambe* v *Eames* (1871), they do not readily impose a trust. However, this is a marginal case - though more likely fully secret - and the better student will deal with both alternatives.

   i) If half secret - there must be communication and acceptance before or at the time of the will and this has clearly been the case with A. The gift will be to them as joint tenants (because they are trustees), so A's acceptance will bind B (*Re Stead*). Note, however, that B has in any event accepted the terms of the trust before the will by accepting a sealed envelope containing those details before the will was made - *Re Keen, Re Boyes* (1884) ('a ship sailing under sealed orders'). The trust is therefore prima facie valid and neither A nor B can keep the money. However, whether they hand it on to the beneficiary (C and hence D) or whether it results to the testator's next of kin depends on whether it matters that the intended beneficiary (C) died before the testator. *Re Gardner (No 2)* (1923) says that the estate of a beneficiary obtains their intended interest under a half secret trust even if that beneficiary dies before the testator. However, this may be wrong as it appears that secret trusts do not come into existence until the testator dies and, therefore, people who die before him are not really beneficiaries - they have no interest when they die. If *Re Gardner (No 2)* is wrong, the money results to the next of kin and not C's estate (D).

ii) If fully secret - the date of communication is irrelevant so long as it is before the testator's death. Given that A (directly) and B (by means of accepting the envelope) have both accepted the trust it is irrelevant whether the gift to them was as joint tenants or tenants in common. They are both bound. Hence the question is the same as above viz, whether *Re Gardner (No 2)* is correct. In the case of fully secret trusts, it is rather more certain that the trust does not arise until the testator's death and therefore anybody who dies before him can have no claim. The money goes to the testator's next of kin.

Question 2

'Purpose trusts are either charitable or non-charitable. If they are charitable, they are free from many constraints which apply to private trusts and, if they are non-charitable, they are subject to constraints from which other private trusts are free.'

Develop and illustrate this proposition by reference to the relevant authorities.

University of London LLB Examination
(for External Students) Law of Trusts June 1991 Q2

General comment

This is a cleverly worded question and many students will fall into the trap of simply describing the 'beneficiary principle' and/or the law of charities. However, the question asks about the consequence of something being charitable or non-charitable rather than how the law defines those categories. It requires good knowledge of both areas of the law and is an object lesson in why a student should never omit these topics from her or his revision.

Skeleton solution

Definition of purpose trusts - essential invalidity contrasted with essential validity of charities - Perpetuity rule - problems of enforcement - tax benefits - trustee's powers - use of cy-près.

Suggested solution

Normally trusts must have certain objects (*Re Endacott* (1960)). Generally, this means that a trust must either be for the benefit of human beneficiaries (*Re Astor*

(1952)) or fall within the definition of charity. To the first rule (the need for human beneficiaries), there are only limited exceptions - sometimes known as the anomalous exceptions of *Re Endacott* or 'trusts of imperfect obligation' viz, trusts for the erection and maintenance of monuments and graves (*Re Hetherington* (1989) or *Bourne* v *Keane* (1919) or *Re Caus* (1934)), trusts for the maintenance of specific animals (*Re Dean* (1889)) and the trusts in *Re Thompson* (1934) for the promotion of fox-hunting. Reference must also be made to the rule in *Re Denley* (1969), that only those non-charitable purpose trusts that are 'abstract or impersonal' are void and, therefore, a trust which 'directly or indirectly' benefits ascertainable individuals may still be valid. However, herein lies the first and foremost distinction between charitable and non-charitable purpose trusts - the former are valid, the great majority of the latter are void. This is the greatest 'constraint' to which non-charitable purpose trusts are subject and which obviously does not apply to charitable purpose trusts or private trusts which have a human beneficiary.

a) *Valid non-charitable purpose trusts and private trusts*

The major difference between these two types of trust is that valid non-charitable purpose trusts (*Endacott* exceptions and *Re Denley*) have difficulty satisfying the perpetuity rule. To be valid, these purpose trusts must not last longer than the perpetuity period ie, they can exist only for a certain maximum duration. This is often expressed as 'the rule against perpetual trusts'. This perpetuity period is 'a life in being plus twenty-one years' ie the length of the life of any person named in the document establishing the trust plus 21 years after their death. However, because these trusts are normally established by will, the 'life in being' is usually the testator (now dead) and therefore the period is only 21 years. It seems that such a trust satisfies the perpetuity period only if it is possible to say at the outset that it will definitely not last longer than the perpetuity period, which means in effect that the will or deed must contain a clause such as 'for so long as the law allows' or 'for 21 years' or 'for the perpetuity period' - *Leahy* v *Attorney-General for New South Wales* (1959); *Re Denley*. (NB *Re Drummond* (1988) gives a different test viz, whether the capital sum could be spent within the period, but this is probably not correct.) This is a difficult test to satisfy and certainly is a 'constraint' on the validity of such trusts. Pure private trusts (those with a human beneficiary) usually have no difficulty meeting this test and, in any event, have the benefit of the Perpetuities and Accumulations Act 1964. Valid purpose trusts cannot rely on the provisions of this Act to save what would otherwise be void for perpetuity under the common law - s15(4) PAA 1964. It is also clear (at least for the *Endacott* exceptions), that valid purpose trusts suffer from problems of enforcement - there is no beneficiary who has an interest to go to court to compel the trustees to carry out the trust. This is why these trusts are known as 'trusts of imperfect obligation' - because the trustee's obligation is imperfect. This is often circumvented by giving the residuary legatees of the will (if any) the power (but not the duty) to apply to the court to enforce the trust. But, this is obviously unsatisfactory because such residuary legatees would be entitled to the capital sum if the trust did fail and, therefore, it is not in their interest to see the trust performed. In pure private trusts, there is a beneficiary both capable and willing to ensure that the trustees carry out their duties.

b) *Charitable trusts and private trusts*

It is often said that the main difference between private trusts and charitable trusts is that the former must have certainty of objects whilst the latter does not. This is not strictly true. Private trusts must satisfy the certainty of objects rule by having human beneficiaries - *Re Astor* (1952). Charities, however, need not satisfy this rule, but must satisfy a much less stringent certainty of objects rule viz, they must fall within the category of purposes recognised by the law as charitable. This is the purpose of the *Pemsel* (1891) categories of aged, impotent, infirm; advancement of religion; advancement of education; and other purposes beneficial to the community. So, to be charitable a trust must satisfy an 'objects test' even though one less stringent than private trusts. Other advantages enjoyed by charitable trusts over private trusts are first, that charities are not subject to the perpetuity rule - they can last for ever; secondly, that charitable trusts are exempt from many taxes, rates and excise duties - the fiscal advantages which are worth about 660 million pounds a year (1991); thirdly, that charitable trustees can act by majority vote, whereas private trustees must usually act unanimously; and fourthly, that surplus assets of charitable trusts fall under the cy-pres doctrine whereas private trusts are governed by the law of resulting trusts. Charities are, however, subject to one constraint not placed upon private trusts viz, that charities must be for the public benefit. So, for charities, the purpose must be generally *beneficial* to the community *and*, for every charity except those for the relief of the poor, must benefit the public at large (or a section thereof) - *Re Compton* (1945), *Dingle* v *Turner* (1972), *Williams Trustees* v *IRC* (1947).

Question 3

a) 'Constructive trusts show the conscience of equity at work.'

Discuss.

b) Jack and Jill have for the last two years been living together in a flat. Jill had been the tenant of the flat for several years when, last year, the landlord offered to grant a 99-year lease to Jill at a nominal rent for £20,000, a price that was low by reason of the fact that Jill was a protected sitting tenant. Jill agreed but at her request the 99-year lease was granted to Jack who provided the whole of the £20,000. On the open market and with vacant possession, the leasehold flat would fetch £40,000 and Jack, having become disenchanted with Jill, is talking of selling and keeping the entire proceeds.

Advise Jill as to her interest, if any, in the flat or its future proceeds, on the assumption that her tenancy came to an end when Jack purchased.

University of London LLB Examination
(for External Students) Law of Trusts June 1991 Q3

General comment

This is a question that invites in part (a) a general description of the meaning and scope of constructive trusts. A good question to begin with and which lends itself to a second class mark. Part (b) is straightforward case law.

Skeleton solution

Trust or remedy - America vs England - standard categories of constructive trust - *Pettitt* v *Pettitt* - *Lloyds Bank* v *Rosset* - relationship to resulting trusts.

Suggested solution

a) Constructive trusts are often said to be at the cutting edge of a court's equitable jurisdiction. It is true that the 'constructive trust' is perceived by many to be an all-embracing remedy which the courts may use at their discretion to remedy 'inequitable' conduct by an individual, and this is indeed reinforced by the fact that constructive trusts are exempt from the normal formalities relating to the creation and operation of trusts - see s53(2) of the Law of Property Act 1925.

However, it is also clear that there is no set meaning to the term 'constructive trust' and that the many and various situations in which they can arise may defy definition. Some jurists argue that one feature common to all cases of constructive trust is that no person can be a constructive trustee (and hence there can be no constructive trust) unless he or she is the legal owner of property at the time the court imposes the trust. Such a 'definition' would seem to rule out 'knowing assistance' cases as examples of constructive trusts (because the person knowingly assisting does not have and does not acquire legal title). Another purported distinction is between the 'English' and 'American' constructive trusts, and herein lies the heart of the issue whether 'constructive trusts show the conscience of equity at work'.

The so-called 'English' approach sees constructive trusts as substantive trusts; that is, there are beneficiaries, trustees and those trustees have substantive duties of holding and administering the trust property just as if they had been constituted trustees under an express settlement. The consequence of this theoretical approach is that the court can impose a constructive trust only in certain reasonably defined situations. This does not mean that constructive trusts are not concerned with 'conscience', but rather that equity will remedy unconscionable behaviour only if certain conditions are satisfied. Examples of such constructive trusts are the rule that a trustee must not make a profit from his trust (*Keech* v *Sandford* (1726)); the rules of knowing receipt and assistance (*Lipkin Gorman* v *Karpnale* (1987), *AGIP (Africa)* v *Jackson and Others* (1989)); the rule that equity will not allow a statute to be an instrument of fraud (*Rochefoucauld* v *Boustead* (1897)); the law of secret trusts (possibly - see *Ottaway* v *Norman* (1972)); the rule that a person cannot retain the benefit of a criminal act (*Davitt* v *Titcumb* (1990)); the law of mutual wills (*Re Cleaver* (1981)); and the rule that a vendor holds property on constructive trusts for a purchaser under a constructive trust, even before transfer of the property, if the contract for sale is specifically enforceable (*Lysaght* v *Edwards*

(1876)). All of these are cases where the court has imposed a trust to prevent inequity, but where the law has developed a reasonable certain set of rules to establish when this has occurred.

The 'American' view, on the other hand, sees the constructive trust as a flexible 'weapon' or 'remedy' which the court may use to prevent or redress inequitable conduct in any situation at any time. It is often known as the 'remedial constructive trust'. Furthermore, not only are there little restrictions on the circumstances in which such a trust can be imposed, but also the nature of this type of constructive trust is quite different. This constructive trust is clearly not substantive; the only duty which the constructive trustee will be under will be to return the trust property to its 'rightful' owner, ie the person to whom the court thinks in all fairness it should belong. It is a method of compelling a person to return property when they have been unjustly enriched. A good example in English law is *Chase Manhattan Bank* v *Israeli-British Bank* (1981), a case often considered under the law of tracing, but more properly regarded as one of unjust enrichment or remedial constructive trust because of the absence of any recognisable fiduciary relationship between the parties. A similar approach was gaining ground in the law of matrimonial or quasi-matrimonial property where, under the guidance of *Grant* v *Edwards* (1986), the court adopted a flexible, result-oriented approach to ownership of property on the break-up of a stable relationship. This has been somewhat restricted by *Lloyds Bank* v *Rosset* (1988) which preferred the more defined 'English view'.

All in all then, it is true on one level to say that constructive trusts are the conscience of equity at work. Their purpose is to ensure that the legal owner of property should not unlawfully deprive another of his or her property. However, the more interesting question is how flexible this jurisdiction really is. In recent years, the courts of this country have been moving towards a more relaxed attitude to the use of constructive trusts and, in this sense, we can agree with the quotation in the question.

b) There are a number of possible answers to the question whether Jill has an interest in the flat or the proceeds of sale thereof. The first, most obvious, and clearly incorrect view is that Jill has no interest in the leasehold of the flat because legal title to the flat is in Jack's name alone. This is the presumption at law but, of course, it can be rebutted by showing that Jill has an interest by virtue of a resulting or constructive trust on the *Pettitt* v *Pettitt* (1970), *Lloyds Bank* v *Rosset* model. It is clear, however, that no resulting trust can arise in Jill's favour because she has not contributed to the purchase price of the flat - it is purchased entirely with Jack's money. Indeed, the fact that Jack has legal title and that he alone provided the purchase money could go a long way to proving his sole ownership. However, this is unlikely because it appears that Jack is behaving inequitably and may be subject to a constructive trust in Jill's favour.

There are, perhaps two ways in which Jill could establish an interest - either of the whole or part - to the flat by virtue of a constructive trust. First, she could seek to show that there was a common intention between herself and Jack that she should have an interest in the flat plus some act of detriment by her in reliance on that promise - *Lloyds Bank* v *Rosset*. On the facts, it may be possible to deduce such a common intention from the fact that she was offered the tenancy but insisted that it be given formally to Jack. Unless this was tantamount to a gift, there is little to explain such action unless Jill did have such intention. Her detriment would be similar to that in *Tanner* v *Tanner* (1975) in that she has given up the sure protection of a protected tenancy under the Rent Acts, as well as the chance of the leasehold at a low price. If this is the case, the extent of Jill's interest would be commensurate with the terms of the common intention - which could be that she have all the property (subject to repayment to Jack of his money) or some proportion thereof. However, this may be a rather complicated way of looking at the situation and the second angle of approach may be more helpful. Simply, Jack is now seeking to take advantage of the fact that he has an absolute conveyance in his favour and that there is no trust in writing as there should under s53(1)(b) LPA 1925. He is, in essence, attempting to use a statute (s53 LPA) as an instrument of fraud; cf *Rochefoucauld* v *Boustead*. This is established as above viz, the flat was offered to Jill because she was a sitting tenant and at a low price because that tenancy was protected. This is clearly a case for equitable intervention and Jack will hold the flat on constructive trust for Jill, quite possibly as sole owner subject to Jack's right of repayment; cf *Hussey* v *Palmer* (1972).

Question 4

By her will, Celia, after appointing Tug and Tow to be her executors and trustees, left her residuary estate to them upon trust to divide it into two equal parts and to hold such parts upon the following trusts:

a) As to one part, upon trust to pay the income thereof to her husband, Henry, for life upon protective trusts and subject thereto upon trust for such of her children as should attain the age of 25;

b) As to the other part, upon trust in equal shares for such of her children as should be living when her youngest child attains the age of 18.

Celia died last year leaving Henry and three children surviving, Tom, Dick, and Harriet, aged 3, 14 and 21.

Advise Tug and Tow:

i) Whether they may have recourse to the trust income of either fund to pay school fees for Dick;

ii) Whether they may apply trust capital from either fund to enable Harriet to purchase a fast food franchise (a business in which she has five years' experience);

iii) Pending the attainment by Tom of the age of 18, what they should do with the income of fund b);

iv) In the event of Henry's bankruptcy, what they should do with the income of fund a).

University of London LLB Examination
(for External Students) Law of Trusts June 1991 Q4

General comment

Questions on a trustee's power of maintenance or advancement are often difficult and always involve complicated factual situations. They repay careful reading and should be attempted only if you have a clear understanding of the difference between the powers and a sure grasp of the concept of 'intermediate income'.

Skeleton solution

Maintenance - s31 Trustee Act 1925 - protective trusts - prior interests. Advancement - s32 Trustee Act 1925 - meaning of 'benefit'.

Suggested solution

This problem concerns the trustees' powers of maintenance and advancement. The power of maintenance is the power to apply income of a trust fund for the maintenance, education or benefit of an infant beneficiary - the trustees being unable to give the infant his or her share of the income because the infant cannot give a valid receipt. The power of advancement is the power to give a beneficiary part of the capital sum under a trust which he or she would receive (but is not yet entitled to) should he or she fulfil the terms of the trust, eg, reach a specified age. In this case, as there is neither an express power of maintenance or advancement, the trustees' powers arise under s31 and s32 of the Trustee Act 1925. These powers have not been expressly excluded.

i) *Dick's school fees*

The issue here is whether the trustees may exercise the statutory power of maintenance in Dick's favour by using part of the income from either part of the trust to pay his school fees. Clearly, there is a prima facie chance that the power may be exercisable as Dick is under 18 and he is one of the beneficiaries of both trusts. Again, there is no doubt that the proposed purpose is within s31 TA 1925 as this specifically authorises income to be paid for an infant beneficiary's 'maintenance, education or benefit'. However, the major problem is whether the income arising from Dick's share is actually available for his use. In other words, whether Dick is entitled to the income; sometimes expressed as 'whether the gift or trust carries the intermediate income'.

The income from Part One of the trust is not available to Dick as there is a prior interest - the income is to be paid to Henry under the protective trust. There can be no maintenance from this part.

The income from Part Two may well be available for Dick's maintenance. There is not a deferred gift, but rather a gift contingent on a future event. The gift is therefore either or both (we are not told) a contingent residuary gift of realty and/or personalty. A contingent gift of residuary personalty carries all income earned from the testator's death until the beneficiary actually becomes entitled - *Re Adams* (1893). Further, under s175 of the Law of Property Act 1925, contingent residuary gifts of freehold land (leasehold being personalty for these purposes) will carry the intermediate income. Thus there can be maintenance from this part.

ii) The issue here is whether the trustees may exercise their power of advancement in Harriet's favour. This depends on whether s32 of the Trustee Act is applicable. Advancement is the payment of capital sums to a beneficiary before the time comes when he or she is actually entitled to the fund, although under s32 only half the capital sum due to Harriet can be paid by way of advancement. An immediate problem is whether the proposed use of the capital is for the 'advancement or benefit' of Harriet within s32, for if it is not, the power cannot be exercised. Following *Pilkington* v *IRC* (1964), where a wide definition was given to 'advancement and benefit', it seems likely that the proposed use is within the section, especially since this is intended to be Harriet's career and is not speculative due to her previous experience. The question therefore arises whether the other conditions of s32 are fulfilled. Section 32 enables trustees to advance capital held on trust for any beneficiary (infant or adult), with any interest in the property (contingent, deferred or vested). Thus, the trustee may advance up to one half of the capital from Part Two of the fund to Harriet, even though she may never actually receive an interest (eg because she dies before the youngest child is 18). However, where there are prior interests - as with Henry's life interest under Part One of the fund - the trustees may only advance capital if the person with the prior interest is of full age and gives his written consent s32(1)(c).

iii) Pending the attainment of 18 by Tom, the youngest child, (at which date the trust property can be distributed) s31(2) of the Trustee Act directs that the residue of income from each beneficiary's share not applied for their maintenance while they are a minor should be accumulated by investment during the minority. This becomes available for their future maintenance.

iv) The creation of the trust in Part One of the fund is designed clearly to fall within s33 of the Trustee Act. Under this section, if income is directed to be held on 'protective trusts' for the benefit of any person for their life (as here), then the income is held on the trusts set out in the section. This is simply a shorthand way of establishing an effective protective trust. In the event of a bankruptcy - which would terminate the life interest - the income is to be held on trust for the maintenance, support or benefit of all or any of the following: a) the former life tenant (called the 'principal beneficiary' - Henry) and his spouse and issue OR b) if the principal beneficiary has no spouse or issue, the principal beneficiary and the persons who would be entitled to the capital if the principal beneficiary were dead. All of Henry, Tom, Dick and Harriet are within b) and Henry and possibly the children if they are his issue are within a).

Question 5

By a settlement made by Smith, the trustees, Dum and Dee, were directed to hold a trust fund consisting of shares and debentures in Alpha plc, a public limited company, and certain government stock, on trust to pay the income to Adam for life remainder to his children. The settlement contains no special investment clause except a provision that, before making any change of investment, the trustees should first obtain the consent in writing of Smith.

In 1987, Dum and Dee, with the consent in writing of Smith, sold the shares in Alpha to one of themselves, Dum, for £200,000 (their quoted value) and invested the proceeds in the purchase of shares in Beta plc, another public limited company.

In 1988, Dum and Dee, with the consent in writing of Smith, sold the government stock for £500,000 (its quoted value) and invested the proceeds in the purchase of freehold offices in Docklands.

In 1989, Dum and Dee, without the consent of Smith but with the encouragement of Adam, sold the debentures in Alpha plc for £100,000 (their market value) and invested the proceeds in shares in Delta plc, another public limited company.

The shares in Alpha plc are now worth £300,000; the shares in Beta plc are now worth £100,000; the shares in Delta plc are now worth £200,000 and the freehold offices are worth £250,000.

Advise a) Adam's children, b) Dum and Dee jointly as trustees, and c) Dum individually, as to their respective legal positions.

University of London LLB Examination
(for External Students) Law of Trusts June 1991 Q5

General comment

This is a typical question on liability for breach of trust, especially since it involves some consideration of powers of investment. Such questions usually look much harder than they actually are and should be attempted by any candidate with a reasonable knowledge of the law of personal liability of trustees.

Skeleton solution

Personal liability for breach of trusts - standard of care - measure of damages - remedies and defences. Some knowledge of Trustee Investment Act 1961.

Suggested solution

The issues raised in this question concern the individual liabilities of trustees for breach of trust - both collectively and individually - as well as the possible remedies available to a beneficiary whose interest has been adversely affected by such breach. It is, of course, the duty of trustees to invest trust property so that income will be produced for the beneficiaries (eg *Stone* v *Stone* (1869)) and trustees will be liable for failing to do so within a reasonable time of the establishment of the trust. This is not the case here. However, trustees may also be liable for breach of trust for investing contrary to their powers of investment or by failing to meet the standard of care required of trustees when dealing with beneficiaries' property. These are the matters in issue here. There are no express powers of investment in this case and therefore, the power of investment is governed by the Trustee Investment Act 1961. It is unlikely that the requirement of Smith's consent excludes the statutory power (if it did there would be no power to invest!), but rather places an additional limit on the trustees in the exercise of the powers under the Act. This means that the trustees cannot exercise the powers of investment under the Act without Smith's consent, but also that Smith's consent cannot make lawful an investment which the Act does not authorise.

215

Of course, if investment is undertaken (which in this case, if at all must be under the Act), the trust fund must be divided into two equal parts - the narrower range and the wider range part. This is a precondition of the exercise of investment powers under the Act and it is clear that on sale of any of the existing investments of this particular fund, the fund would have to be divided. (NB there is no breach of trust merely by retaining unauthorised investments when the trust was created, because this is not *investment*).

a) The sale of the shares in Alpha to one of the trustees - Dum - and the investment of the proceeds in Beta plc. Adam's children are beneficiaries under the trust and are therefore concerned by the fact that the value of the investment has halved after the sale of Alpha shares and the purchase of Beta shares. However, in order to establish liability for breach of trust - so as to recover the difference in value - they must establish some breach of trust. It is clear that there has been no breach of any express stipulation, for Smith's consent has been obtained. However, there is no indication that the fund has been divided into two halves as required by the Act and, therefore, the investment in Beta shares may be unauthorised. Likewise, there is no indication whether Beta plc fulfils the conditions stipulated in the Trustee Act for investment in public companies (viz not less than £1 million share capital, dividend paid on relevant shares for preceding five years, shares quoted on Stock Exchange, shares fully paid and incorporated in the UK).

Again, trustees investing in wider range investments must obtain and consider advice (s6(2)) as to the suitability of the investment and its suitability in the overall investment profile of the trust. Importantly, however, there is also the general duty of care imposed on trustees when investing trust money. The trustee must act as an ordinary prudent man of business would act if he were minded to make investments on behalf of other people - *Re Whitely* (1886). If any or all of these breaches of trust have occurred, it is clear that both Dum and Dee will be jointly and severally liable to make good the loss to the trust fund, ie the difference between the value of the unauthorised/unwarranted/imprudent investment and the value of the fund before such investment was purchased - *Fry* v *Fry* (1859). Here, £100,000.

In addition, however, Dum may have incurred further liability as constructive trustee because of his purchase of the trust property. Under the 'self-dealing' rule a trustee must not be both a vendor and purchaser of the trust property and any such sale is voidable at the instance of the beneficiaries within a reasonable time - irrespective of how fair the transaction may have been, *ex parte Lacey* (1802). Smith's consent is irrelevant as it is the beneficiaries' interests that are prejudiced. If Adam's children act within a reasonable time, Dum will be held constructive trustee of the Alpha shares, including their increase in value. It is thus better for the children to pursue this avenue, as they would effectively have an asset worth £300,000, instead of an asset worth £100,000 (Beta shares) plus the £100,000 damages awarded for breach above. If Dum is bankrupt or otherwise unable to meet this constructive trust liability, it may be that Dee could be held liable for his co-trustee's breach of trust either because he was in 'wilful default' within s30 Trustee Act or because he failed in his own duty to supervise Dum.

b) This case is much clearer. A trustee may only invest money in the purchase of land if he is expressly authorised by the trust instrument or by some other statutory provision such as the Settled Land Act, see eg *Re Power* (1947). Neither of these is applicable here and therefore there has been a breach of trust and the trustees are jointly and severally liable for the loss. Smith's consent does not absolve the trustees as, as explained above, the consent is in addition to the requirements of the Trustee Investment Act. It does not replace them.

c) The same general considerations apply to the purchase of Delta shares with the money obtained from the sale of Alpha investments as were relevant in a) above. It is, however, clear that the provisions of the 1961 Act have been breached because the Alpha debentures were Part II narrower range investments and the proposed Delta investments could only be Part III wider range. The income from the sale of narrower range investments should be invested in investments authorised under that Part.

Similarly, Smith's consent has not been obtained and so there is a breach of the clear terms of the trust. Adam's encouragement does not affect his children's ability to sue for breach of trust for any loss sustained, but it would be open to the trustees to plead his instigation as a bar to a claim made by him - eg *Life Association of Scotland* v *Siddall* (1861). Moreover, under s62 Trustee Act 1925, the trustees may seek to impound Adam's beneficial interest to help meet their liability on the ground that Adam instigated or requested a breach of trust with knowledge that he was so doing - *Re Somerset* (1894). This is in effect a form of indemnity for the trustees. They may also try to plead s61 TA, on the grounds that they should be excused liability being (in relation to this breach) honest, reasonable and ought fairly to be excused. This is unlikely given their deliberate disregard of the consent requirement.

Question 6

a) In what circumstances may a trustee be remunerated for his services to the trust?

b) Consider the application of the maxim *delegatus non potest delegare* in the context of a trustee of a personalty settlement who wishes:

   i) to go abroad for a period which may be between six to eighteen months;

   ii) to delegate to a stockbroker the power at his discretion to make changes of investment with a view to producing balanced gains in capital and income;

   iii) in exercise of an express power to revoke the trusts of the settlement and declare other trusts for the benefit of all or any of the same beneficiaries, to vest part of the trust fund in other trustees upon discretionary trusts for the beneficiaries.

University of London LLB Examination
(for External Students) Law of Trusts June 1991 Q6

General comment

This is a straightforward question on the law of trustee remuneration and the law of delegation of duties and powers. It is unusual to find these two topics mixed in one question, but such is the trend in recent years.

Skeleton solution

Brady v *Ford* - trustee remuneration - the six exceptions - s25 Trustee Act 1925 - s23 Trustee Act 1925.

Suggested solution

a) It is a fundamental principle of the law of trusts that a trustee must not place himself in a position where his interest and duty conflict - Lord Hershell in *Bray* v *Ford* (1896). One aspect of this principle is the rule that a trustee is in general under a duty to act without remuneration. Trusteeship is essentially gratuitous because the trustee's duty is to effectively administer the trust, but his own self interest would be to gain more personal remuneration by drawing out the time spent on trust work. However, this does not mean that there is anything unlawful in a trustee being paid for his work: rather, it is that such remuneration will not be paid unless the trustee can point to some rule of law or trust provision that authorises such payment for work done. In general, a trustee may be remunerated for his services in the following situations:

   i) Where there is an express remuneration clause in the trust instrument. Although such a clause will receive a strict interpretation (*Re Gee* (1948)), such clauses are today common especially where it is the intention that professional trustees (eg a bank) be appointed.

   ii) A trustee may receive remuneration under a contract for services made with a beneficiary. However, the trustee must provide some new consideration for his remuneration as promising to fulfil the trust duties is not enough - he is already obliged to do this.

   iii) There are a number of ad hoc statutory provisions which provide that payment may be made to special kinds of trustee; eg s42 Trustee Act 1925 in respect of corporate trustees and the Judicial Trustee Act 1896.

   iv) A trustee is entitled to keep any remuneration received by virtue of his administering trust assets situated abroad, if such is received without his volition - *Re Northcote's Will Trusts* (1949).

   v) Under the rule in *Cradock* v *Piper* (1850) a solicitor trustee is entitled to receive the normal profit-costs for his work done as solicitor to the trust on behalf of himself and his co-trustees in legal proceedings, provided that the costs are not more than would have been incurred by the trust if the solicitor had been acting only for his co-trustees and not himself.

   vi) A trustee may be awarded remuneration under the inherent jurisdiction of the court to ensure the smooth and efficient administration of the trust - *Re Duke of Norfolk's ST* (1981). Remuneration will be ordered if it would be for the benefit of the administration of the trust and can include varying the remuneration actually authorised. The court must consider all factors, but especially the need to protect beneficiaries from unscrupulous trustees.

In all other cases, a trustee will be called to account as constructive trustee for any payment received by virtue of his position as trustee. He can, however, be reimbursed for expenses - s30(2) Trustee Act 1925 and *Hardoon v Belilas* (1901).

b) As a general rule, a trustee cannot delegate his responsibility under the trust for taking decisions. The trustee is in effect a delegate of the settler, and the rule is that a delegate cannot delegate - hence the Latin maxim in the question. To this sweeping statement of principle there are, however, a number of exceptions, all of them designed to facilitate the better administration of the trust.

i) Under s25 of the Trustee Act 1925 as amended, a trustee may delegate all or any of his powers to another for a period of up to one year, providing that the delegate is not the sole remaining co-trustee (unless a trust corporation). This is essentially a power of attorney and must be granted by written instrument signed by the trustee and witnessed. Written notice must be given to the other trustees. However, the delegation cannot be for longer than a year and if any loss arises through default of the delegate the trustee will be liable as if the default had been his own. All powers may be delegated under s25.

ii) It is an established rule of equity that a trustee can employ an agent to perform certain administrative (ministerial) acts on his behalf. The rule was encapsulated in *Speight* v *Gaunt* (1883) where the court held that trustees employing agents in the course of business were not liable for the default of the agent if the employment of that agent was such as would be done by an ordinary prudent man of business. Hence, trustees can employ solicitors, stockbrokers, valuers etc. However, there are some limitations to this rule: notably that the trustee must only employ agents for work within the normal scope of the agent's responsibilities - *Fry* v *Tapson* (1884) - and most importantly that only ministerial acts can be delegated under the equitable rules and not the taking of decisions. In this case, if all we had was the old law, then it is probable (but see below) that the stockbroker could not be given the power to make investment decisions, but only the power to carry out the general policy of investment decided by the trustees, ie to act ministerially: cf *Rowland* v *Witherden* (1851). However, according to Maugham J in *Re Vickery* (1931), s23(1) of the Trustee Act has altered this situation by permitting a trustee to employ an agent whether there is any real necessity or not. According to this case, the power to appoint agents in s23 extends to giving those agents the power to take policy decisions in respect of the trust - such as investment decisions. However, this is a controversial view and not widely accepted for it would take away the heart of trusteeship. Such a power is clearly given in s23(2) for certain trust assets abroad and this would indicate that it was not intended to be given under s23(1). Finally, however, perhaps we could argue in our case that in fact this is only a ministerial delegation - not a policy delegation - in that the stockbroker is given power to invest in order to fulfil the overall policy of the trust of achieving a balance between income and capital growth. It is arguable that such a delegation would fall within the narrow view of s23(1).

iii) An aspect of the general rule against delegation already considered is that the person to whom a power is given must in effect exercise that power. A donee of a power cannot delegate the choice involved inherent in that power to another - *Re Morris's Settlement* (1951). In this case, the trustee has been given a power to revoke the trust and declare other trusts for the benefit of all or any of the same beneficiaries. However, in the absence of any express authorisation allowing the trustee to re-appoint the trust property on discretionary trusts, the trustee is not entitled to establish new trustees with discretions as to the choice of beneficiaries. The issue is similar to that decided in *Re Hay* (1981) where trustees had power to appoint to such persons or purposes in their discretion except for a limited excluded class. They attempted to use this power to establish themselves as trustees on a discretionary trust for the same object. This was held void as the power demanded an appointment, not a further delegation of the power of choice. A fortiori where the person with the power tries to exercise that power by giving somebody else the discretion.

Question 7

Under the terms of the will of a testator who died in 1983, a fund of £3,000,000 was left to trustees upon trust to distribute the capital amongst such charitable or worthy causes and in such shares as the trustees should in their absolute discretion think fit and the residuary estate was left to the XY Charity. On various dates since the testator's death, the trustees dealt with the fund as follows:

i) £1m was paid to the AB hospital which spent £500,000 on dialysis machines and computer equipment and invested the balance in government stock which is now worth £550,000;

ii) £1m was paid to the CD University which applied the money towards the cost of a new library building. The total cost of the building was £2m;

iii) £1m was paid to the EF Foundation for the Relief of Poverty. It paid this sum into its bank account which at the time was £200,000 in credit. The following day, the EF Foundation drew out £500,000 and applied it in providing hotel accommodation for the homeless. One week later, it received a donation of £500,000 and paid this sum into its account. Since then, further sums have been drawn out and the present credit balance is £400,000.

Advise the XY Charity.

University of London LLB Examination
(for External Students) Law of Trusts June 1991 Q7

General comment

For anyone with even a passing knowledge of the law of tracing, this is a good question to answer. It really revolves around *Re Diplock* and the examiner might well think in retrospect that the question was too easy.

Skeleton solution

Tracing - conditions - *Re Diplock* - *Re Oatway* - personal remedies - loss of tracing.

Suggested solution

The issues raised in this question are similar in many respects to those discussed in the landmark decision on the law of equitable tracing - *Re Diplock* (1948). We are asked to advise the XY Charity, obviously with a view to this charity (as residuary legatees) recovering any assets wrongly paid out by the executors. Our first priority is, therefore, to establish that the executors/trustees of the testator have wrongfully distributed the assets subject to the trust. There is no difficulty in this. The trust is expressed to be for 'such charitable or worthy causes' as the trustees think fit. However, in order to be charitable a trust has to be exclusively charitable. As seen in *Chichester Diocesan Fund* v *Simpson* (1944) (concerning the will of Caleb Diplock), a trust for 'charitable or benevolent' purposes was held void on the grounds that the trustees could choose objects which were benevolent but not charitable in law. The same is true in our case and the gift is not charitable, not being exclusively devoted thereto. Thus, the trustees have wrongfully distributed the funds. Can the XY Charity recover the property?

The first point to note is that the XY Charity as residuary legatee must sue the trustees personally. They will be liable personally for all the loss, although with such large sums it is unlikely that they could meet this liability in full. Only, however, when they have exhausted this remedy (eg the trustees are bankrupt) may the XY Charity resort to tracing in equity and the *Re Diplock* special in personam remedy.

Equitable tracing

The conditions for the existence of the right to trace in equity were reasonably clearly laid down in *Re Diplock*; there must have been a fiduciary relationship and the plaintiff must have an equitable proprietary interest in the property he or she is seeking to trace. In this case, there clearly is a fiduciary relationship between the XY Charity and the trustees (note the relationship does not have to be between the immediate parties to the action) and as residuary legatees the charity has an equitable interest in the trust. Both the conditions are satisfied.

i) *The money paid to AB Hospital*

The hospital has given no consideration for the payment of the £1 million and therefore cannot avoid tracing on the ground of being a bona fide purchaser for value. Of course, if the AB Hospital had notice of the breach of trust, they would be constructive trustee of the property and liable to repay the money in full. Assuming however no notice, they are innocent volunteers. *Re Diplock* makes it

221

clear that if the innocent volunteer has retained the plaintiff's property (more correctly the property in which the plaintiff has a proprietary interest) in recognisable form - even if different from the original form - then the plaintiff may trace to it and recover. Here specific property has been purchased - dialysis machines/computers and government stock. Subject to the general rule that an equitable remedy will not be permitted to do inequity, the XY Charity can recover this property, or in the case of the equipment ask that its monetary equivalent be returned. Further, in the case of the government stock, it appears from *Re Tilley* (1967) that the plaintiff may be able to claim the increase in value of the property, ie the extra £50,000. This is because tracing is a right in rem - a right to the thing which is your property irrespective of the value it holds at the moment. Note, however, that *Re Tilley* was decided in the context of an action against a trustee and the court may adopt a more lenient attitude where the tracing is against an innocent third party, especially if that third party has used skill and judgment to increase the value of the property. There is an argument that the profit should be shared: cf *Boardman* v *Phipps* (1967).

ii) Again, prima facie tracing is available. The University again appears to be an innocent volunteer. However, in *Re Diplock*, some of the money had been spent on the alteration of old buildings and the erection of new ones. The Court of Appeal held that in these circumstances no action would lie because it would be inequitable to force an innocent third party to surrender such an asset, especially where the innocent party also contributed substantially to the cost of the property with its own money - as here. Essentially, the plaintiff's property has become untraceable, although this is something of a fiction because if the defendant had been the original trustee it is clear that the plaintiff would have had an enforceable charge over the property as a reflection of its interest (cf *Re Oatway* (1903)).

iii) Where an innocent volunteer mixes trust money (ie XY's) in a bank account with his own money - as here - the court in *Re Diplock* decided that a beneficiary did not deserve the special protection afforded by the rule in *Re Hallet* (1880) which applied to mixing by trustees. The rule in *Clayton's Case* (1816) applies so that the money spent on untraceable assets (here the hotel accommodation) is spent on the basis of 'first in first out'. Thus, the first £200,000 of the £500,000 spent on hotel accommodation was EF's own money, the next £300,000 belonged to XY. EF then received £500,000 by donation and the balance in the account stands at £400,000. Under the rule in *Clayton*, this £400,000 must be the remains of the last £500,000 to go into the account (ie last in, last out). It therefore belongs entirely to EF and XY has no claim under tracing to the balance in the account.

In personam

If the personal action against the trustees and equitable tracing fails to secure the return of trust property - as is likely in our case - the XY Charity can fall back on the special in personam remedy of *Re Diplock*. This is a remedy of last resort and it appears to be available only when there has been a wrongful distribution of assets under a will (or possibly a liquidated company - *Re J Leslie Engineers Co Ltd* (1976)). In effect, it means that although XY cannot receive back its specific property by means of tracing, it can sue the recipients of that property personally for its value. What is more, it is clear from *Re Diplock* that there is no defence of 'change of position' (ie that the money has been innocently spent) to this action and therefore the three charities will be liable. Note, however, that if this action is really a species of unjust enrichment, the case of *Lipkin Gorman* v *Karpnale* (1987) may provide some comfort, for in that case the House of Lords has recently held that the defence of 'change of position' is available to an unjust enrichment claim.

Question 8

a) In what circumstances, if any, may the administration of an English trust be transferred abroad (in the sense of the trust fund being invested in overseas investments and the trustees being non-UK residents)?

b) Under the terms of a settlement, investments worth £500,000 are held upon trust to hold the income on protective trusts for Mary during her life and subject thereto for such of her children as attain the age of 21 in equal shares.

Mary is a widow aged 50 and has three children aged 18, 20 and 23. Mary and her children are all agreed that they would like to terminate the trust and divide the investments amongst themselves in agreed shares.

Consider whether this may be done i) without an application to the court, and ii) by making such an application.

University of London LLB Examination
(for External Students) Law of Trusts June 1991 Q8

General comment

This is quite a technical question, on the edge of the syllabus and probably would not be attempted by many students. It is quite straightforward in itself and does involve some of the more familiar Variation of Trusts Act problems.

Skeleton solution

Variation of Trusts Act - adult beneficiaries - infant beneficiaries. Meaning of 'benefit' - tax saving - *Re Weston*.

Suggested solution

a) There are various reasons why the trustees of an English trust may wish the investment funds of the trust to be transferred abroad and the management of the trust be placed in the hands of foreign trustees. The most obvious is, of course, that the beneficiaries intend to live in the foreign jurisdiction or, at least, intend to have some real and genuine link with that jurisdiction. It is clear, however, that another important reason why such a move might wish to be made is for the purpose of minimising the tax liability of the trust. This is particularly evident in cases where it is desired to move the investment and administration of the trust to 'off-shore' tax havens, such as the Channel Isles or the Isle of Man.

It is of course perfectly possible for the trust instrument to contain a power authorising the trustees both to invest overseas and, if appropriate, transfer the administration of the trust to foreign trustees. The exercise of such a power may, or may not, be made dependent on the consent of the beneficiaries. Similarly, the appointment of a foreign trustee may be made without any need to have recourse to the court if all the beneficiaries are of full age, sui juris and consent to the changes - as in *Re Whitehead's Will Trusts* (1971).

However, in the normal case, it is clear that a trust can only be 'exported' if the terms of the trust can be varied so as to meet the requirements of the foreign law and to authorise the appointment of foreign trustees. All adult beneficiaries who are sui juris can, of course, consent for themselves to such a variation and if they are the only beneficiaries no problem arises. This is, however, unlikely for the trust is likely to include infant beneficiaries or even persons not yet born who will become such beneficiaries - eg future children of the settlor. Such persons cannot consent to a variation as they have no legal capacity and so application must be made to the court under the Variation of Trusts Act 1958 for approval on their behalf.

Under this Act, the court has the power to approve variations on behalf of four classes of persons - persons unborn (eg future children), infants, any person who has a discretionary interest under a protective trust, and any person who would be a member of a class of beneficiaries at a future date, where the class is ascertainable only at a future time. However, in order to be able to approve a variation on behalf of these persons (*except* a person with an interest under a discretionary trust), the court must be satisfied that the proposed variation is for their 'benefit'. This is the most difficult hurdle to overcome when asking for the approval of a variation which transfers the trust property and the administration of the trust abroad.

The most potent and obvious type of benefit is financial benefit and if the tax saving resultant on such a move is substantial then the court would find it difficult to deny that there is 'benefit' within the Act. Similarly, if the beneficiaries are emigrating permanently to a foreign jurisdiction then there may well be an additional intangible benefit in exporting the trust, as in *Re Seale* (1961) and *Re Windeatt's Will Trusts* (1969). Problems do arise, however, if the link with the foreign jurisdiction is tenuous because it is clear that the court must consider moral and social benefit as well as that which is financial. The leading authority here is *Re Weston* (1969) where the Court of Appeal refused consent on behalf of infant beneficiaries to a resettlement of the trusts in Jersey - the object being legitimate tax avoidance. According to the court, 'there are many things in life more worthwhile than money. One of these is to be brought up in this our England, which is still "the envy of less happier lands". I do not believe that it is for the benefit of children to be uprooted from England and transported to another country simply to avoid tax.' There is here, of course, a certain reluctance to approve variations whose sole purpose is tax avoidance ('the avoidance of tax may be lawful, but it is not yet a virtue'), but there is the greater point that the court's responsibility goes beyond fiscal considerations and approval must not be given where such would imperil the 'true welfare' of the children, born or unborn. It is, in essence, that the court must balance fiscal considerations with rather more intangible 'benefits'. Of course, the decision becomes easier if the beneficiaries can demonstrate a genuine link with the new jurisdiction. Finally, we must note that the court has power to order a *variation* of trust - it does not have power to consent to a complete re-settlement on completely new trusts which change the whole 'substratum' of the original scheme - *Re Ball's Settlement* (1968). This would, of course, depend on the terms of the proposed variation.

i) Under this protective trust, Mary is the life tenant and her children are entitled in remainder. All the children are adult, but not all have obtained vested interests. However, under a protective trust it is difficult for the beneficiaries to effect a variation without recourse to the court. First, the rule in *Saunders* v *Vautier* (1841) is inapplicable because not all of the beneficiaries are of full age, sui juris and together absolutely entitled. This is because under a protective trust governed by s33 of the Trustee Act (as this appears to be), when or if the life tenant's interest ends (eg due to an act of bankruptcy), the income is to be paid to the life tenant, his or her spouse and any issue *or* the persons absolutely entitled (the three children). The problem is that a potential and future spouse of Mary would have an interest under the trust - as would any future children - a possibility despite Mary's age. Thus, there are persons with contingent and future interests who would need to consent, but cannot.

ii) Application to the court to vary may be made in a number of ways, although only the last of these is relevant in the circumstances of this case. A court has inherent power to vary the terms of the trust in cases of absolute necessity to preserve the value of trust property eg *Re New* (1901). This is not relevant here. Likewise, the extended jurisdiction to make variations in the administration of the trust which are 'expedient' under s57(1) of the Trustee Act does not assist in this case. Section 57 authorises changes in terms relating to administration of the trust, not changes in beneficial interests. The clearest ground for approaching the court is to gain approval for a variation under the Variation of Trusts Act. As seen above, the court may approve a variation on behalf of incompetent persons and persons who had a discretionary interest under a protective trust. In this case, the court could approve the application on behalf of the unborn children (provided it was satisfied that it was for their benefit) and on behalf of any person who would acquire an interest under the discretionary trusts which would arise if the protective trusts should determine (such as a future spouse) and to this class of persons the requirement of benefit does not apply.

HLT GROUP PUBLICATIONS FOR THE LLB EXAMINATIONS

Our publications, written by specialists, are used widely by students at universities, polytechnics and colleges throughout the United Kingdom and overseas.

Textbooks
These are designed as working books to provide students with a valuable framework on which to base their studies. They are updated each year to reflect new developments and changing trends.

Casebooks
These are designed as companion volumes to the Textbooks and incorporate important cases, statutes as appropriate, and other material, together with detailed commentaries.

Revision Workbooks
For first degree law students, these provide questions and answers for all topics in each law subject. Every topic has sections on key points, recent cases and statutes, further reading etc.

Suggested Solutions
These are available to past London University LLB examination papers and provide the student with an invaluable revision aid and an insight into the techniques essential to examination success.

The books listed below can be ordered through your local bookshops or obtained direct from the publisher using this order form. Telephone, Fax or Telex orders will also be accepted. Quote your Access or Visa card numbers for priority orders. To order direct from the publisher please enter the cost of the titles you require, fill in the despatch details and send it with your remittance to The HLT Group Ltd.

ORDER FORM

LLB PUBLICATIONS	TEXTBOOKS		CASEBOOKS		REVISION WORKBOOKS		SUG. SOL. 1985/90		SUG. SOL. 1991	
	Cost £	£	Cost £	£	Cost £	£	Cost £	£	Cost £	£
Administrative Law	17.95		18.95				9.95		3.00	
Commercial Law Vol I	18.95		18.95		9.95		9.95		3.00	
Commercial Law Vol II	17.95		18.95							
Company Law	18.95		18.95		9.95		9.95		3.00	
Conflict of Laws	16.95		17.95							
Constitutional Law	14.95		16.95		9.95		9.95		3.00	
Contract Law	14.95		16.95		9.95		9.95		3.00	
Conveyancing	17.95		16.95							
Criminal Law	14.95		17.95		9.95		9.95		3.00	
Criminology	16.95						+3.00		3.00	
English Legal System	14.95		12.95				*7.95		3.00	
Equity and Trusts	14.95		16.95		9.95		9.95		3.00	
European Community Law	17.95		18.95		9.95		+3.00		3.00	
Evidence	17.95		17.95		9.95		9.95		3.00	
Family Law	17.95		18.95		9.95		9.95		3.00	
Jurisprudence	14.95				9.95		9.95		3.00	
Labour Law	15.95									
Land Law	14.95		16.95	·	9.95		9.95		3.00	
Public International Law	18.95		17.95		9.95		9.95		3.00	
Revenue Law	17.95		18.95		9.95		9.95		3.00	
Roman Law	14.95									
Succession	17.95		17.95		9.95		9.95		3.00	
Tort	14.95		16.95		9.95		9.95		3.00	

* 1987–1990 papers only   + 1990 papers only

cut along dotted line

DETAILS FOR DESPATCH OF PUBLICATIONS

Please insert your full name below

[   ]

Please insert below the style in which you would like the correspondence from the Publisher addressed to you

TITLE Mr, Miss etc.   INITIALS   SURNAME/FAMILY NAME

[| |]

Address to which study material is to be sent (please ensure someone will be present to accept delivery of your Publications).

[   ]

POSTAGE & PACKING

You are welcome to purchase study material from the Publisher at 200 Greyhound Road, London W14 9RY, during normal working hours.

If you wish to order by post this may be done direct from the Publisher. Postal charges are as follows:

UK   - Orders over £30: no charge. Orders below £30: £2.50. Single paper (last exam only): 50p
OVERSEAS - See table below

The Publisher cannot accept responsibility in respect of postal delays or losses in the postal systems.

DESPATCH All cheques must be cleared before material is despatched.

SUMMARY OF ORDER   Date of order: [   ]

				£
		Cost of publications ordered:		
		UNITED KINGDOM:		
OVERSEAS:	TEXTS		Suggested Solutions (Last exam only)	
	One	Each Extra		
Eire	£4.00	£0.60	£1.00	
European Community	£9.00	£1.00	£1.00	
East Europe & North America	£10.50	£1.00	£1.00	
South East Asia	£12.00	£2.00	£1.50	
Australia/New Zealand	£13.50	£4.00	£1.50	
Other Countries (Africa, India etc)	£13.00	£3.00	£1.50	
			Total cost of order:	

Please ensure that you enclose a cheque or draft payable to **THE HLT GROUP LTD** for the above amount, or charge to ☐ Access ☐ Visa ☐ American Express

Card Number [| | | | | | | | | | | | | | | | | |]

Expiry Date ....   Signature ....

NOTES

NOTES

NOTES

NOTES